Commercial Pilot

ORAL EXAM GUIDE

JASON BLAIR
Based on original text by Michael D. Hayes

ELEVENTH EDITION

COMPREHENSIVE PREPARATION
FOR THE FAA CHECKRIDE

AVIATION SUPPLIES & ACADEMICS, INC.
NEWCASTLE, WASHINGTON

Commercial Pilot Oral Exam Guide
Eleventh Edition
by Jason Blair
based on original text by Michael D. Hayes

Aviation Supplies & Academics, Inc.
7005 132nd Place SE
Newcastle, Washington 98059
asa@asa2fly.com | 425-235-1500 | asa2fly.com

See the Reader Resources at **asa2fly.com/oegc** for additional information and updates relating to this book.

ASA-OEG-C11
ISBN 978-1-64425-343-4

Additional formats available:
eBook EPUB ISBN 978-1-64425-344-1
eBook PDF   ISBN 978-1-64425-345-8

Printed in the United States of America
2028   2027   2026   2025   2024   9 8 7 6 5 4 3 2 1

Library of Congress Cataloging-in-Publication Data
Names: Blair, Jason, author. | Hayes, Michael D., author.
Title: Commercial pilot oral exam guide : comprehensive preparation for the FAA
   checkride / Jason Blair based on original text by Michael D. Hayes.
Other titles: Commercial oral exam guide | Oral exam guide
Description: Eleventh edition. | Newcastle, Washington : Aviation Supplies & Academics,
   Inc., [2024] | First edition published 1992 entitled: Commercial oral exam guide by
   Michael D. Hayes.
Identifiers: LCCN 2023041544 (print) | LCCN 2023041545 (ebook) | ISBN 9781644253434
   (trade paperback) | ISBN 9781644253441 (epub) | ISBN 9781644253458 (pdf)
Subjects: LCSH: United States. Federal Aviation Administration—Examinations—Study
   guides. | Aeronautics, Commercial—Examinations—Study guides. | Aeronautics—
   Examinations, questions, etc. | Airplanes—Piloting—Examinations—Study guides. |
   Oral examinations. | LCGFT: Study guides.
Classification: LCC TL546.5 .B53 2023 (print) | LCC TL546.5 (ebook) | DDC
   629.132/5216076—dc23/eng/20231212
LC record available at https://lccn.loc.gov/2023041544
LC ebook record available at https://lccn.loc.gov/2023041545

Contents

Contents

Introduction

The *Commercial Pilot Oral Exam Guide* is a comprehensive guide designed for pilots who are involved in training for the Commercial Pilot Certificate. It was originally designed for use in a Part 141 flight school but quickly became popular with those training under Part 61 who were not affiliated with an approved school. This guide will also prove beneficial to pilots who wish to refresh their knowledge or who are preparing for a flight review.

The *Commercial Pilot—Airplane Airman Certification Standards* (FAA-S-ACS-7) specifies the areas in which knowledge and skills must be demonstrated by the applicant before issuance of a pilot certificate or rating. The *Commercial Pilot Oral Exam Guide* is designed to evaluate a pilot's knowledge of those areas.

Commercial pilots are professionals engaged in various flight activities for compensation or hire. Because of their professional status, they should exhibit a significantly higher level of knowledge than a private pilot. This guide assumes that the pilot has the prerequisite knowledge necessary for Private Pilot certification and attempts to cover only those advanced areas of knowledge necessary for Commercial Pilot certification. A review of the information presented within this guide along with a general review of the *Private Pilot Oral Exam Guide* (ASA-OEG-P) should provide the necessary preparation for the oral section of an FAA Commercial Pilot checkride or recertification check.

In this guide, questions and answers are organized into nine chapters which represent those areas of knowledge required for the practical test. At any time during the practical test, an examiner may ask questions pertaining to any of the subject areas within these divisions. Based on intensive debriefings conducted after Commercial Pilot checkrides, we have provided you with the questions or topics commonly asked along with the information or the appropriate reference necessary for a knowledgeable response. Additionally,

Chapter 10 includes scenario-based questions to help you prepare for typical scenarios that the examiner may present as part of your oral exam.

This guide may be supplemented with other comprehensive study materials as noted in parentheses after each question. For example: (FAA-H-8083-25). The abbreviations for these materials and their titles are listed below. Be sure that you use the latest revision of these references when reviewing for the test. Also, check the ASA website at asa2fly.com/oegc for the most recent updates to this book due to changes in FAA procedures and regulations as well as for Reader Resources containing additional relevant information and updates.

14 CFR Part 1	*Definitions and Abbreviations*
14 CFR Part 3	*General Requirements*
14 CFR Part 21	*Certification Procedures for Products and Articles*
14 CFR Part 23	*Airworthiness Standards: Normal Category Airplanes*
14 CFR Part 43	*Maintenance, Preventive Maintenance, Rebuilding, and Alteration*
14 CFR Part 47	*Aircraft Registration*
14 CFR Part 61	*Certification: Pilots, Flight Instructors, and Ground Instructors*
14 CFR Part 67	*Medical Standards and Certification*
14 CFR Part 91	*General Operating and Flight Rules*
14 CFR Part 93	*Special Air Traffic Rules*
14 CFR Part 95	*IFR Altitudes*
14 CFR Part 99	*Security Control of Air Traffic*
14 CFR Part 110	*Certification and Operations: General Requirements*
14 CFR Part 119	*Certification: Air Carriers and Commercial Operators*
49 CFR Part 830	*NTSB, Notification and Reporting of Aircraft Accidents or Incidents and Overdue Aircraft*
49 CFR Part 1544	*TSA, Aircraft Operator Security: Air Carriers and Commercial Operators*
49 CFR Part 1552	*TSA, Civil Aviation Security, Flight Schools*

AC 20-105	*Reciprocating Engine Power-Loss Accident Prevention and Trend Monitoring*
AC 21-40	*Guide for Obtaining a Supplemental Type Certificate*
AC 23-8	*Flight Test Guide for Certification of Part 23 Airplanes*
AC 39-7	*Airworthiness Directives*
AC 43-12	*Preventive Maintenance*
AC 61-65	*Certification: Pilots and Flight and Ground Instructors*
AC 61-67	*Stall and Spin Awareness Training*
AC 61-107	*Aircraft Operations at Altitudes Above 25,000 Feet Mean Sea Level or Mach Numbers Greater than .75*
AC 61-134	*General Aviation Controlled Flight into Terrain Awareness*
AC 61-142	*Sharing Aircraft Operating Expenses in Accordance with 14 CFR §61.113(c)*
AC 68-1	*BasicMed*
AC 90-66	*Non-Towered Airport Flight Operations*
AC 90-100	*U.S. Terminal and En Route Area Navigation (RNAV) Operations*
AC 90-109	*Transition to Unfamiliar Aircraft*
AC 90-114	*Automatic Dependent Surveillance–Broadcast Operations*
AC 91-37	*Truth in Leasing*
AC 91-63	*Temporary Flight Restrictions (TFR) and Flight Limitations*
AC 91-73	*Parts 91 and 135 Single-Pilot, Flight School Procedures during Taxi Operations*
AC 91-74	*Pilot Guide: Flight in Icing Condition*
AC 120-12	*Private Carriage vs. Common Carriage of Persons or Property*
AC 120-80	*Firefighting of General and High-Energy In-Flight Fires*

(continued)

AFM/POH	*Airplane Flight Manuals and Pilot's Operating Handbooks*
AIM	*FAA Aeronautical Information Manual*
AWC	*Aviation Weather Center*
Chart Supplement	*US Chart Supplements*
drs.faa.gov	*Dynamic Regulatory System—Order 8900.1*
FAA AME	*FAA Guide for Aviation Medical Examiners: Pharmaceuticals (Therapeutic Medications)*
FAA FRAT	*FAA Fly Safe Fact Sheet: Flight Risk Assessment Tools*
faa.gov	*Federal Aviation Administration website*
FAA-H-8083-1	*Aircraft Weight and Balance Handbook*
FAA-H-8083-2	*Risk Management Handbook*
FAA-H-8083-3	*Airplane Flying Handbook*
FAA-H-8083-9	*Aviation Instructor's Handbook*
FAA-H-8083-15	*Instrument Flying Handbook*
FAA-H-8083-16	*Instrument Procedures Handbook*
FAA-H-8083-19	*Plane Sense: General Aviation Information*
FAA-H-8083-25	*Pilot's Handbook of Aeronautical Knowledge*
FAA-H-8083-28	*Aviation Weather Handbook*
FAA-H-8083-30	*Aviation Maintenance Technician Handbook—General*
FAA-H-8083-31	*Aviation Maintenance Technician Handbook—Airframe*
FAA-H-8083-32	*Aviation Maintenance Technician Handbook—Powerplant*
FAA OTC Med Guide	*Over-the-Counter (OTC) Medications Reference Guide*
FAA-P-8740-13	*Engine Operation for Pilots*
FAA-P-8740-35	*All About Fuel*
FAA-P-8740-36	*Proficiency and the Private Pilot*
FAA-P-8740-44	*Impossible Turn*
FAA: Pilots and Medication	*FAA Fly Safe Fact Sheet: Pilots and Medication*

FAA Safety	*FAA Safety Briefing Magazine/Fly Safe Fact Sheets*
FAA-S-ACS-7	*Commercial Pilot—Airplane Airman Certification Standards*
GADLG	*General Aviation Dry Leasing Guide*
go.usa.gov/xkhJK	*Flight Risk Assessment Tool (FRAT) library*
NOTAMs	*Notices to Air Missions*
P/CG	*Pilot/Controller Glossary (from AIM)*
SAFO	*FAA Safety Alert for Operators*
TSA	*Transportation Security Administration*
USRGD	*FAA Aeronautical Chart User's Guide*

Most of these documents are available on the FAA's website (faa.gov). Additionally, many of the publications are reprinted by ASA (asa2fly.com) and are available from aviation retailers worldwide.

A review of the information and references presented within this guide should provide the necessary preparation for the FAA Commercial Pilot checkride.

Pilot
Qualifications

A. Privileges and Limitations

1. **What are the eligibility requirements for a Commercial Pilot (airplane) Certificate?** (14 CFR 61.123)

    a. Be at least 18 years of age.

    b. Be able to read, speak, write, and understand the English language.

    c. Hold at least a Private Pilot Certificate.

    d. Hold at least a current Third Class Medical Certificate.

    e. Received the required ground and flight training endorsements.

    f. Pass the required knowledge and practical tests.

    g. Meet the aeronautical experience requirements.

2. **What are the aeronautical experience requirements for a Commercial Pilot Certificate?** (14 CFR 61.129)

    A person who applies for a Commercial Pilot Certificate with an Airplane Category and Single-Engine Class Rating must log at least 250 hours of flight time as a pilot that consists of at least:

    a. 100 hours in powered aircraft, of which 50 hours must be in airplanes.

    b. 100 hours of PIC flight time, which includes at least:
       - 50 hours in airplanes.
       - 50 hours in cross-country flight of which 10 hours must be in airplanes.

    c. 20 hours of training on the areas of training listed in §61.127(b)(1) that includes at least 10 hours of instrument training. Five of the 10 hours of instrument training must be in a single-engine airplane.

    d. 10 hours of training in a complex, turbine-powered, or technically advanced airplane (TAA), or any combination thereof.

    e. 10 hours of solo flight time in a single-engine airplane or 10 hours of flight time performing the duties of pilot-in-command in a single-engine airplane with an authorized instructor on board (either of which may be credited towards the flight time requirement under §61.129[a][2]), on the areas of operation listed under §61.127(b)(1) that include—

- One cross-country flight of not less than 300 NM total distance, with landings at a minimum of three points, one of which is a straight-line distance of at least 250 NM from the original departure point. However, if this requirement is being met in Hawaii, the longest segment need only have a straight-line distance of at least 150 NM; and
- 5 hours in night VFR conditions with 10 takeoffs and 10 landings (with each landing involving a flight in the traffic pattern) at an airport with an operating control tower.

Exam Tip: The evaluator may ask you to demonstrate that you're current and eligible to take the practical test. The examiner will need to see documented flight and ground instruction time (a commonly forgotten documentary requirement) to show that all experience requirements have been met. This may require documenting items beyond what the standard logbook includes. Take the time to detail this in your logbook, extra training records, or through other methods to ensure that you can provide documentation of all requirements to avoid having to reschedule the practical test

3. What privileges apply to a commercial pilot?
(14 CFR 61.133)

A person who holds a Commercial Pilot Certificate may act as PIC of an aircraft:

a. Carrying persons or property for compensation or hire.

b. For compensation or hire.

Note: 14 CFR §61.133 also states that a commercial pilot must be qualified and comply with the applicable parts of the regulations that apply to the particular operation being conducted (e.g., Part 121 or 135).

4. What does the term *commercial operator* refer to?
(14 CFR Part 1)

A commercial operator is a person who, for compensation or hire, engages in the carriage by aircraft in air commerce of persons or property, other than as an air carrier or foreign carrier under the authority of 14 CFR Part 375. It is worth noting that this relates to the pilot acting as a commercial operator, something they may do as a Commercial Pilot Certificate holder. There is a difference between a pilot acting in accordance with their commercial pilot privileges versus an aircraft acting in a commercial carriage capacity. A pilot may act commercially in private carriage within commercial pilot privileges while an aircraft or its operation is not engaged in commercial carriage that would constitute holding out or public carriage of passengers or property for hire. Payment is not limited to currency, but could also include anything of value such as services, goods, or trade. A pilot who is acting as a pilot in consideration of gaining benefit of any sort may be considered to be acting in a commercial capacity.

5. **Explain the difference between your commercial pilot privileges and the operational authority required to conduct a flight for compensation or hire.** (AC 61-142)

The privileges and limitations conferred on pilots are separate and distinct from the operational authority required to conduct the flights. A person who holds an ATP Certificate or Commercial Pilot Certificate may act as PIC of an aircraft operated for compensation or hire and may carry persons or property for compensation for hire if done in accordance with an operator certificate under Part 119. If the aircraft is generating revenue or benefit, it is also considered to be acting commercially. Unless a valid exception from operational certification applies, in order to "hold out" as being able to transport persons or property for compensation or hire, a commercial pilot or ATP must be operating in accordance with an air carrier certificate or operating certificate under 14 CFR Part 119. These are typically operated then under Part 121 or Part 135 operational approvals.

Note: Even though a Commercial Pilot Certificate allows a pilot to be compensated for their services, it must be done in one of the areas of exception or under private carriage conditions. It does not allow them to act as an air carrier or commercial operator without first obtaining an air carrier or operating certificate.

6. **Would being both the pilot and the provider of an aircraft to someone for compensation or hire require the pilot to also be in possession of a Part 119 operating certificate?** (FAA Safety)

Generally, if you are being compensated for providing a service to another person and have operational control of the aircraft in which that service is provided, you are required to have been issued an operating certificate to conduct that operation under Part 135, or Parts 121 or 125 if larger aircraft and more complex operations are involved.

7. Define the term *operational control.* (AC 91-37, 14 CFR 1.1)

As defined in 14 CFR §1.1, operational control "with respect to a flight, means the exercise of authority over initiating, conducting, or terminating a flight." This should not be construed with the pilot-in-command, as operational control may be held by an operator, an owner, or other entity hiring and directing the pilot. Operational control involves three basic areas: flight crew, aircraft, and flight management.

8. What is common carriage? (AC 61-142, AC 120-12)

Common carriage refers to the carriage of passengers or cargo as a result of advertising the availability of the carriage to the public. A carrier becomes a common carrier when it "holds itself out" to the public, or a segment of the public, as willing to furnish transportation within the limits of its facilities to any person who wants it. There are four elements in defining a common carrier:

a. A holding out or a willingness,

b. to transport persons or property,

c. from place to place,

d. for compensation or hire.

A pilot may indicate their ability to provide commercial pilot services within the constraints of a Commercial Pilot Certificate held, but may not indicate a willingness to fly any and all comers or broadly provide commercial carriage availability to the general public.

9. What actions by a pilot would constitute holding out? (AC 61-142, AC 120-12)

Holding out is accomplished by any means that communicates to the public that a transportation service is indiscriminately available to the members of that segment of the public that it is designed to attract. There is no specific rule or criteria as to how holding out is achieved. Instead, holding out is determined by assessing the available facts of a specific situation. Advertising in any form raises the question of holding out.

10. What are examples of factors that the FAA would consider in determining whether an operator is holding out? (AC 61-142)

The FAA would consider whether an operator is using:

a. *Agents, agencies, or salespeople*—individuals who may obtain passenger traffic from the general public and collect them into groups to be carried by the operator.

b. *Print publications*—advertising in newspapers, magazines, directories, brochures, posters, or any other type of publication is the most direct means of holding out.

c. *Internet*—the internet has a virtually unlimited audience and an advertisement published on the internet would not meet the criteria of a limited and defined group and, in most instances, would be considered to be holding out.

d. *Websites*—posting of a flight on a website accessible to the general public, or a segment of the general public, is considered holding out.

e. *Social media*—to avoid being considered to be holding out, a pilot would need to be reaching out to a defined and limited group of people with whom he or she has an ongoing, pre-existing relationship apart from expense sharing.

f. *Apps*—the use of applications on mobile or electronic devices to advertise flights for cost sharing under 14 CFR §61.113(c) is considered holding out.

g. *Email*—an email among close friends, asking to share operating expenses, may be acceptable. However, sending an email to every friend, acquaintance, colleague, or contact may be considered holding out.

h. *Personal solicitation and reputation/course of conduct*—physically holding out, without advertising, where the pilot gains a reputation of serving all, is sufficient to constitute an offer to carry all customers.

i. *Sharing aircraft operating expenses (such as flight-sharing apps)*—The FAA noted the following in its *FAA Safety Briefing* magazine: Generally, if you're being compensated for providing a service to another person and have "operational control" of the aircraft that the service is provided with, you're going to have to be issued a 14 CFR part 119 certificate to conduct that operation under 14 CFR part 135 (or part 121 or 125 if larger aircraft or more complex operations are involved). "In most instances where compensation is provided, the FAA has determined that this level of safety can only be achieved when the operation is conducted by at least a commercial pilot flying under the provisions of an operating certificate," explains Paul Greer, an attorney in the FAA's Office of the Chief Counsel. "The public has an expectation that both the pilot and the operator will meet a standard of competence and provide a level of safety higher than that provided by a private pilot operating solely under the general operating requirements of part 91." For more information, a pilot can review FAA Advisory Circular 61-142, *Sharing Aircraft Operating Expenses in Accordance with 14 CFR §61.113(c)*.

11. **Are there commercial operations that a commercial pilot could conduct that do not require the issuance of a Part 119 certificate?** (14 CFR Part 119.1)

A Part 119 certificate is not required when conducting:

a. Student instruction.

b Non-stop commercial air tours (14 CFR §119.1(e)(2)).

c. Ferry or training flights.

d. Crop dusting, seeding, spraying, or bird chasing.

e. Banner towing.

f. Aerial photography or survey.

g. Firefighting.

h. Powerline or pipeline patrol.

i. Carrying persons for the purpose of intentional parachute operations.

j. Emergency mail service.

k. Carriage of candidates in elections (14 CFR §91.321).

Note: This list is a list of commercial aircraft operations that are exempted from requiring an air carrier certificate for a commercial pilot to conduct these activities. It should be noted that these are instances when the *aircraft* is operating commercially. When an aircraft is not acting commercially, such as in private carriage, this does not preclude the pilot from acting commercially as a pilot in accordance with their certificate privileges.

12. **Determine if either of the following two scenarios are common carriage operations and, if so, why?**

    Scenario 1: **I am a local businessperson and require a package to be flown to a distant destination ASAP. I will pay you to fly my airplane to deliver this package.**

    Scenario 2: **I am a local businessperson and require a package to be flown to a distant destination ASAP. You reply that you can do the job for a fee. You promptly line up a local rental aircraft you're checked out in and deliver the package.**

    Scenario 2 would be considered common carriage as an operation because you are holding out by having a general willingness to provide a customer with both an aircraft over which you exercise operational control (sourcing for the carriage of, in this case, goods) and the pilot services for compensation or hire.

    In Scenario 1, you are not in operational control of the aircraft and are just being paid for your pilot services to fly the aircraft for the owner.

13. **Determine if either of the following scenarios would be considered private carriage and thus a Commercial Pilot Certificate holder would be allowed to accept compensation for a flight they conduct.**

    Scenario 1: **A pilot who owns his own aircraft has recently had his medical certificate suspended. The pilot normally flies himself to business meetings and has asked you as a pilot to fly the aircraft for him until he can get his medical back. The pilot will pay you a daily rate to fly the aircraft while he attends meetings.**

    Scenario 2: **A pilot who owns her own aircraft has a friend who would like to use the aircraft to get to some meetings. The pilot offers access to the aircraft and your pilot services packaged for an hourly operation rate to the friend, who will pay for the use.**

    In Scenario 1, the pilot is acting on his Commercial Pilot Certificate privileges, and the aircraft and its operational control remains with the owner who is securing (hiring) a pilot to fly for them. This is private carriage. In Scenario 2, the owner is providing a package of pilot and aircraft for compensation, which would constitute holding out and would require a commercial operator certificate. While the aircraft is not yours, you are acting as a part of the package that is being held out for profit that includes compensation for both the aircraft and the pilot, both of which would be acting commercially in this case.

14. **What are the three types of operations that require a Part 119 certificate?** (14 CFR 119.5)

    A Part 119 certificate is required for each person conducting or intending to conduct:

    a. Operations as a direct air carrier.

    b. Operations as a U.S. commercial operator.

    c. Operations when common carriage is not involved as an operator of U.S. registered civil airplanes with a seat configuration of 20 or more passengers or a maximum payload capacity of 6,000 pounds or more (Part 125).

15. **What are the two basic types of certificates issued to applicants under Part 119?** (14 CFR 119.5, drs.faa.gov)

    a. *Air carrier certificate*—this certificate is issued to applicants who plan to conduct interstate, foreign, or overseas transportation, or to carry mail.

    b. *Operating certificate*—this certificate is issued to applicants who plan to conduct intrastate common carriage operations and certain applicants who do not conduct common carriage operations (i.e., Part 125 private carriage operations). See 14 CFR §119.5 and Order 8900.1 Volume 2, Chapter 2, Section 2-128 for additional information.

16. **What are the four types of operations that do not involve common carriage?** (14 CFR 110.2, 119.3)

    14 CFR §119.3 defines operations not involving common carriage to mean any of the following:

    a. Non-common carriage.

    b. Operations in which persons or cargo are transported without compensation or hire.

    c. Operations not involving the transportation of persons or cargo.

    d. Private carriage.

(continued)

Note: Non-common carriage and private carriage are commercial because they involve compensation or hire. Operations in which persons or cargo are transported without compensation or hire and operations not involving the transportation of persons or cargo, are non-commercial.

17. Define the terms *non-common carriage* and *private carriage*. (drs.faa.gov)

Non-common carriage—Involves the carriage of persons or property for compensation or hire, but there is no holding out. Non-common carriage operations require the issuance of an operating certificate. Operations are conducted under Parts 125 or 135, depending on the type of aircraft, seating configuration, and payload capacity.

Private carriage—Involves the carriage of persons or property for compensation or hire with limitations on the number of contracts. The carriage of persons or property for compensation or hire under a contractual business arrangement between the operator and another person or organization, which did not result from the operator's holding out or offering service, is considered to be private carriage. Private carriage operations require the issuance of an operating certificate. Operations are conducted under Parts 125 or 135, depending on the type of aircraft, seating configuration, and payload capacity.

18. What are several examples of non-common carriage operations that involve the transportation of persons or property and may involve compensation, but are conducted under Part 91? (14 CFR 91.501)

Part 91 Subpart F applies to large and turbine-powered multi-engine airplanes and fractional ownership program aircraft. 14 CFR §91.501 sets conditions on the amount and types of compensation for these operations. Examples include:

a. Flights conducted by the operator of an airplane for the operator's own personal transportation, or the transportation of guests.

b. Carriage of company officials, employees, and guests on an airplane operated under a time sharing, interchange, or joint ownership agreement.

c. Carriage of property (except mail) incidental to business (limited compensation for expenses).

d. Carriage of a group (with common purpose) when there is no charge, assessment, or fee.

e. Fractional ownership.

19. A lease involving an aircraft is sometimes referred to as a wet lease or a dry lease. Explain the difference. (AC 91-37, 14 CFR 110.2)

Wet lease—Any leasing arrangement whereby a person agrees to provide an entire aircraft and at least one crewmember. A wet lease is a commercial arrangement whereby an aircraft owner leases both the aircraft and at least one crewmember to another person for his or her exclusive use for a specified period or a defined number of flights. The lessor maintains operational control. A common example of a wet lease would be the charter of an aircraft and crew to a passenger(s) by a certificated charter operator conducting operations under Part 135.

Dry lease—The leasing of an aircraft without the crew is considered to be a dry lease and the lessee exercises operational control of the aircraft. When dry leasing, you do not need an operating certificate as long as you do not carry persons or property for compensation or hire. For larger aircraft operating under Part 125, review §125.1 for the certificate requirements of your intended operation.

20. Describe a common form of a dry lease. (GADLG)

Types of dry leases include rental agreements and, in aircraft, trust arrangements and operating agreements. Under a dry lease, the compensation being paid is typically in the form of a rental payment in exchange for the lessee's own use (whether the lessee is a pilot or a passenger who has hired a pilot) of the equipment being rented, analogous to obtaining a rental car for one's ground transportation needs.

21. Why is it important to understand the difference between a wet lease and a dry lease? (AC 91-37)

The regulations that govern an aircraft's operation will be different depending on who has operational control of the flight and whether the aircraft was wet leased or dry leased. With certain exceptions, such as 14 CFR §91.501(c), an aircraft operated under a wet lease agreement is required to have an air carrier certificate and conduct operations under Parts 121 or 135 regulations. When operating under a dry lease, the lessee is not required to have an air carrier certificate and may operate under the less restrictive Part 91 regulations.

22. Briefly describe the following regulations: 14 CFR Part 91 Subpart F, 119, 121, 125, and 135.

Part 91 Subpart F—Generally, corporate operations not involving common carriage are governed by Part 91, Subpart F.

Part 119—Consolidates the certification and operations specifications (ops specs) requirements for persons who operate in common carriage under Parts 121 and 135. Part 119 also lists operations that do not require an air carrier or commercial operating certificate.

Part 121—Establishes the regulations for air carriers flying for compensation or hire. Part 121 operations require issuance of an air carrier certificate and associated ops specs.

Part 125—Establishes a uniform set of certification and operational rules for large airplanes having a seating capacity of 20 or more passengers or a maximum payload capacity of 6,000 pounds or more, when common carriage is not involved. These rules substantially upgrade the level of safety applicable to large airplanes formerly operated under Part 91.

Part 135—Governs commuter or on-demand operations; requires issuance of an air carrier or operating certificate and associated ops specs.

23. **What limitation is imposed on a newly certificated commercial airplane pilot if that person does not hold an Instrument Rating?** (14 CFR 61.133)

The pilot must hold an Instrument Rating in the same category and class, or the Commercial Pilot Certificate that is issued is endorsed with a limitation prohibiting the following:

a. The carriage of passengers for hire in airplanes on cross-country flights in excess of 50 nautical miles.

b. The carriage of passengers for hire in airplanes at night.

Note: It should be noted that the FAA in legal interpretations has confirmed that this is a limitation of 50 nautical miles from the point of origin—not limiting flight legs to 50 nautical miles and then continuing flight.

24. **To act as a required pilot flight crewmember of a civil aircraft, what must a pilot have in his/her physical possession or readily accessible in the aircraft?** (14 CFR 61.3)

a. A pilot certificate (including any special purpose pilot authorization or temporary certificate).

b. A government-issued photo identification that includes one of the following: a U.S. or foreign-issued passport; a driver's license issued by a U.S. state, the District of Columbia, or territory or possession of the United States; a government identification card issued by the federal government, a state, the District of Columbia, or a territory or possession of the United States; a U.S. Armed Forces' identification card; a credential that authorizes unescorted access to a security identification display area at an airport regulated under 49 CFR Part 1542; or another form of identification that the FAA Administrator finds acceptable.

c. An appropriate medical certificate.

25. If a certificated pilot changes his/her permanent mailing address and fails to notify the FAA Airman Certification Branch of the new address, for how long may the pilot continue to exercise the privileges of his/her pilot certificate? (14 CFR 61.60)

30 days after the date of the move.

26. If a pilot certificate is accidentally lost or destroyed, a pilot could continue to exercise the privileges of that certificate provided he or she follows what specific procedure? (14 CFR 61.29)

An airman may request a replacement certificate by contacting the FAA's Airmen Certification branch. The airman will make an application for replacement of a lost or destroyed certificate issued under Part 61 to the Department of Transportation, Federal Aviation Administration, either in paper format or using the FAA's online Airmen Services website. At this site, an airman may obtain a document that allows them to operate with temporary authority in accordance with their certification privileges and/or limitations for up to 60 days until a replacement certificate is received. Using the Airmen Services website, airmen may change the status of their address releasability, change their address, order a replacement certificate, remove a social security number as a certificate number, request temporary authority to exercise certificate privileges, or request verification of certificate privileges.

27. To act as PIC of a high-performance aircraft, what flight experience requirements must be met? (14 CFR 61.31)

A high-performance airplane is an airplane with an engine of more than 200 horsepower. To act as PIC of a high-performance airplane, a person must have:

a. Received and logged ground and flight training from an authorized instructor in a high-performance airplane, or in a full flight simulator or flight training device that is representative of a high-performance airplane;

b. Been found proficient in the operation and systems of that airplane; and

c. Received a one-time endorsement in the pilot's logbook from an authorized instructor who certifies the person is proficient to operate a high-performance airplane.

28. What is the definition of a *complex airplane*? (14 CFR 61.1)

A complex airplane is defined as an airplane that has a retractable landing gear, flaps, and a controllable pitch propeller, including airplanes equipped with an engine control system consisting of a digital computer and associated accessories for controlling the engine and propeller, such as a full authority digital engine control (FADEC).

29. What are the requirements to act as PIC of a complex airplane? (14 CFR 61.31)

To act as PIC of a complex airplane, you must have:

a. Received and logged ground and flight training from an authorized instructor in a complex airplane, or in a full flight simulator or flight training device that is representative of a complex airplane, and been found proficient in the operation and systems of the airplane; and

b. Received a one-time endorsement in your logbook from an authorized instructor who certifies that you are proficient to operate a complex airplane.

30. To act as PIC of a pressurized aircraft, what flight experience requirements must be met? (14 CFR 61.31)

To act as PIC of a pressurized aircraft (an aircraft that has a service ceiling or maximum operating altitude, whichever is lower, above 25,000 feet MSL), a person must have received and logged ground and flight training from an authorized instructor and obtained an endorsement in the person's logbook or training record from an authorized instructor who certifies the person has:

a. satisfactorily accomplished the ground training, which includes high-altitude aerodynamics, meteorology, respiration, hypoxia, etc.; and

b. received and logged training in a pressurized aircraft, or in a full flight simulator or flight training device representative of a pressurized aircraft, and obtained an endorsement in the person's logbook or training record from an authorized instructor who found the person proficient in the operation of pressurized aircraft (must include normal cruise flight above 25,000 feet MSL, emergency procedures for rapid decompression, and emergency descent procedures).

31. Is a pilot required to have a high altitude endorsement to fly a pressurized aircraft if the pilot will not be flying above 25,000 feet MSL (FL250)? (14 CFR 61.31)

14 CFR §61.31(g) notes that "no person may act as pilot in command of a pressurized aircraft (an aircraft that has a service ceiling or maximum operating altitude, whichever is lower, above 25,000 feet MSL), unless that person has received and logged ground training from an authorized instructor and obtained an endorsement in the person's logbook or training record from an authorized instructor who certifies the person has satisfactorily accomplished the ground training." The regulation stipulates that the endorsement is required if the aircraft is capable of operating at that altitude, not just if the pilot actually flies the aircraft to that altitude.

32. To act as PIC of a tailwheel airplane, what flight experience requirements must be met? (14 CFR 61.31)

No person may act as PIC of a tailwheel airplane unless that person has received and logged flight training from an authorized instructor in a tailwheel airplane and received an endorsement in the person's logbook from an authorized instructor who found the person proficient in the operation of a tailwheel airplane. The flight training must include at least the following maneuvers and procedures: normal and crosswind takeoffs and landings, wheel landings, and go-around procedures.

33. What is a technically advanced airplane (TAA)? (14 CFR 61.129)

Unless otherwise authorized by the FAA Administrator, a technically advanced airplane (TAA) must be equipped with an electronically advanced avionics system that includes the following installed components:

a. An electronic primary flight display (PFD) that includes, at a minimum, an airspeed indicator, turn coordinator, attitude indicator, heading indicator, altimeter, and vertical speed indicator;

b. An electronic multifunction display (MFD) that includes, at a minimum, a moving map using Global Positioning System (GPS) navigation with the aircraft position displayed;

c. A two-axis autopilot integrated with the navigation and heading guidance system; and

d. The display elements described in items (a) and (b) above must be continuously visible.

34. What counts as cross-country flight time? (14 CFR 61.1)

Technically, cross-country flight has many definitions that may include travel to a "point-in-space" when being used for ATP certificate experience requirements, landing at an airport different from the one from which the takeoff was made, or travel greater than 50 miles away from the point of origin. For the purposes of airman certificates and rating the definition in 14 CFR §61.1 is critical. It states that, "For the purpose of meeting the aeronautical experience requirements (except for a rotorcraft category rating), for a private pilot certificate (except for a powered parachute category rating), a commercial pilot certificate, or an instrument rating, or for the purpose of exercising recreational pilot privileges (except in a rotorcraft) under §61.101(c), time acquired during a flight" ...must include "a point of landing that was at least a straight-line distance of more than 50 nautical miles from the original point of departure." This is a critical point that is commonly missed by students and their instructors. A conservative student or pilot applies this to all of their cross-country flight time logging and would only log "cross-country" flight time when they have departed from an airport and landed at another airport that is greater than 50 nautical miles from the original departure airport.

35. When would a commercial pilot be required to hold a type rating? (14 CFR 61.31)

According to 14 CFR §61.31, a person who acts as a PIC of any of the following aircraft must hold a type rating for that aircraft:

a. Large aircraft (gross weight over 12,500 pounds, except lighter-than-air).

b. Turbojet-powered airplanes.

c. Other aircraft specified by the Administrator through aircraft type certificate procedures.

Note: Some aircraft manufacturers require type ratings for specific makes and models of aircraft even if they are less than 12,500 pounds gross weight.

36. **With respect to certification, privileges, and limitations of airmen, define the terms *category*, *class*, and *type*.** (14 CFR Part 1)

   Category—a broad classification of aircraft (e.g., airplane, rotorcraft, glider, etc.)

   Class—a classification of aircraft within a category having similar operating characteristics (e.g., single-engine land, multi-engine land, etc.)

   Type—a specific make and basic model of aircraft including modifications that do not change its handling or flight characteristics (e.g., DC-9, B-737, etc.)

37. **Can a pilot with a Commercial Pilot Certificate and Multi-Engine Land Rating carry passengers in a single-engine airplane?** (14 CFR 61.31)

   No. Unless the pilot holds a category, class, and type rating (if a class and type rating is required) that applies to that aircraft, the pilot may not act as PIC in this situation.

38. **Can a commercial pilot carry a passenger in an aircraft operated in formation flight?** (14 CFR 91.111)

   No person may operate an aircraft, carrying passengers for hire, in formation flight.

39. **Can a commercial pilot carry passengers in a restricted, limited, or experimental category aircraft?** (14 CFR 91.313, 91.315, 91.317, and 91.319)

   No person may operate a restricted, limited, or experimental category aircraft carrying persons or property for hire.

40. **When may a commercial pilot log flight time as second-in-command time?** (14 CFR 61.51)

   According to 14 CFR §61.51, a pilot may log second-in-command time only for that flight time during which that person:

   a. Is qualified according to the second-in-command requirements of 14 CFR §61.55, and occupies a crewmember station in an aircraft that requires more than one pilot by the aircraft's type certificate; or

b. Holds the appropriate category, class, and instrument rating (if an instrument rating is required for the flight) for the aircraft being flown, and more than one pilot is required under the type certification of the aircraft or the regulations under which the flight is being conducted.

Operational limitations such as an operation requiring a two-person crew per an operator certificate as issued by the FAA in a Part 135 operation would be an example of an instance where an aircraft may not require two crew per the aircraft's type certificate, but the regulations under which the flight is conducted could require two crew members.

41. **While you are performing a preflight inspection on your aircraft, an Inspector from the FAA introduces herself and says she wants to conduct a ramp inspection. What documents are you required to show the inspector?** (14 CFR 61.3)

Each person who holds an airman certificate, medical certificate, authorization, or license required by Part 61 must present it and their photo identification for inspection upon a request from the Administrator; an authorized NTSB representative; any federal, state, or local law enforcement officer; or an authorized representative of the TSA.

42. **Can an individual who holds a Commercial Pilot Certificate fly under 14 CFR Part 91 for an owner of an aircraft as a commercial pilot?** (14 CFR 91.147)

Yes, as long as the owner does not receive compensation for the transportation of passengers or property on any of the flights. Although the owner delegates functions of operational control to the commercial pilot, the owner still has full legal responsibility for the pilot's actions. This would constitute a "private carriage" flight and the pilot would be allowed to fly it as a commercial pilot.

43. What compliance in addition to a Commercial Pilot Certificate must a pilot ensure is in place before offering commercial air tour flights in a local area?
(14 CFR 91.147)

A pilot who wants to offer commercial air tour operations (scenic tours), as allowed by 14 CFR §91.147 within a 25 nautical mile radius, must additionally apply for and receive a Letter of Authorization from the responsible FAA Flight Standards office and must register and implement a drug and alcohol testing program.

44. You hold a Commercial Pilot Certificate and also own an aircraft. Can you rent or lease your aircraft out to friends and then have them employ you as their pilot to fly them to their destinations? Explain.

Generally, a pilot who provides a "package" of aircraft and pilot services must have an operator certificate to conduct these operations. As you are in operational control of the aircraft and are providing it for compensation or hire, it is considered holding out for compensation. In this case, the aircraft and the pilot would both be considered to be acting "commercially" and would typically require an operating certificate.

45. Can a Commercial Pilot Certificate holder be employed by a 14 CFR Part 121 certificate holder (an airline)?
(14 CFR 121.436)

The FAA regulations require that no certificate holder may use nor may any pilot act as pilot-in-command of an aircraft (or as second in command of an aircraft in a flag or supplemental operation that requires three or more pilots) unless the pilot holds an Airline Transport Pilot Certificate. This could be a full ATP or a Restricted ATP Certificate, but a pilot would not be allowed to act as a crewmember in a Part 121 operated flight on a Commercial Pilot Certificate.

B. Currency Requirements

1. What are the requirements to remain current as a commercial pilot? (14 CFR 61.56, 61.57)

a. Within the preceding 24 months, the pilot must have accomplished a flight review given in an aircraft for which that pilot is rated by an authorized instructor and received a logbook endorsement certifying that the person has satisfactorily completed the review.

b. To carry passengers, a pilot must have made, within the preceding 90 days:

- Three takeoffs and landings as the sole manipulator of flight controls of an aircraft of the same category and class and, if a type rating is required, of the same type.

- If the aircraft is a tailwheel airplane, the landings must have been made to a full stop in a tailwheel airplane.

- If operations are to be conducted during the period beginning 1 hour after sunset and ending 1 hour before sunrise, with passengers on board, the PIC must have made at least three takeoffs and three landings to a full stop during that period in an aircraft of the same category, class, and type (if a type is required) of aircraft to be used.

Exam Tip: Many examiners will ask you to apply currency requirements to switching makes and models of aircraft. For example, they might ask, "If you did your takeoffs and landings in a DA40, would you be current to take passengers in a Piper Cherokee?" Many applicants confuse make and model of aircraft with "type" as applied to requiring a type rating. The examiner may also follow this with questions regarding "proficiency" in a particular make and model of aircraft and personal minimums.

Note: Takeoffs and landings required by this regulation may be accomplished in a flight simulator or flight training device that is approved by the Administrator and used in accordance with an approved course conducted by a certificated training center. Exceptions exist for the recent flight experience requirements for pilots employed by a Part 119 certificate holder authorized to conduct operations under Parts 125, 121, and 135. See §§125.281 and 125.285, 121.436 and 121.439, and 135.243 and 135.247.

(continued)

Exam Tip: The evaluator may ask you to demonstrate that you're current and eligible to take the practical test. When preparing for your practical test, verify that you have the required hours and that you're current, and don't forget to double-check all of your endorsements. Make sure that you have totaled all of the logbook columns and that the entries make sense.

2. **Is a commercial pilot required to log all flight time?** (14 CFR 61.51)

Not all flight time is required to be logged. A pilot needs only to document and record aeronautical experience required for meeting the recent flight experience requirements of Part 61. This must be done in a manner acceptable to the FAA Administrator, as needed to document the training and aeronautical experience used to meet the requirements for a certificate, rating, or flight review of Part 61. A pilot may elect to forgo logging of any time not required to meet these experience or currency documentation requirements.

3. **When logging flight time in your logbook, what minimum information is required for each entry?** (14 CFR 61.51)

Each person must enter the following information for each flight or lesson logged:

a. *General*—date; total flight time or lesson time; location where the aircraft departed and arrived, or for lessons in a flight simulator or flight training device, the location where the lesson occurred.

b. *Type of pilot experience or training*—solo; pilot-in-command; second-in-command; flight and ground training received from an authorized instructor; training received in a flight simulator, flight training device, or aviation training device from an authorized instructor.

c. *Conditions of flight*—day or night; actual instrument; simulated instrument conditions in flight, a flight simulator, flight training device, or aviation training device.

4. As a commercial pilot, you obtain a job flying freight at night. Does your night currency count towards your currency to carry passengers during the day? (14 CFR 61.57)

Yes, provided that the landings at night were accomplished (within the preceding 90 days) in the same category, class and type (if a type rating is required) of the aircraft you will fly during the day.

5. Explain the difference between being current and being proficient. (FAA-H-8083-2, FAA-P-8740-36)

Being current means that a pilot has accomplished the minimum FAA regulatory requirements within a specific time period to exercise the privileges of their certificate. It means that the pilot is legal to make a flight, but it does not necessarily mean that the pilot is proficient or competent to make that flight.

Proficient could be viewed as a way of measuring the health of the skills that would be required to complete an intended flight. This might go well beyond the basic regulatory requirements that must be met to be "current" for a flight operation. It would include consideration of the degree of competence or skill, knowledge, and judgment required to safely complete an intended flight. Proficient might be a consideration that changes for different types of operations and recency of experience for a pilot.

6. How will establishing a personal minimums checklist reduce risk? (FAA-H-8083-25)

Professional pilots live by the numbers, and so should you. Pre-established hard numbers can make it a lot easier to make a smart go/no-go or divert decision than does a vague sense that you can probably deal with the conditions you face at any given time. In addition, a written set of personal minimums can make it easier to explain tough decisions to passengers who are, after all, trusting their lives to your aeronautical skill and judgment.

Exam Tip: The evaluator will ask you if you have established your own personal minimums. Prior to the checkride, complete a personal minimums worksheet if you have not already done so. Also, at some point during the test, the evaluator may present you with a scenario to determine if you will actually adhere to your personal minimums, so be prepared. For a copy of the FAA's "Personal Minimums Worksheet," see faasafety.gov.

7. **How can using a flight risk assessment tool (FRAT) help pilots better determine risk factors relating to their proficiency and the conditions of an intended flight?** (go.usa.gov/xkhJK, FAA FRAT)

   Although designs can vary, flight risk assessment tools (FRATs) allow a pilot to evaluate a series of questions including both their personal experience and the conditions related to an intended flight. In response to the questions, a pilot can more fully evaluate questions related to the PAVE model (Pilot, Aircraft, enVironment, and External pressures) to evaluate a total risk score as calculated. This can help a pilot become more aware of total risk for an intended flight and allow mitigation or elimination of risk factors.

8. **How can flying an unfamiliar aircraft or an aircraft with unfamiliar avionics or flight display systems increase the total risk of a flight?** (FAA-H-8083-25, AC 90-109)

   Pilot familiarity with all equipment is critical in optimizing both safety and efficiency. If a pilot is unfamiliar with any aircraft systems, this will add to workload and may contribute to a loss of situational awareness. This level of proficiency is critical and should be looked upon as a requirement, not unlike carrying an adequate supply of fuel. As a result, pilots should consider unfamiliarity with the aircraft and its systems a hazard with high risk potential. Discipline is key to success.

9. **You are currently en route to your destination and the sun has set. When can you begin logging flight time as night flight time?** (14 CFR Part 1)

   Night is defined as the time between the end of evening civil twilight and the beginning of morning civil twilight, as published in the Air Almanac and converted to local time. All flight time that occurs during this period of time is considered night flight time.

10. **What are the minimum currency requirements for a commercial pilot carrying passengers and flying under IFR?** (14 CFR 61.57)

   For a pilot to fly with passengers under IFR conditions, the pilot must meet the currency requirements of 14 CFR §61.56 and §61.57. In a general sense, the pilot must have had a flight review within the preceding 24 calendar months; be current for passenger carriage in the category, class, and type (if a type rating is required) of aircraft to be operated for day or night currency with more than three takeoffs and landings conducted in the preceding 90 days; and have completed at least six instrument approaches, tracking and navigating, and a hold or completed an instrument proficiency check within the preceding six calendar months.

11. If a pilot has accomplished a proficiency check or added a rating to their pilot certificate within the preceding 24 months, is the pilot still required to accomplish a flight review? (14 CFR 61.56)

If a pilot completes the addition of a pilot certificate or rating, it may be used to meet flight review requirements in the United States, provided it meets the requirements set forth in 14 CFR §61.56 (more than 1 hour of ground and 1 hour of flight time).

If a pilot adds a new pilot certificate or rating during the 24-month period, the flight review requirements for the new certificate or rating can also satisfy the flight review requirement for all other certificates held by the pilot.

12. The ratings on your Commercial Pilot Certificate indicate Airplane, Single-Engine, and Multi-Engine Land. After a quick review of your logbook, you determine that you're current to carry passengers in a multi-engine airplane. Are you also current to carry passengers in a single-engine airplane? (14 CFR 61.57)

No. Currency requirements under 14 CFR §61.57 require the pilot to conduct takeoffs and landings in an aircraft of the same category, class, and type (if a type rating is required). Since a multi-engine aircraft is a different class than a single-engine aircraft, the takeoffs and landings would not result in the pilot being current to take passengers in a single-engine aircraft.

C. Medical Certificates

1. What regulations apply to medical certification?

14 CFR Part 67, Medical Standards and Certification.

2. What class of medical certificate is required to exercise the privileges of a Commercial Pilot Certlficate? (14 CFR 61.23)

A pilot is required to have a valid and current First or Second Class Medical Certificate issued by the FAA to exercise the privileges of a Commercial Pilot Certificate. While a pilot may operate as a private, sport, or recreational pilot while the holder of a Commercial Pilot Certificate using BasicMed or a Third Class Medical Certificate, they may not exercise commercial pilot privileges unless their First or Second Class Medical is current.

3. What is the duration of a Second Class Medical Certificate for operations requiring a Commercial Pilot Certificate? (14 CFR 61.23)

Second class privileges of a Second Class Medical Certificate expire at the end of the last day of the 12th month after the month of the date of examination shown on the medical certificate.

4. Where can you find a list of the medical conditions that would disqualify you from obtaining or holding a medical certificate? (14 CFR Part 67)

The standards for medical certification are contained in Part 67. There are 15 conditions that are considered disqualifying by history of clinical diagnosis.

5. As a flight crewmember, you discover you have high blood pressure. You are in possession of a current medical certificate. Can you continue to exercise the privileges of your certificate? (14 CFR 61.53)

No; Regulations prohibit a pilot from exercising the privileges of a medical certificate while the pilot has a known medical condition that would make the issuance of that medical certificate invalid. A pilot who develops a medical condition that puts their ability to meet medical certificate requirements in question should contact an Aviation Medical Examiner for further information or review.

6. **Are flight crew members allowed to use any medications while performing their required duties?** (14 CFR 61.53, FAA: Pilots and Medication, FAA AME)

The regulations prohibit pilots from performing crewmember duties while taking medication or receiving other treatment for a medical condition that results in the person being unable to meet the requirements for the medical certificate necessary for the pilot operation. A pilot is recommended to review the FAA's approved medications list and suggested wait times for any medication they may take prior to making a flight while taking any medication. If in question, a pilot is recommended to contact an Aviation Medical Examiner (AME) for further advice.

7. **Can a pilot exercise Commercial Pilot Certificate privileges if they are currently complying with medical requirements using BasicMed?** (AC 68-1)

The FAA indicates that as a pilot, "you may not fly for compensation or hire" when operating under BasicMed.

Airworthiness
Requirements

2

A. Aircraft Certificates and Documents

1. **What documents are required on board an aircraft prior to flight?** (14 CFR 91.203, 91.9)

Supplements (14 CFR §91.9)

Placards (14 CFR §91.9)

Airworthiness Certificate (14 CFR §91.203)

Registration Certificate (14 CFR §91.203)

Radio Station License—if operating outside of U.S.; FCC regulation (47 CFR §87.18)

Operating limitations—AFM/POH and supplements, placards, markings (14 CFR §91.9)

Weight and balance data—current (14 CFR §23.2620)

Exam Tip: During the practical test, your evaluator may wish to examine the various required aircraft documents (SPARROW) during the preflight inspection, as well as the currency of any aeronautical charts, EFB data, etc., on board the aircraft. Prior to the test, verify that all of the necessary aircraft documentation, manuals, placards, onboard databases, charts, etc., are current and available.

2. **Are the AFM supplements required to be on board the airplane?** (14 CFR 91.9)

Yes, the airplane flight manual (AFM) supplements are required to be on board the airplane. The AFM is a critical document provided by the aircraft manufacturer, and it contains essential information about the safe operation of the specific aircraft model. The AFM supplements, also known as "supplemental manuals" or "supplemental type certificates (STC)," provide additional information that supplements the content of the main AFM.

14 CFR §91.9 states that each person operating an aircraft must have the appropriate AFM, approved manual material, markings, and placards on board the aircraft. This includes any required AFM supplements that apply to that particular aircraft. The presence of these documents is necessary to ensure that the pilot and the crew have access to all the necessary information for safe and compliant flight operations.

Some common examples of AFM supplements or STCs include those related to avionics upgrades, modifications, or changes to the aircraft's operating limitations. These supplements often provide specific operating procedures, performance data, and limitations that apply to the aircraft after the modification or alteration.

Before each flight, pilots should ensure that the aircraft is equipped with the required documents, including the AFM and any relevant supplements, to comply with regulatory requirements and promote safe and efficient flight operations. Additionally, it is essential to keep these documents up to date and replace them as necessary to ensure the information provided remains current and accurate.

3. What is an airworthiness certificate? (FAA-H-8083-25)

An airworthiness certificate is issued by the FAA to all aircraft that have been proven to meet the minimum requirements of Part 21 and that are in condition for safe operation. Under any circumstances, the aircraft must meet the requirements of the original type certificate or it is no longer airworthy. Airworthiness certificates come in two different classifications: standard airworthiness and special airworthiness.

4. The two most common categories under which an aircraft airworthiness certificate is issued to an aircraft are Normal and Utility. What does each mean?

a. *Normal category*—Aircraft structure capable of withstanding a load factor of 3.8 Gs without structural failure. Applicable to aircraft intended for non-aerobatic operation.

b. *Utility category*—Aircraft structure must be capable of withstanding a load factor of 4.4 Gs. This would usually permit limited aerobatics, including spins (if approved for the aircraft).

Note: Some aircraft have operating limitations listed at varying weight levels for each category of operation.

5. Does an airworthiness certificate have an expiration date? (FAA-H-8083-25)

No. A standard airworthiness certificate remains valid for as long as the aircraft meets its approved type design, is in a condition for safe operation, and the maintenance, preventative maintenance, and alterations are performed in accordance with Parts 21, 43, and 91.

6. Where must the airworthiness certificate be located?
(14 CFR 91.203, FAA-H-8083-19)

The airworthiness certificate must be displayed in the cabin or at the cockpit entrance so that it is legible and visible to passengers or crew.

7. For an aircraft to be considered airworthy, what two conditions must be met? (14 CFR 3.5, FAA-H-8083-19)

a. The aircraft must conform to its type design (type certificate). Conformity to type design is attained when the required and proper components are installed to be consistent with the drawings, specifications, and other data that are part of the type certificate. Conformity includes applicable STCs and field-approval alterations.

b. The aircraft must be in a condition for safe operation, referring to the condition of the aircraft with relation to wear and deterioration. For an aircraft to be operated with inoperative equipment, it must be permitted in accordance with an approved minimum equipment list, kinds of operation list, or have been deemed airworthy and returned to service by an FAA-approved maintenance provider.

8. Explain how a pilot determines if an aircraft conforms to its approved type design and is in a condition for safe operation. (14 CFR Parts 21, 43 and 91)

a. To determine that the aircraft conforms to its type design, a pilot must determine that the maintenance, preventive maintenance, and alterations have been performed in accordance with Parts 21, 43, and 91 and that the aircraft is registered in the United States. The pilot does this by ensuring that all required inspections, maintenance, preventive maintenance, repairs, and alterations have been appropriately documented in the aircraft's maintenance records. If any inoperative equipment is present, it must have been appropriately returned to service.

b. To determine that the aircraft is in condition for safe operation, the pilot conducts a thorough preflight inspection of the aircraft for wear and deterioration, structural damage, fluid leaks, tire wear, inoperative instruments and equipment, etc. If an unsafe condition exists or inoperative instruments or equipment are found, the pilot uses the guidance in 14 CFR §91.213 for handling the inoperative equipment.

9. Who is responsible for ensuring that an aircraft is maintained in an airworthy condition? (14 CFR 91.403)

The owner or operator of an aircraft is primarily responsible for maintaining an aircraft in an airworthy condition. The pilot-in-command is responsible for verifying that this has been completed prior to a flight.

10. What are airworthiness directives? (FAA-H-8083-25)

An airworthiness directive (AD) is the medium the FAA uses to notify aircraft owners and other potentially interested persons of unsafe conditions that may exist because of design defects, maintenance, or other causes, and to specify the conditions under which the product may continue to be operated. Airworthiness directives are regulatory in nature, and compliance is mandatory. It is the aircraft owner's or operator's responsibility to ensure compliance with all pertinent ADs. Airworthiness directives may be found on the FAA's website at www.faa.gov/regulations_ policies/airworthiness_directives and drs.faa.gov.

11. What are the three types of airworthiness directives issued by the FAA? (AC 39-7)

The FAA issues three types of ADs: (1) notice of proposed rulemaking (NPRM), followed by a final rule; (2) final rule; request for comments; and (3) emergency ADs.

12. When are Emergency ADs issued? (FAA-H-8083-19)

An Emergency AD is issued when an unsafe condition exists that requires immediate action by an owner/operator. The intent of an Emergency AD is to rapidly correct an urgent safety-of-flight situation. All known owners and operators of affected U.S.-registered aircraft or those aircraft that are known to have an affected product installed will be sent a copy of an Emergency AD.

Exam Tip: ADs and Recurring ADs—be capable of finding and explaining the status of all ADs and recurring ADs that exist for your aircraft. Locate and tab prior to the practical test.

13. **While reviewing the aircraft logbooks, you discover that your aircraft is not in compliance with an AD's specified time or date. Are you allowed to continue to operate that aircraft until the next required maintenance inspection? Do the regulations allow any kind of buffer?** (AC 39-7)

    The belief that AD compliance is only required at the time of a required inspection (e.g., at a 100-hour or annual inspection) is not correct. The required compliance time/date is specified in each AD, and no person may operate the affected product after expiration of that stated compliance time without an Alternative Method of Compliance (AMOC) approval for a change in compliance time. While a recurring AD due time or hours may be reset by the maintenance provider during an annual or 100-hour inspection, it is not permitted to delay such an AD compliance requirement until such an inspection is completed. The specific requirements of the AD must be complied with. In some cases, short intervals of 50 or even 25 hours between compliance inspections or actions may be required for recurring ADs.

14. **What are Special Airworthiness Information Bulletins? Are they regulatory?**

    A Special Airworthiness Information Bulletin (SAIB) is an information tool that alerts, educates, and makes recommendations to the aviation community. An SAIB contains non-regulatory information and guidance that does not meet the criteria for an AD. Guidance on when to use an SAIB and how to develop and issue an SAIB is provided in FAA Order 8110.100. Additional information can be found at drs.faa.gov.

15. **What is a *type certificate data sheet*?** (FAA-H-8083-30)

    The FAA issues a type certificate when a new aircraft, engine, propeller, etc., is found to meet safety standards set forth by the FAA. The type certificate data sheet (TCDS) lists the specifications, conditions, and limitations under which airworthiness requirements were met for the specified product, such as engine make and model, fuel type, engine limits, airspeed limits, maximum weight, minimum crew, etc. Information on the TCDS by make and model can be found on the FAA website at drs.faa.gov.

16. What is a *supplemental type certificate* (STC)?
(FAA-H-8083-3, FAA-H-8083-30, AC 21-40)

An STC is the FAA's approval of a major change in the type design of a previously approved type-certificated product. The certificate authorizes an alteration to an airframe, engine, or component that has been granted an approved type certificate. Sometimes alterations are made that are not specified or authorized in the TCDS. When that condition exists, an STC will be issued. STCs are considered a part of the permanent records of an aircraft and should be maintained as part of that aircraft's logs.

17. What is an aircraft registration certificate?
(FAA-H-8083-25)

Before an aircraft can be flown legally, it must be registered with the FAA Aircraft Registry. The Certificate of Aircraft Registration, which is issued to the owner as evidence of the registration, must be carried in the aircraft at all times.

18. Does an aircraft's registration certificate have an expiration date? (14 CFR 47.31, 47.40)

Yes. A Certificate of Aircraft Registration issued in accordance with 14 CFR §47.31 expires seven years after the last day of the month in which it was issued. A temporary Certification of Registration is valid for no more than 90 days after the date the applicant signs the application.

19. Where can you find information on the placards and marking information required to be in the airplane?
(FAA-H-8083-25, 14 CFR 91.9, 14 CFR 23.1541)

The principal source of information for identifying the required airplane flight manuals, approved manual materials, markings, and placards is the TCDS or aircraft specification issued for each airplane eligible for an airworthiness certificate. The required placards are also reproduced in the "Limitations" section of the AFM or as directed by an AD. Additional placards and marking requirements may also be found in supplemental documents or aircraft supplemental type certificate authorizations.

20. Is an airplane flight manual (AFM) or pilot's operating handbook (POH) required to be on board all aircraft? (14 CFR 91.9)

14 CFR §91.9 requires that all U.S.-registered aircraft have available in the aircraft a current, approved AFM, or if applicable, any combination of approved manual materials, markings, and placards. Generally, all aircraft manufactured after March 1, 1979, must have an AFM. For airplanes type-certificated at gross weights of 6,000 pounds or under which were not required to have an AFM, the required information may be an AFM or any combination of approved manual material, markings, and placards. These materials must be current and available in the airplane during operation.

B. Aircraft Maintenance Requirements

1. What are the required tests and inspections to be performed on an aircraft? Include inspections for IFR. (14 CFR 91.171, 91.207, 91.403, 91.409, 91.411, 91.413, 91.417)

Annual inspection within the preceding 12 calendar months (14 CFR §91.409)

Airworthiness directives and life-limited parts complied with as required (14 CFR §§91.403, 91.417)

VOR equipment check every 30 days (for IFR ops) (14 CFR §91.171)

100-hour inspection, if used for hire or flight instruction in aircraft CFI provides (14 CFR §91.409)

Altimeter, altitude reporting equipment, and static pressure systems tested and inspected (for IFR ops) every 24 calendar months (14 CFR §91.411)

Transponder tests and inspections, every 24 calendar months (14 CFR §91.413)

Emergency locator transmitter, operation and battery condition (1 cumulative hour use or 50% useful life) inspected every 12 calendar months (14 CFR §91.207)

Exam Tip: Be prepared to locate all of the required inspections, ADs, life-limited parts, etc., in the aircraft and engine logbooks and be able to determine when the next inspections are due. Create an aircraft status sheet that indicates the status of all required inspections, ADs, life-limited parts, etc., and/or use post-it notes to tab the specific pages in the aircraft and engine logbooks. Write the due date of the next inspection on the post-it note. All maintenance records should be thoroughly inspected well before your checkride, and checked again the day of your exam, to confirm the aircraft is in an airworthy condition to fly.

2. What is an annual inspection and which aircraft are required to have annual inspections? (FAA-H-8083-25)

An annual inspection is a complete inspection of an aircraft and engine, required by the regulations, and is required to be completed every 12 calendar months on all certificated aircraft. It must be completed by an FAA Inspection Authorized (IA) A&P mechanic.

3. What aircraft are required to have 100-hour inspections? (FAA-H-8083-25, 14 CFR 91.409)

a. All aircraft under 12,500 pounds (except turbojet/turbopropeller-powered multi-engine airplanes and turbine-powered rotorcraft) used to carry passengers for hire.

b. Aircraft used for flight instruction for hire.

4. If an aircraft is operated for hire, is it required to have a 100-hour inspection as well as an annual inspection? (14 CFR 91.409)

Yes; if an aircraft is operated for hire, it must have a 100-hour inspection as well as an annual inspection when due. If not operated for hire, it must have an annual inspection only.

5. **A 100-hour inspection was due at 3302.5 hours. The 100-hour inspection was actually done at 3309.5 hours. When is the next 100-hour inspection due?** (FAA-H-8083-25)

   The 100-hour inspection is due every 100 hours of flight time for certain aircraft used for hire or flight instruction. It must be conducted within 10 hours before or after the 100-hour mark.

   In this case, the 100-hour inspection was due at 3302.5 hours, and it was actually done at 3309.5 hours. Completion of the 100-hour inspection after it was due does not extend the date for the next required inspection beyond when it would have originally been due; therefore, the next inspection will still be due 100 hours from when the previous inspection was due, unless the inspection was signed off as an annual inspection by an inspection authorized mechanic.

   Therefore, the next 100-hour inspection will be due at 3302.5 + 100 = 3402.5 hours.

6. **If an aircraft has been on a schedule of inspection every 100 hours, under what condition may it continue to operate beyond the 100 hours without a new inspection?** (14 CFR 91.409)

   The 100-hour limitation may be exceeded by not more than 10 hours while en route to a place where the inspection can be done. The excess time used to reach a place where the inspection can be done must be included in computing the next 100 hours of time in service.

7. **If the annual inspection date has passed, can an aircraft be operated to a location where the inspection can be performed?** (FAA-H-8083-25)

   An aircraft overdue for an annual inspection may be operated under a special flight permit issued by the FAA for the purpose of flying the aircraft to a location where the annual inspection can be performed. However, all applicable ADs that are due must be complied with before the flight.

8. **If an aircraft is being maintained under an FAA-accepted and approved progressive maintenance inspection program, must the aircraft's owner additionally complete annual inspections?** (14 CFR 91.409)

A progressive inspection schedule must ensure that the aircraft, at all times, will be in an airworthy condition and will conform to all applicable FAA aircraft specifications, type certificate data sheets, airworthiness directives, and other approved data. As long as this is maintained, it may be allowed in lieu of 100-hour and annual inspection requirements. Should the owner or operator discontinue compliance with an approved program, they shall immediately notify the responsible Flight Standards office and an annual inspection will be due within 12 calendar months after the last complete inspection of the aircraft under the progressive inspection plan was completed.

9. **While inspecting the engine logbook of the aircraft you are planning to fly, you notice that the engine has exceeded its TBO. Is it legal to fly this aircraft?** (AC 20-105)

Time between overhaul (TBO) is computed by the engine manufacturer and is a reliable estimate of the number of hours the engine could perform reliably within the established engine parameters and still not exceed the service wear limits for overhaul for major component parts such as the crankshaft, cam shaft, cylinders, connecting rods, and pistons. TBO times are make and model specific and the recommended overhaul times are usually identified in the engine manufacturer's Service Bulletin or Letter. For 14 CFR part 91 operations compliance to the TBO time is not a mandatory maintenance requirement, however for engines in 14 CFR Part 121 or 135 service, TBO compliance is mandatory.

10. If a pilot finds that their aircraft has inoperative equipment that requires a special flight permit (ferry permit) to be issued to fly the aircraft to where maintenance can be conducted, may the pilot allow passengers to accompany them on the flight? (14 CFR 21.197; drs.faa.gov)

In addition to issuing the special flight permit, the FAA office may include other limitations for the flight to be conducted and additional requirements or limitations for flight crew. Typically, this will limit the operation to "required flight crew only" to conduct the flight safely. This would mean in most cases that a special flight permit would not allow a pilot to carry passengers on a flight.

11. What are special flight permits, and when are they necessary? (14 CFR 91.213, 14 CFR 21.197)

A special flight permit may be issued for an aircraft that may not currently meet applicable airworthiness requirements but is capable of safe flight. These permits are typically issued for the following purposes:

a. Flying an aircraft to a base where repairs, alterations or maintenance are to be performed, or to a point of storage.

b. Delivering or exporting an aircraft.

c. Production flight testing new-production aircraft.

d. Evacuating aircraft from areas of impending danger.

e. Conducting customer demonstration flights in new-production aircraft that have satisfactorily completed production flight tests.

12. How are special flight permits obtained? (FAA-H-8083-25)

If a special flight permit is needed, assistance and the necessary forms may be obtained from the local FSDO or Designated Airworthiness Representative (DAR).

13. **After aircraft inspections have been made and defects have been repaired, who is responsible for determining that the aircraft is in an airworthy condition?** (14 CFR 91.7)

    The PIC of a civil aircraft is responsible for determining whether that aircraft is in a condition for safe flight. The PIC shall discontinue the flight when unairworthy, mechanical, electrical, or structural conditions occur.

14. **What regulations apply concerning the operation of an aircraft that has had alterations or repairs that may substantially affect its operation in flight?** (14 CFR 91.407)

    No person may operate or carry passengers in any aircraft that has undergone maintenance, preventative maintenance, rebuilding, or alteration that may have appreciably changed its flight characteristics or substantially affected its operation in flight until an appropriately rated pilot with at least a Private Pilot Certificate

    a. Flies the aircraft;

    b. Makes an operational check of the maintenance performed or alteration made; and

    c. Logs the flight in the aircraft records.

15. **What is a *kinds of operations equipment list* (KOEL)?** (14 CFR 23.1583, AC 23-8)

    A KOEL identifies the systems and equipment upon which type certification for each kind of operation was predicated (i.e., day or night VFR, day or night IFR, icing conditions) and which must be installed and operable for the particular kind of operation indicated. The KOEL is located in the Limitations section of the FAA-approved AFM. A KOEL is typically applicable to a specific make and model of aircraft and therefore differs from a MEL, which is applicable only to a specific make and model aircraft by serial and registration numbers (e.g., BE-200, N12345).

16. What is a *minimum equipment list* (MEL)?
(FAA-H-8083-25)

An MEL is a precise listing of instruments, equipment and procedures that allows an aircraft to be operated under specific conditions with inoperative equipment. An MEL is the specific inoperative equipment document for a particular make and model aircraft by serial and registration numbers (e.g., BE-200, N12345). An FAA-approved MEL includes only those items of equipment that the FAA deems may be inoperative and still maintain an acceptable level of safety with appropriate conditions and limitations. A pilot should consider a MEL a "permission to operate with inoperative" list. Any items outside of this list and outside the conditions set forth should be considered required to be operational.

Note: Do not confuse an MEL with the aircraft's equipment list. They are not the same.

17. Can a pilot legally conduct flight operations with known inoperative equipment on board? (14 CFR 91.213)

Yes, under specific conditions. 14 CFR Part 91 describes acceptable methods for the operation of an aircraft with certain inoperative instruments and equipment that are not essential for safe flight. These acceptable methods are:

a. Operation of an aircraft with a minimum equipment list (MEL), as authorized by 14 CFR §91.213(a), or

b. Operation of an aircraft without a MEL under 14 CFR §91.213(d)

c. Operation of an aircraft within allowed inoperative equipment scenarios as allowed by a manufacturer's provided kinds of operation equipment list (KOEL).

Exam Tip: Know this regulation well; unfamiliarity with 14 CFR §91.213 is a common weakness of applicants at all levels. You will need to demonstrate that you know this regulation and how to apply it. A best way to think about inoperative equipment is to operate as if an MEL or KOEL is a "permission to operate with inoperative" allowance if something inoperative is found. In absence of this, an aircraft with inoperative equipment will typically require a maintenance provider to determine whether the aircraft can be returned to airworthiness and continued operation is allowed.

18. **What limitations apply to aircraft operations conducted using the deferral provision of 14 CFR §91.213(d)?** (FAA-H-8083-25)

When inoperative equipment is found during preflight or prior to departure, the decision should be to cancel the flight, obtain maintenance prior to flight, or defer the item or equipment. Maintenance deferrals are not used for inflight discrepancies. The manufacturer's AFM/POH procedures are to be used in those situations.

19. **During the preflight inspection in an aircraft that doesn't have a MEL, the pilot notices that an instrument or equipment item is Inoperative. Describe how the pilot will determine If the aircraft is still airworthy for flight.** (14 CFR 91.213(d), FAA-H-8083-25)

The pilot in this case will need to evaluate if the aircraft is able to be operated with the inoperative equipment. This will be done in the following order:

a. Is the inoperative equipment required for the day, night, or IFR flight requirements by regulation?

b. Is inoperative equipment allowed to be inoperative by any MEL or KOEL document that allows the pilot to operate in the specific conditions while inoperative?

c. Is the inoperative equipment required to be operational by an AD?

If the answer to any of items a, b, or c above is "yes," the aircraft is not considered airworthy and maintenance is required before it can be flown.

d. Is the equipment required according to the aircraft's type certificate data sheet?

e. Is the equipment such that it was installed in the equipment list as delivered from the manufacturer?

(continued)

f. Is the equipment installed in accordance with a supplemental type certificate (STC)?

If the answer to any of items d, e, or f is "yes," a maintenance provider will need to address the concern and determine if the aircraft can be made airworthy. With this, a logbook entry would be required. If the equipment will not be fixed, the equipment will need to be disabled, placarded as "inoperative," and a logbook entry made.

g. Is the inoperative equipment able to be fixed by the pilot?

If the answer to item g is "yes," then the inoperative equipment is something that falls under the preventive maintenance allowances for a pilot to address, and the pilot may fix it and return the aircraft to an airworthy condition after properly logging the fix in the maintenance logs.

In a general sense, if some equipment is inoperative, and an MEL or KOEL does not give the pilot a path to operate with such equipment inoperative, it will require maintenance and documentation before the aircraft will be allowed to be operated.

20. For an aircraft with an approved MEL, explain the decision sequence a pilot would use after discovering the position lights are inoperative. (FAA-H-8083-25)

With an approved MEL, if the position lights were discovered inoperative prior to a daytime flight, the pilot would make an entry in the maintenance record or discrepancy record provided for that purpose. The item is then either repaired or deferred in accordance with the MEL. Upon confirming that daytime flight with inoperative position lights is acceptable in accordance with the provisions of the MEL, the pilot would leave the position lights switch OFF, open the circuit breaker (or whatever action is called for in the procedures document), and placard the position light switch as INOPERATIVE.

21. Explain the limitations that apply to aircraft operations being conducted using an MEL. (FAA-H-8083-25)

The use of an MEL for a small, non-turbine-powered airplane operated under Part 91 allows for the deferral of inoperative items or equipment. The FAA considers an approved MEL to be an STC issued to an aircraft by serial number and registration number. Once an operator requests an MEL, and a Letter of Authorization (LOA) is issued by the FAA, then the MEL becomes mandatory for that aircraft. All maintenance deferrals must be done in accordance with the terms and conditions of the MEL and the operator-generated procedures document.

22. **What types of inoperative equipment may a pilot/operator fix or what maintenance may they perform on an aircraft without an FAA maintenance certificate?** (14 CFR Part 43 Appendix A)

    14 CFR Part 43, Appendix A, Paragraph c, offers a list of preventive maintenance work a pilot/operator may complete on an aircraft. This list includes a range of tasks such as changing a navigation light bulb, charging or changing an aircraft battery, or even changing a tire and completing an oil change. While the pilot still needs to complete a logbook entry when doing this maintenance, these items are available for a pilot to fix if found inoperative or to service if desired.

23. **What instruments does the FAA require by regulation for all aircraft to have operational during VFR day flight operations?** (14 CFR 91.205)

    For VFR flight during the day, the following instruments and equipment are required:

    Anticollision light system—aviation red or white for small airplanes certificated after March 11, 1996

    Tachometer for each engine

    Oil pressure gauge for each engine

    Manifold pressure gauge (for each altitude engine, i.e., turbocharged)

    Altimeter

    Temperature gauge for each liquid-cooled engine

    Oil temperature gauge for each air-cooled engine

    Fuel gauge indicating the quantity in each tank

    Flotation gear—if operated for hire over water beyond power-off gliding distance from shore

    (continued)

Landing gear position indicator, if the airplane has
retractable gear

Airspeed indicator

Magnetic direction indicator

Emergency locator transmitter (if required by 14 CFR §91.207)

Safety belts (and shoulder harnesses for each front seat in aircraft
manufactured after 1978)

24. **Explain how you will deactivate an item or system that
has become inoperative on your airplane. Can you
deactivate any item or system in the airplane? What is
required?** (FAA-H-8083-25)

A pilot may deactivate and make inoperative a piece of equipment
on an aircraft only under certain conditions. First, it must be
allowed to be deactivated under an established and approved MEL
or KOEL.

Outside of that condition, a maintenance provider will need to
conduct and document any work that would result in the disabling
and placarding of any inoperative equipment before the aircraft
could be returned to an airworthy condition.

25. **What instruments does the FAA require by regulation
for all aircraft to have operational during VFR night flight
operations?** (14 CFR 91.205)

For VFR flight at night, all the instruments and equipment for VFR
day flight are required, plus the following:

Fuses—one spare set or three fuses of each kind required
accessible to the pilot in flight

Landing light—if the aircraft is operated for hire

Anticollision light system—approved aviation red or white

Position lights—(navigation lights)

Source of electrical energy—adequate for all installed electrical
and radio equipment

26. Aircraft maintenance records must include what information? (14 CFR 91.417)

Aircraft maintenance records must include a comprehensive set of information to document the maintenance and airworthiness history of the aircraft. These records play a crucial role in ensuring that the aircraft is properly maintained and in compliance with aviation regulations. Here are the key types of information that must be included in aircraft maintenance records:

a. *Aircraft identification*—The records should identify the specific aircraft by its registration number or tail number, make, model, and serial number.

b. *Maintenance and inspection entries*—Detailed records of all maintenance and inspections performed on the aircraft, including the date of the maintenance, the type of work performed, and the name of the person or organization conducting the maintenance.

c. *AD compliance*—Documentation of compliance with all applicable airworthiness directives (ADs) and service bulletins.

d. *Component overhauls and repairs*—Records of major component overhauls, repairs, or replacements, such as engine overhauls, propeller overhauls, and avionics upgrades.

e. *Modifications and alterations*—Records of any modifications or alterations made to the aircraft, including supplemental type certificates (STCs) and field approvals.

f. *Weight and balance information*—Documents related to weight and balance computations and any changes to the aircraft's weight and balance data.

g. *Logbook entries*—The aircraft's logbooks, which include the airframe logbook, engine logbook, and propeller logbook, should contain detailed entries of all maintenance activities and inspections.

h. *Life-limited components*—Records of life-limited components, such as engine components with a specified lifespan, and documentation of compliance with replacement intervals.

i. *Repairs and damage history*—Records of any repairs made to the aircraft due to damage or accidents, including the extent of the damage and the repair work performed.

(continued)

j. *Release to service*—The signature and certificate number of the individual or organization releasing the aircraft to service after maintenance or inspections.

k. *Compliance with service bulletins and service letters*— Documentation of compliance with any non-mandatory manufacturer service bulletins or service letters.

l. *Engine and propeller time*—Accurate records of engine and propeller time since new or since the last overhaul.

Aircraft maintenance records are required to be kept in an organized and easily accessible manner, typically within the aircraft's logbook system. These records serve as a vital historical reference for the aircraft's maintenance and help establish its airworthiness for regulatory compliance and safety purposes. Properly maintained and comprehensive maintenance records contribute to safe flight operations and ensure the aircraft's continued airworthiness.

27. What is the purpose of FAA Form 337? (FAA-H-8083-25)

FAA Form 337, titled "Major Repair and Alteration," is used for the approval and documentation of major repairs or alterations to aircraft in the United States. The purpose of this form is to ensure that significant changes or repairs made to an aircraft are properly evaluated, approved, and recorded by the Federal Aviation Administration (FAA). The FAA requires strict compliance with the regulations and standards to maintain the safety and airworthiness of the aircraft.

Key purposes of FAA Form 337 include:

a. *Approval of major repairs or alterations*—The form is used to seek approval from the FAA for significant modifications or repairs that may affect the aircraft's performance, structure, or systems. These alterations could include changes to the airframe, engine, avionics, electrical systems, and more.

b. *Documentation*—The form serves as a detailed record of the work performed, including the description of the alteration or repair, the method of compliance with the applicable regulations, and the inspection and approval process.

c. *Airworthiness compliance*—By completing FAA Form 337, the person or organization performing the repair or alteration certifies that the work complies with the appropriate FAA regulations and standards. It ensures that the aircraft remains in an airworthy condition.

d. *Accountability and safety*—The form helps maintain accountability for the work done on the aircraft and ensures that any major changes are documented and properly inspected by an authorized individual or entity.

e. *Legal and regulatory compliance*—The completion and submission of FAA Form 337 demonstrates compliance with FAA regulations and guidelines for major repairs and alterations, as outlined in 14 CFR Part 43.

It is crucial for aircraft owners, mechanics, or repair facilities to complete and submit FAA Form 337 whenever a major repair or alteration is performed on the aircraft.

28. **How can you determine if all applicable airworthiness directives have been complied with for your airplane? Where can you find them?** (FAA-H-8083-25, 14 CFR 91.417)

Most maintenance providers provide a list of applicable, complied with, and recurring ADs for a specific aircraft that can be reviewed as a part of the aircraft's maintenance logs. A pilot can also check this list by referencing the FAA's Dynamic Regulatory System website (drs.faa.gov) and looking up the ADs for a specific make and model of aircraft, engine, or other installed components.

29. **If a pilot arrives at an aircraft and finds that its landing light has burned out, may the pilot change that light or must they have a maintenance provider complete this action?** (AC 43-12)

A pilot is allowed to change a landing light in accordance with 14 CFR Part 43, Appendix A. The pilot may change the light but is required to make required maintenance log entries documenting the change before the aircraft is returned to service.

30. **A pilot determines that an airworthiness directive for a seat rail track inspection must be checked every 100 hours. The aircraft has flown 102 hours but is not yet due for its annual inspection. Can the aircraft continue to be operated until the annual inspection or must the aircraft have maintenance prior to that inspection?** (14 CFR 91.403)

    ADs that have specific due times are not allowed to be deferred until a next inspection time. In this case, the pilot would need to have a mechanic conduct the inspection prior to the annual inspection if the pilot desires to continue operating the aircraft.

31. **A pilot finds that an AD inspection is required on the engine's exhaust system every 50 hours. The pilot typically conducts their own oil changes at 50-hour intervals and does so in accordance with allowed preventive maintenance. Can the pilot also complete the AD inspection while doing the oil change, or is a maintenance provider required to complete the AD inspection?** (14 CFR 91.403)

    While a pilot may complete an oil change in accordance with 14 CFR Part 43, Appendix A, the pilot would not be able to complete the AD inspection on the exhaust system. A maintenance provider would be required to complete the AD compliance inspection.

32. **As PIC, you have the responsibility for determining whether your aircraft is in a condition for safe flight. After completing a flight, how can procedures regarding discrepancy records or squawk sheets affect the total risk of a flight?** (FAA Safety)

    Procedures regarding discrepancy records or "squawk sheets" play a crucial role in aviation safety and can significantly impact the total risk of a flight. As the pilot-in-command (PIC), you are responsible for determining whether the aircraft is in a condition for safe flight. Here's how discrepancy records and squawk sheets affect flight risk:

    a. *Safety assessment*—Discrepancy records or squawk sheets document any reported issues or problems with the aircraft. As the PIC, reviewing these records is essential before each flight to assess the aircraft's airworthiness. Ignoring or neglecting reported discrepancies can lead to serious safety issues during flight, potentially endangering passengers and crew.

b. *Aircraft airworthiness*—The presence of unresolved discrepancies on the squawk sheet can indicate that the aircraft may not be in an airworthy condition. If there are outstanding issues that haven't been addressed, it could affect the aircraft's performance, handling, or systems during the flight. This could increase the risk of an incident or accident.

c. *Maintenance follow-up*—The squawk sheet serves as a communication tool between flight crews and maintenance personnel. Properly documenting discrepancies allows maintenance teams to address the reported issues promptly and perform necessary repairs or inspections. Neglecting to report discrepancies may delay necessary maintenance actions, potentially escalating risk.

d. *Flight planning*—Reviewing the squawk sheet before a flight helps the PIC factor in any unresolved issues when planning the flight. This ensures that any limitations or considerations related to the aircraft's condition are accounted for, enhancing overall flight safety.

e. *Legal and regulatory compliance*—Properly documenting discrepancies in the squawk sheet is not only a safety best practice but may also be a regulatory requirement. Failure to report certain issues could lead to non-compliance with aviation regulations, resulting in potential penalties or legal consequences.

f. *Safety culture*—Encouraging a robust safety culture that emphasizes reporting and addressing discrepancies is essential for enhancing flight safety. Open communication and a willingness to address and resolve issues contribute to a safer operating environment.

To mitigate risk, pilots should actively review squawk sheets, encourage reporting of discrepancies, and work collaboratively with maintenance personnel to address and resolve any issues before the next flight. By doing so, pilots contribute to the overall safety and operational efficiency of the aircraft.

Weather
Information

3

A. Weather Theory

1. Most of the Earth's weather occurs in what region of the atmosphere? (FAA-H-8083-28)

Most of the Earth's weather occurs in the troposphere, which begins at the Earth's surface and extends up to approximately 36,000 feet. As the gases in this layer decrease with height, the air becomes thinner and the temperature decreases from about 15°C (59°F) to -56.5°C (-70°F).

2. What are the standard temperature and pressure values for sea level? (FAA-H-8083-28)

15°C (59°F) and 29.92 inHg (1013.2 mb).

3. What are isobars? (FAA-H-8083-28)

An isobar is a line on a weather chart that connects areas of equal or constant barometric pressure.

4. If the isobars are relatively close together on a surface weather chart or a constant pressure chart, what information will this provide? (FAA-H-8083-28)

The spacing of isobars on these charts defines how steep or shallow a pressure gradient is. When isobars are spaced very close together, a steep pressure gradient exists, which indicates higher wind speeds. A shallow pressure gradient (isobars not close together) usually means wind speeds will be lower.

5. What does dew point mean? (FAA-H-8083-28)

Dew point is the temperature to which a sample of air must be cooled to attain the state of saturation.

6. How does fog form? (FAA-H-8083-28)

Fog forms when the temperature and dewpoint of the air become identical (or nearly so). This may occur through cooling of the air to a little beyond its dewpoint (producing radiation fog, advection fog, or upslope fog), or by adding moisture and thereby elevating the dewpoint (producing frontal fog or steam fog).

7. **What factor primarily determines the type and vertical extent of clouds?** (FAA-H-8083-28)

   The stability of the atmosphere.

8. **Explain the difference between a stable atmosphere and an unstable atmosphere. Why is the stability of the atmosphere important?** (FAA-H-8083-25, FAA-H-8083-28)

   The stability of the atmosphere depends on its ability to resist vertical motion. A stable atmosphere makes vertical movement difficult, and small vertical disturbances dampen out and disappear. In an unstable atmosphere, small vertical air movements tend to become larger, resulting in turbulent airflow and convective activity. Instability can lead to significant turbulence, extensive vertical clouds, and severe weather.

9. **How can you determine the stability of the atmosphere?** (FAA-H-8083-28)

   When temperature decreases uniformly and rapidly as you climb (approaching 3°C per 1,000 feet), you have an indication of unstable air. If the temperature remains unchanged or decreases only slightly with altitude, the air tends to be stable. When air near the surface is warm and moist, suspect instability.

10. **List the effects of stable and unstable air on clouds, turbulence, precipitation and visibility.** (FAA-H-8083-28)

	Stable	Unstable
Clouds	Stratiform	Cumuliform
Turbulence	Smooth	Rough
Precipitation	Steady	Showery
Visibility	Fair to Poor	Good

11. **State the general characteristics in regard to the flow of air around high-pressure and low-pressure systems in the Northern Hemisphere.** (FAA-H-8083-28)

    Low pressure—inward, upward, and counterclockwise.

    High pressure—outward, downward, and clockwise.

12. **If your route of flight takes you toward a low-pressure system, in general what kind of weather can you expect? What if you were flying toward a high-pressure system?** (FAA-H-8083-28)

A low-pressure system is characterized by rising air, which is conducive to cloudiness, precipitation and bad weather. A high-pressure system is an area of descending air, which tends to favor dissipation of cloudiness and good weather.

13. **Describe the different types of fronts.** (FAA-H-8083-28)

Cold front—occurs when a mass of cold, dense, and stable air advances and replaces a body of warmer air.

Occluded front—A frontal occlusion occurs when a fast-moving cold front catches up with a slow-moving warm front. The two types are the cold front occlusion and warm front occlusion.

Warm front—The boundary area formed when a warm air mass contacts and flows over a colder air mass.

Stationary front—When the forces of two air masses are relatively equal, the boundary or front that separates them remains stationary and influences the local weather for days. The weather is typically a mixture of both warm and cold fronts.

14. **What are the general characteristics of the weather a pilot would encounter when operating near a cold front? A warm front?** (FAA-H-8083-25)

Cold front—As the front passes, expected weather can include towering cumulus or cumulonimbus, heavy rain accompanied by lightning, thunder and/or hail; tornadoes possible; during passage, poor visibility, winds variable and gusting; temperature/dew point and barometric pressure drop rapidly.

Warm front—As the front passes, expected weather can include stratiform clouds, drizzle, low ceilings and poor visibility; variable winds; rise in temperature.

Note: The weather associated with a front depends on the amount of moisture available, the degree of stability of the air that is forced upward, the slope of the front, the speed of frontal movement, and the upper wind flow.

15. What is a trough? (FAA-H-8083-28)

A trough (also called a trough line) is an elongated area of relatively low atmospheric pressure. At the surface, when air converges into a low, it cannot go outward against the pressure gradient, and it cannot go downward into the ground; it must go upward. Therefore, a low or trough is an area of rising air. Rising air is conducive to cloudiness and precipitation; hence the general association of low pressure and bad weather.

16. What is a ridge? (FAA-H-8083-28)

A ridge (also called a ridge line) is an elongated area of relatively high atmospheric pressure. Air moving out of a high or ridge depletes the quantity of air; therefore, these are areas of descending air. Descending air favors dissipation of cloudiness; hence the association of high pressure and good weather.

17. Define the term *ceiling*. (FAA-H-8083-28)

The term "ceiling" in aviation refers to the height above the ground or water at which the lowest layer of clouds or obscuring phenomena (such as fog or smoke) covers more than half of the sky. It represents the lowest point at which the sky becomes obscured, limiting vertical visibility.

18. If the temperature is +16°C at an elevation of 1,600 feet, and a standard (average) temperature lapse rate exists, what will the approximate freezing level be? (FAA-H-8083-28)

To determine the approximate freezing level, we need to consider the standard temperature lapse rate, which is approximately 2°C per 1,000 feet of altitude gain.

If we were at 1,600 feet MSL at ground level at our airport and the current temperature was 16°C, we could do the following math.

16°C ÷ 2°C per 1,000 feet = 8

8 × 1,000 feet would leave us with an expected altitude of 8,000 feet above ground level (AGL) where we would experience the freezing level.

(continued)

We could then add our current elevation of 1,600 feet MSL to the 8,000 feet AGL number to give us an expected mean sea level (MSL) freezing level.

1,600 + 8,000 = 9,600 MSL freezing level

B. Obtaining Weather Information

1. What service does the FAA provide for pilots to obtain a weather briefing? (AIM 7-1-2)

The FAA provides the Flight Service program which provides weather briefings to pilots through its Flight Service Stations (FSS) by phone 1-800-WX-BRIEF and online (through Leidos Flight Service) at 1800wxbrief.com.

2. What are the two main categories of sources of weather data? (FAA-H-8083-28)

Federal government—the FAA and National Weather Service (NWS) collect weather observations. The NWS analyzes the observations and produces forecasts and the FAA and NWS disseminate observations, analyses, and forecasts through a variety of systems. The Federal Government is the only approval authority for sources of weather observations (e.g., contract towers and airport operators).

Commercial weather information providers—these entities repackage proprietary weather products based on NWS information with formatting and layout modification but make no material changes to the weather information. Other commercial providers produce forecasts, analyses, and other proprietary weather products which may substantially differ from the information contained in NWS products.

3. Does the weather data provided by commercial and/or third-party vendors satisfy the preflight action required by 14 CFR §91.103? (AIM 7-1-3)

Pilots and operators should be aware that weather services provided by entities other than the FAA, NWS, or their contractors may not meet FAA/NWS quality control standards. Operators and pilots contemplating using such services should request and/or review an appropriate description of services and provider disclosure. This should include, but is not limited to, the type of weather product (e.g., current weather or forecast weather), the currency of the product (product issue and valid times), and the relevance of the product. When in doubt, consult with an FAA Flight Service Specialist.

4. What type of weather briefings are available from an FSS briefer? (AIM 7-1-5)

Standard briefing—Request anytime you are planning a flight and you have not received a previous briefing or have not received preliminary information through mass-dissemination media; e.g., TIBS, TWEB, etc.

Abbreviated briefing—Request when you need information to supplement mass-disseminated data, update a previous briefing, or when you need only one or two items.

Outlook briefing—Request whenever your proposed time of departure is six or more hours from the time of the briefing. This is for planning purposes only.

Inflight briefing—Request when needed to update a preflight briefing.

5. What pertinent information should a weather briefing include? (AIM 7-1-5)

a. Adverse conditions.

b. VFR flight not recommended.

c. Synopsis.

d. Current conditions.

e. Enroute forecast.

f. Destination forecast.

g. Winds aloft.

h. Notices to Air Missions (NOTAMs).

i. ATC delay.

j. Pilots may obtain the following from FSS briefers upon request: information on special use airspace (SUA) and SUA-related airspace, including alert areas, MOAs, MTRs (IFR, VFR, VR, and SR training routes), warning areas, and ATC assigned airspace (ATCAA); a review of the printed NOTAM

publication; approximate density altitude data; information on
air traffic services and rules; customs/immigration procedures;
ADIZ rules; search and rescue; GPS RAIM availability for 1
hour before to 1 hour after ETA or a time specified by the pilot;
and other assistance as required.

**6. What is a Flight Information Services–Broadcast
(FIS-B)?** (FAA-H-8083-25, AIM 7-1-9)

Flight Information Services–Broadcast (FIS-B) is a ground
broadcast service provided through the Automatic Dependent
Surveillance–Broadcast (ADS-B) services network over the 978
MHz UAT data link. The FAA FIS-B system provides pilots and
flight crews of properly equipped aircraft with a flight-deck display
of aviation weather and aeronautical information.

**7. Can onboard datalink weather (FIS-B) be useful
in navigating an aircraft safely around an area of
thunderstorms?** (FAA-H-8083-28, AIM 7-1-9)

Weather data linked from a ground weather surveillance radar
system is not real-time information; it displays recent rather than
current conditions. This data is typically updated every 5 minutes,
but can be as much as 15 minutes old by the time it displays in
the cockpit. Therefore, FIS aviation weather products are not
appropriate for tactical avoidance of severe weather such as
negotiating a path through a weather hazard area. The best use
of onboard weather information is to utilize it to make strategic
weather decisions, not tactical ones.

8. What is ATIS? (AIM 4-1-13)

Automatic Terminal Information Service (ATIS) is the continuous
broadcast of recorded noncontrol information in selected high
activity terminal areas. Its purpose is to improve controller
effectiveness and to relieve frequency congestion by automating
the repetitive transmission of essential but routine information. The
information is continuously broadcast over a discrete VHF radio
frequency or the voice portion of a local NAVAID, and updated
upon the receipt of any official hourly and special weather.

9. **What type of information is provided in an ATIS broadcast?** (AIM 4-1-13)

   Information includes the time of the latest weather sequence, ceiling, visibility, obstructions to visibility, temperature, dew point (if available), wind direction (magnetic), and velocity, altimeter, other pertinent remarks, instrument approach and runway in use.

10. **When the ceiling/sky, visibility, and obstructions to vision are omitted in the ATIS, what condition is indicated?** (AIM 4-1-13)

    The absence of a sky condition or ceiling and/or visibility on ATIS indicates a sky condition or ceiling of 5,000 feet or above and visibility of 5 miles or more. A remark may be made on the broadcast, "the weather is better than 5000 and 5," or the existing weather may be broadcast.

11. **While en route, how oan a pilot obtaln updated weather information?** (FAA-H-8083-25)

    a. Flight Service on 122.2 and appropriate remote communication outlet (RCO) frequencies.

    b. ATIS, Automated Surface Observing System (ASOS), or Automated Weather Observing System (AWOS) broadcasts along your route of flight.

    c. Air Route Traffic Control Center (ARTCC) broadcasts—AWW, Convective SIGMET, SIGMET, AIRMET, Urgent PIREP, and CWA alerts are broadcast once on all frequencies, except emergency.

    d. Datalink weather—cockpit display of FIS-B information.

    e. ATC (workload permitting).

    Exam Tip: Be prepared to demonstrate how you would obtain inflight weather advisories and updates, and how you would communicate with a FSS specialist while en route.

12. Can ATC assist you in avoiding clouds along your route of flight? (AIM 7-1-12)

Yes, air traffic control (ATC) can assist pilots in avoiding clouds along their route of flight. ATC provides a range of services to assist pilots with weather-related concerns and to help ensure safe and efficient flight operations. Here are some ways in which ATC can assist in avoiding clouds:

a. *Weather information*—ATC provides pilots with up-to-date weather information, including current weather reports and forecasts along the planned route. This information can include cloud bases and tops, visibility, and other weather hazards that may affect the flight.

b. *Deviation instructions*—If a pilot encounters adverse weather conditions or wants to avoid clouds, they can request deviations from their assigned route. ATC may approve these requests, providing alternative headings or altitudes to help pilots avoid areas of significant weather.

c. *Altitude changes*—ATC can approve altitude changes to help pilots climb or descend to a different flight level, potentially avoiding cloud layers or adverse weather conditions.

d. *Radar services*—In certain airspace, ATC may provide radar services to help pilots navigate around areas of significant weather. Radar assistance can be particularly useful for avoiding thunderstorms or other convective weather phenomena.

e. *Coordination with other facilities*—If pilots are navigating through a large airspace area, ATC can coordinate with adjacent facilities to provide the best routing and weather avoidance assistance.

f. *Real-time updates*—ATC can relay real-time weather updates or warnings to pilots, including information about rapidly developing weather conditions that might not have been available during preflight planning.

C. Aviation Weather Reports and Forecasts

1. What is a METAR? (FAA-H-8083-28)

The aviation routine weather report (METAR) is the weather observer's interpretation of the weather conditions at a given site and time. There are two types of METARs: a routine METAR that is transmitted every hour and an aviation selected special weather report (SPECI). This is a special report that can be given at any time to update the METAR for rapidly changing weather conditions, aircraft mishaps, or other critical information

Example:

METAR KOKC 011955Z AUTO 22015G25KT 180V250 3/4SM R17L/2600FT +TSRA BR OVC010CB 18/16 A2992 RMK AO2 TSB25 TS OHD MOV E SLP132

2. Describe several types of weather observing programs available. (AIM 7-1-12)

Manual observations—With only a few exceptions, these reports are from airport locations staffed by FAA personnel who manually observe, perform calculations, and enter their observations into the communication system.

ASOS/AWOS—The primary U.S. surface weather observing systems. Both systems provide continuous minute-by-minute observations that generate METARs and other aviation weather information. Transmitted over a discrete VHF radio frequency or the voice portion of a local NAVAID, and receivable to a maximum of 25 NM from the station and a maximum altitude of 10,000 feet AGL. Observations made without human intervention will include the modifier "AUTO" in the report data. A maintenance indicator ($) is coded when an automated system detects that maintenance is needed on the system.

3. What are PIREPs and where are they usually found? (FAA-H-8083-28)

A pilot report (PIREP) provides valuable information regarding the conditions as they actually exist in the air—information which cannot be gathered from any other source. Pilots can confirm the height of bases and tops of clouds, locations of wind shear and turbulence, and the location of inflight icing. There are two types of PIREPs: routine or "UA," and urgent or "UUA." PIREPs should be given to the ground facility with which communications are established (i.e., FSS, ARTCC, or terminal ATC). Altitudes are MSL, visibilities SM, and distances in NM. PIREPs are available from ATC, FSS, and on the internet at aviationweather.gov/data/pirep/.

4. What are Terminal Aerodrome Forecasts (TAFs)?
(FAA-H-8083-28)

A TAF is a concise statement of the expected meteorological conditions significant to aviation for a specified time period within 5 SM of the center of the airport's runway complex (terminal). The TAFs use the same weather codes found in METAR weather reports, in the following format:

a. *Type of reports*—A routine forecast (TAF); an amended forecast (TAF AMD), or a corrected forecast (TAF COR).

b. *ICAO station identifier*—4-letter station identifier.

c. *Date and time of origin*—The date/time of the forecast follows the terminal's location identifier and shows the day of the month in two digits, and the time in which the forecast is completed and ready for transmission in four digits, appended with a Z to denote UTC. *Example:* 061737Z—the TAF was issued on the 6th day of the month at 1737 UTC.

d. *Valid period date and time*—The first two digits are the day of the month for the start of the TAF, followed by two digits that indicate the starting hour (UTC). The next two digits indicate the day of the month for the end of the TAF, and the last two digits are the ending hour (UTC) of the valid period. Scheduled 24- and 30-hour TAFs are issued four (4) times per day, at 0000, 0600, 1200, and 1800Z. *Example:* A 00Z TAF issued on the 9th of the month and valid for 24 hours would have a valid period of 0900/0924.

e. *Forecasts*—Wind, visibility, significant and vicinity weather, cloud and vertical obscuration, non-convective low-level wind shear, and forecast change indicators (FM, TEMPO and PROB).

5. **From which primary source should information be obtained regarding expected weather at the ETA If your destination airport does not have a TAF?** (FAA-H-8083-28)

The Graphical Forecast Analysis (GFA).

6. **Describe the GFA.** (AIM 7-1-4)

The GFA is a set of web-based graphics that provide observations, forecasts, and warnings that can be viewed from 14 hours in the past to 15 hours in the future. The GFA covers the continental United States (CONUS) from the surface up to Flight Level 480 (FL480). Wind, icing, and turbulence forecasts are available in 3,000-foot increments from the surface up to 30,000 feet MSL, and in 6,000-foot increments from 30,000 feet MSL to 48,000 feet MSL. Turbulence forecasts are also broken into LO (below FL180) and HI (at or above FL180) graphics. A maximum icing graphic and maximum wind velocity graphic (regardless of altitude) are also available. The GFA can be viewed at aviationweather.gov/gfa.

7. **What are the four types of inflight aviation weather advisories?** (AIM 7-1-6)

Inflight aviation weather advisories are forecasts to advise enroute aircraft of the development of potentially hazardous weather. The four types are the SIGMET (WS), the convective SIGMET (WST), the AIRMET (WA; text or graphical product), and the center weather advisory (CWA). All heights are referenced MSL, except in the case of ceilings (CIG) which indicate AGL.

8. **What is a convective SIGMET?** (FAA-H-8083-28)

Convective SIGMETs (WST) imply severe or greater turbulence, severe icing and low-level wind shear. They may be issued for any convective situation which the forecaster feels is hazardous to all categories of aircraft. Bulletins are issued hourly at H+55, and special bulletins are issued at any time as required and updated at H+55. The text of the bulletin consists of either an observation and a forecast, or just a forecast (valid for up to 2 hours):

(continued)

a. Severe thunderstorms due to:
   - Surface winds greater than or equal to 50 knots.
   - Hail at the surface greater than or equal to ¾ inches in diameter.
   - Tornadoes.

b. Embedded thunderstorms.

c. A line of thunderstorms.

d. Thunderstorms that produce precipitation levels greater than or equal to heavy-intensity precipitation, affecting 40 percent or more of an area at least 3,000 square miles.

9. What is a SIGMET (WS)? (AIM 7-1-6)

A SIGMET (WS) advises of weather that is potentially hazardous to all aircraft. SIGMETs are unscheduled products that are valid for 4 hours. However, SIGMETs associated with tropical cyclones and volcanic ash clouds are valid for 6 hours. Unscheduled updates and corrections are issued as necessary. In the conterminous United States, SIGMETs are issued when the following phenomena occur or are expected to occur:

a. Severe icing not associated with thunderstorms.

b. Severe or extreme turbulence or clear air turbulence (CAT) not associated with thunderstorms.

c. Widespread dust storms or sandstorms lowering surface visibilities to below 3 miles.

d. Volcanic ash.

10. What is an AIRMET (WA or G-AIRMET)? (AIM 7-1-6)

An AIRMET is an advisory of significant weather phenomena that describes conditions at intensities lower than those which require the issuance of SIGMETs. They are issued every 6 hours beginning at 0245 UTC. Pilots should use AIRMETs in the preflight and enroute phase of flight to enhance safety. AIRMET information is available in two formats: text bulletins (WA) and graphics (G-AIRMET). Unscheduled updates and corrections are issued as necessary. AIRMETs contain details about IFR, extensive mountain obscuration, turbulence, strong surface winds, icing, and freezing levels.

11. What are the different types of AIRMETs? (AIM 7-1-6)

There are three types of AIRMETs, Sierra, Tango, and Zulu:

a. AIRMET Sierra describes IFR conditions and/or extensive mountain obscurations.

b. AIRMET Tango describes moderate turbulence, sustained surface winds of 30 knots or greater, and/or nonconvective low-level wind shear.

c. AIRMET Zulu describes moderate icing and provides freezing level heights.

12. What is a winds and temperatures aloft forecast (FB)? (FAA-H-8083-28)

Winds and temperatures aloft are forecast for specific locations in the contiguous U.S. and also for a network of locations in Alaska and Hawaii. These forecasts, called FBs, are issued 4 times daily. In an FB, a 4-digit code group shows wind direction, in reference to true north, and wind speed in knots, with an additional 2-digit code group showing forecast temperatures in degrees Celsius. Wind forecasts are not issued for altitudes within 1,500 feet of a location's elevation.

Note: The AWC's website provides a graphical depiction of the FB Winds/Temps forecasts as well as a text version at aviationweather.gov/data/windtemp/.

13. What valuable information can be determined from an FB? (FAA-H-8083-28)

Most favorable altitude—Based on winds and direction of flight.

Areas of possible icing—By noting air temperatures of +2°C to -20°C.

Temperature inversions—A temperature increase with altitude can mean a stable layer aloft reducing the chance for convective activity.

Turbulence—By observing abrupt changes in wind direction and speed at different altitudes.

14. What is a Center Weather Advisory (CWA)?
(FAA-H-8083-28)

Issued by a Center Weather Service Unit (CWSU), this is
an aviation warning for use by aircrews to anticipate and
avoid adverse weather conditions in the enroute and terminal
environments. The CWA is a short-term "nowcast," pinpointing
hazardous weather already causing an impact or expected to cause
an impact within a 2-hour period; therefore it is an inflight advisory
rather than a flight planning tool. CWAs are valid for a maximum
of 2 hours; if conditions are expected to continue beyond the
2-hour valid period, a statement will be included in the CWA.

15. What is a Convective Outlook (AC)? (FAA-H-8083-28)

The AC is a narrative and graphical outlook of the potential for
severe (tornado, wind gusts 50 knots or greater, or hail 1 inch
or greater in diameter) and non-severe (general) convection
and specific severe weather threats during the following 8 days.
It defines areas of marginal risk (MRGL), slight risk (SLGT),
enhanced risk (ENH), moderate risk (MDT), or high risk (HIGH)
of severe weather based on a percentage probability.

**16. What weather product can a pilot use during preflight to
determine forecast cloud tops en route?** (FAA-H-8083-28)

During preflight planning, a pilot can use the Graphical Forecasts
for Aviation (GFA) product to determine forecast cloud tops en
route. The GFA provides valuable graphical representations of
various weather elements, including cloud tops, icing, turbulence,
and more.

The GFA is available online through the Aviation Weather Center
(AWC) website, and it offers several forecast products tailored
specifically for pilots. To access the GFA, pilots can visit the AWC
website and select the appropriate GFA tool. They can then choose
the relevant graphical elements, such as "Cloud Tops," and specify
the desired altitude for the forecast.

The GFA cloud tops product will display forecasted cloud top
heights for different regions along the planned route of flight.
Pilots can use this information to determine the anticipated altitude
of cloud tops and make informed decisions regarding enroute
weather conditions, potential icing hazards, and VFR/IFR flight
planning.

17. What type of aviation forecasts are available in the Forecast section of the GFA? (AIM 7-1-4)

When pilots use the Forecasts resources tool on aviationweather .gov, they have access to information about ceiling and visibility, clouds, precipitation, thunderstorms, temperature, winds, turbulence, and icing. Each of these sections allow a pilot to zoom in on a particular area and review data over time going forward in forecasting.

D. Aviation Weather Charts

1. What is a surface analysis chart? (FAA-H-8083-28)

A surface analysis chart is an analyzed chart of surface weather observations. It depicts the distribution of multiple items, including sea level pressure; the positions of highs, lows, ridges, and troughs; the location and character of fronts; and the various boundaries such as drylines, outflow boundaries, sea-breeze fronts, and convergence lines. The chart is produced eight times daily.

2. Describe a Ceiling and Visibility Analysis (CVA). (FAA-H-8083-28)

A CVA is a real-time analysis (updated every 5 minutes) of current ceiling and visibility conditions across the continental United States. It is intended to aid situational awareness with a quick-glance visualization of current ceiling and visibility conditions across an area or along a route of flight. The CVA provides a viewer-selectable representation of ceiling height (AGL), surface visibility in statute miles, and flight category designation. The overview provided by a CVA should be followed by further examination of METARs, TAFs, AIRMETs, FAs, GFA, and other weather information. The CVA can be found at aviationweather.gov/gfa/#cigvis.

3. Define the terms *LIFR, IFR, MVFR,* and *VFR*. (AIM 7-1-7)

LIFR—Low IFR; ceiling less than 500 feet and/or visibility less than 1 mile.

IFR—Ceiling 500 to less than 1,000 feet and/or visibility 1 to less than 3 miles.

(continued)

MVFR—Marginal VFR; ceiling 1,000 to 3,000 feet and/or visibility 3 to 5 miles inclusive.

VFR—Ceiling greater than 3,000 feet and visibility greater than 5 miles; includes sky clear.

Note: Ceiling is defined as the height above the earth's surface of the lowest layer of clouds, which is reported as broken or overcast, or the vertical visibility into an obscuration.

4. **What information do short-range surface prognostic charts provide?** (FAA-H-8083-28)

Short-range surface prognostic (prog) charts provide a forecast of surface pressure systems, fronts and precipitation for a two-and-a-half day period. They cover a forecast area of the 48 contiguous states and coastal waters. Predicted conditions are divided into five forecast periods: 12, 18, 24, 48, and 60 hours. Each chart depicts a snapshot of weather elements expected at the specified valid time. Charts are issued four times a day and can be used to obtain an overview of the progression of surface weather features during the included periods.

5. **Describe a low-level significant weather chart.** (FAA-H-8083-28)

The low-level significant weather (SIGWX) charts provide a forecast of aviation weather hazards and are primarily intended to be used as guidance products for preflight briefings. The forecast domain covers the CONUS and the coastal waters for altitudes flight level 240 and below. The chart depicts weather flying categories, turbulence, and freezing levels and provides a snapshot of weather expected at the specified valid time. The charts are issued four times per day by the NWS AWC. Two charts are issued: a 12-hour and a 24-hour prog. Both are available at: aviationweather.gov.

Exam Tip: Be prepared to interpret and discuss current and forecast weather along your planned route of flight. The evaluator will expect you to demonstrate your ability to interpret the various aviation weather reports, forecasts, and charts/graphics and make an assessment of how the weather will affect your planned flight.

6. **How are freezing levels depicted on the freezing level graphics chart?** (FAA-H-8083-28)

Freezing level graphics are used to assess the lowest freezing level heights and their values relative to flight paths. The chart uses colors to represent the height in hundreds of feet above mean sea level of the lowest freezing level(s). The initial analysis and 3-hour forecast graphics are updated hourly. The 6-, 9-, and 12-hour forecast graphics are updated every three hours.

7. **Are the wind directions provided on weather charts referenced to magnetic or true north? Explain how you would convert.** (FAA-H-8083-28)

The wind directions provided on weather charts are typically referenced to true north. True north refers to the geographic North Pole, whereas magnetic north is the direction towards the Earth's magnetic North Pole.

Converting wind direction from magnetic to true north involves considering the magnetic variation or declination at a specific location. Magnetic variation is the angular difference between true north and magnetic north at a given location. This value can be positive or negative, depending on the location.

To convert wind direction from magnetic to true north, follow these steps:

a. Determine the magnetic variation using aviation charts to find the magnetic variation at your specific location.

b. Subtract or add the magnetic variation: If the magnetic variation is positive (east), subtract the value from the magnetic wind direction. If the magnetic variation is negative (west), add the value to the magnetic wind direction.

Example: If the wind direction on a weather chart is given as 120 degrees magnetic, and the magnetic variation at your location is +10 degrees, you would subtract 10 degrees from 120 to obtain the true wind direction of 110 degrees.

E. NOTAMs

1. What are NOTAMs? (AIM 5-1-3)

NOTAMs are time critical aeronautical information which is of either a temporary nature or not sufficiently known in advance to permit publication on aeronautical charts or in other operational publications receives immediate dissemination via the National NOTAM System. It includes such information as airport or primary runway closures, changes in the status of navigational aids, ILS's, radar service availability, and other information essential to planned enroute, terminal, or landing operations. Pilots can access NOTAM information via FSS or online via NOTAM Search at notams.aim.faa.gov/notamSearch.

2. Describe the following categories of NOTAMs: Domestic NOTAM (D), Flight Data Center (FDC) NOTAM, International NOTAM, Military NOTAM. (AIM 5-1-3)

a. *Domestic NOTAM (D)*—Information is disseminated for all navigational facilities that are part of the NAS, all public use aerodromes, seaplane bases, and heliports listed in the *Chart Supplement U.S.* publication. NOTAM (D) information includes data such as taxiway closures, personnel and equipment near or crossing runways, and airport lighting aids that do not affect instrument approach criteria, such as VASI.

b. *Flight Data Center (FDC) NOTAM*—Flight information that is regulatory in nature and includes NOTAMs such as amendments to published IAPs, TFRs, ADS-B, TIS-B, FIS-B service availability, WAAS or GPS information, and special notices. Additionally, U.S. Domestic Security NOTAMs are FDC NOTAMs that inform pilots of certain U.S. security activities or requirements.

c. *International NOTAM*—Distributed to more than one country and published in ICAO format. For the most part, International NOTAMs duplicate data found in a U.S. NOTAM (D). International NOTAMs received by the FAA from other countries are stored in the U.S. NOTAM System.

d. *Military NOTAM*—Originated by the U.S. Air Force, Army, Marines, or Navy, and pertain to military or joint-use navigational aids/airports that are part of the NAS. Military NOTAMs are published in the International NOTAM format and should be reviewed by users of a military or joint-use facility.

3. **All (D) NOTAMs will have keywords contained within the first part of the text. What are several examples of these keywords?** (AIM 5-1-3)

RWY, TWY, APRON, AD, OBST, NAV, COM, SVC, AIRSPACE, ODP, SID, STAR, CHART, DATA, IAP, VFP, ROUTE, SPECIAL, SECURITY

4. **Where can NOTAM information be obtained?** (AIM 5-1-1, 5-1-3)
   a. Call Flight Service—1-800-WX-BRIEF
   b. NOTAM Search—notams.aim.faa.gov/notamSearch
   c. Flight Service briefing website—1800wxbrief.com
   d. FIS-B via ADS-B In

Note: The NOTAM (D) and FDC NOTAM products broadcast via FIS-B are limited to those issued or effective within the past 30 days. Except for TFRs, NOTAMs older than 30 days are not provided.

5. **What is a UAS NOTAM?**

NOTAMS for uncrewed aircraft systems (UAS) are becoming more common and are of more importance to pilots in the National Airspace System than they have been historically. They might also potentially be referred to as DROTAMs. These cover areas that might include operations of uncrewed aircraft systems that are operating in the same airspace as other aircraft and are not necessarily prohibited or restricted airspaces.

These NOTAMs are issued by aviation authorities to inform pilots of uncrewed aircraft systems or drones operating in a specific airspace area. The purpose of a UAS NOTAM is to provide a heads-up to crewed aircraft pilots about the presence of drone operations within the designated airspace, promoting situational awareness and safety.

UAS NOTAMs typically include the following information:

a. *Location*—The geographic coordinates or reference points defining the area where drone operations are taking place.

b. *Altitude*—The vertical limits of the drone operation area, indicating the maximum and minimum altitudes where the UAS will be operating.

(continued)

    c. *Time of operation*—The date and time when the drone operation is scheduled to occur or when the airspace will be reserved for UAS activities.

    d. *Type of operation*—Information about the nature of the drone operations, such as aerial photography, surveying, or other specific activities.

    e. *Contact information*—The contact details of the entity or organization responsible for the drone operation, in case pilots need to obtain additional information or coordinate their flights.

UAS NOTAMs are typically published by air traffic control centers, flight service stations, or other relevant aviation authorities.

F. Aviation Weather Hazards

1. What are the three stages of thunderstorm development? (FAA-H-8083-28)

Cumulus stage—The first stage of thunderstorm development is known as the cumulus stage. It begins with the formation of cumulus clouds due to convective uplift of moist air. The air rises, cools, and condenses to form towering cumulus clouds. During this stage, the updrafts within the cloud dominate, carrying moisture and heat upward. However, the downdrafts are generally absent or weak.

Mature stage—The cumulus stage progresses into the mature stage as the thunderstorm intensifies. In this stage, the updrafts and downdrafts within the cloud coexist and strengthen. The updrafts continue to feed the storm, while the downdrafts begin to descend, bringing cooler air and precipitation to the surface. This is the most active stage of the thunderstorm, characterized by heavy rain, lightning, thunder, and possibly hail. The mature stage can last from 10 minutes to an hour or more.

Dissipating stage—The final stage of thunderstorm development is the dissipating stage. During this stage, the storm weakens as the updrafts diminish and the downdrafts dominate. The supply of warm moist air feeding the storm is cut off, causing the thunderstorm to dissipate. The precipitation becomes lighter and more scattered, and the thunderstorm gradually loses its strength and organization. The dissipating stage is marked by the gradual decrease in thunder, lightning, and rainfall.

2. What are the three principal types of thunderstorms? (FAA-H-8083-28)

Single cell—Also called ordinary cell thunderstorms, this type consists of only one cell; they are easily circumnavigated except at night or when embedded in other clouds. Single cell thunderstorms are rare, as almost all thunderstorms are multi-celled.

Multicell (cluster and line)—Consists of a cluster of cells at different stages of their life cycles. As the first cell matures, it is carried downwind, and a new cell forms upwind to take its place. A multicell may have a lifetime of several hours (or more), which makes it tougher to circumnavigate than a single-cell thunderstorm. May have supercells embedded within them.

Supercell—Consists primarily of a single, quasi-steady rotating updraft that persists for an extended period of time. Updraft speeds may reach 9,000 fpm (100 knots). They may persist for many hours (or longer) and their size and persistence make them tough to circumnavigate.

3. When attempting to avoid turbulence around thunderstorms, explain several operational procedures a pilot should never attempt. (AIM 7-1-27)

a. Never land or take off in the face of an approaching thunderstorm. A sudden gust front of low-level turbulence could cause loss of control.

b. Never attempt to fly under a thunderstorm even if you can see through to the other side. Turbulence and wind shear under the storm could be hazardous.

c. Never attempt to fly under the anvil of a thunderstorm. There is a potential for severe and extreme clear air turbulence.

d. Never fly without airborne radar into a cloud mass containing scattered embedded thunderstorms. Scattered thunderstorms not embedded usually can be visually circumnavigated.

e. Never trust the visual appearance to be a reliable indicator of the turbulence inside a thunderstorm.

f. Never assume that ATC will offer radar navigation guidance or deviations around thunderstorms.

g. Never use data-linked Next Generation Radar (NEXRAD) mosaic imagery as the sole means for negotiating a path through a thunderstorm area (tactical maneuvering).

4. **When flying an airplane without onboard thunderstorm detection equipment, describe procedures a pilot can take to avoid thunderstorms and/or the turbulence associated with them.** (AIM 7-1-27)

   a. Remember that the data-linked NEXRAD mosaic imagery shows where the weather was, not where the weather is. The weather conditions may be 15 to 20 minutes older than the age indicated on the display.

   b. Listen to chatter on the ATC frequency for PIREPs and other aircraft requesting to deviate or divert.

   c. Ask ATC for radar navigation guidance or to approve deviations around thunderstorms, if needed.

   d. Use data-linked weather NEXRAD mosaic imagery (i.e., FIS-B) for route selection to avoid thunderstorms entirely (strategic maneuvering).

   e. Advise ATC, when switched to another controller, that you are deviating for thunderstorms before accepting to rejoin the original route.

   f. Always ensure that after an authorized weather deviation, before accepting to rejoin the original route, that the route of flight is clear of thunderstorms.

   g. Avoid by at least 20 miles any thunderstorm identified as severe or giving an intense radar echo. This is especially true under the anvil of a large cumulonimbus.

   h. Circumnavigate the entire area if the area has 6/10 thunderstorm coverage.

   i. Remember that vivid and frequent lightning indicates the probability of a severe thunderstorm.

5. **Can ATC provide inflight assistance in avoiding thunderstorms and severe weather?** (AIM 7-1-12)

   Yes, to the extent possible, controllers will issue pertinent information on weather or chaff areas and assist pilots in avoiding such areas when requested. Pilots should respond to a weather advisory by either acknowledging the advisory or by requesting an alternate course of action as appropriate.

   However, the controller's primary responsibility is to provide safe separation between aircraft. Additional services such as weather avoidance assistance can only be provided to the extent that it doesn't interfere with their primary function. ATC radar limitations and frequency congestion may also limit the controller's capability to assist.

6. **Give some examples of charts and reports useful in determining the potential for and location of thunderstorms along your route.** (FAA-H-8083-28)

   a. *Convective Outlook (AC)*—a narrative and graphical outlook of areas of slight, moderate, or high risk of severe thunderstorms for a 24-hour period.

   b. *Significant Weather Chart (SIGWX)*—provides a forecast of aviation weather hazards; depicts a snapshot of weather expected at the specified valid time.

   c. *Weather radar observations*—(and their resultant images) are graphical displays of precipitation and non-precipitation targets detected by weather radars (NEXRAD). Regional and national radar mosaics can be found on the websites of the NWS, AWC, all NWS weather forecast offices (WFOs), as well as commercial aviation weather providers.

   d. *Convective SIGMETs (WST)*—issued for any convective situation involving severe, embedded, and lines of thunderstorms.

   e. *Pilot reports (PIREPs)*—help determine actual conditions along your planned route of flight.

   f. *Supplementary weather products*—can be used for enhanced situational awareness. Supplementary weather products must only be used in conjunction with one or more NWS primary weather products.

7. **What are microbursts?** (AIM 7-1-24)

   Microbursts are small-scale intense downdrafts which, on reaching the surface, spread outward in all directions from the downdraft center. This causes the presence of both vertical and horizontal wind shears that can be extremely hazardous to all types and categories of aircraft, especially at low altitudes. Due to their small size, short life span, and the fact that they can occur over areas without surface precipitation, microbursts are not easily detectable using conventional weather radar or wind shear alert systems.

8. Where are microbursts most likely to occur?
(AIM 7-1-24)

Microbursts can be found almost anywhere there is convective activity. They may be embedded in heavy rain associated with a thunderstorm or in light rain in benign-appearing virga. When there is little or no precipitation at the surface accompanying the microburst, a ring of blowing dust may be the only visual clue of its existence.

9. What are some basic characteristics of a microburst?
(AIM 7-1-24)

Size—Less than 1 mile in diameter as it descends from the cloud base; can extend 2½ miles in diameter near ground level.

Intensity—Downdrafts as strong as 6,000 feet per minute; horizontal winds near the surface can be as strong as 45 knots resulting in a 90-knot wind shear (headwind to tailwind change for traversing aircraft).

Duration—An individual microburst will seldom last longer than 15 minutes from the time it strikes the ground until dissipation. Sometimes microbursts are concentrated into a line structure, and under these conditions activity may continue for as long as an hour.

10. What types of weather information will you examine to determine if microburst/wind shear conditions might affect your flight? (FAA-H-8083-28)

The following should be examined for clues of potential microburst/wind shear conditions affecting the flight:

TAFs—Examine the terminal forecast for convective activity.

METARs—Inspect for wind shear clues (thunderstorms, rainshowers, blowing dust).

Severe weather watch reports—Check for issuance since severe convective weather is a prime source for microbursts and wind shear.

LLWAS reports—Low Level Windshear Alert System, designed to detect wind shifts between outlying stations and a reference station.

TDWR—Terminal Doppler Weather Radar, deployed at 45 airports across the United States; detects microbursts, gust fronts, wind shifts and precipitation intensities and provides severe weather alerts and warnings to ATC and pilots.

SIGMETs and convective SIGMETs—May provide essential clues.

Visual clues from the cockpit—Heavy rain (in a dry or moist environment) which can be accompanied by curling outflow, a ring of blowing dust or localized dust in general, flying debris, virga, a rain core with rain diverging away horizontally from the rain core, or tornadic features (funnel clouds, tornadoes). At night, lightning may be the only visual clue.

PIREPs—Reports of sudden airspeed changes in the airport approach or landing corridors provide indication of the presence of wind shear.

Airborne weather radar—To detect convective cells.

11. Define *wind shear* and state the areas in which it is likely to occur. (FAA-H-8083-28)

Wind shear is the rate of change of wind velocity (direction and/ or speed) per unit distance; conventionally expressed as vertical or horizontal wind shear. It may occur at any level in the atmosphere but three areas are of special concern:

a. Wind shear with a low-level temperature inversion;

b. Wind shear in a frontal zone or thunderstorm; and

c. Clear air turbulence (CAT) at high levels associated with a jet stream or strong circulation.

12. While on a cross-country flight, you notice a lens-shaped cloud over a mountainous area along your route of flight. What does the presence of this type of cloud indicate? (FAA-H-8083-28)

It indicates the presence of a mountain wave which is an atmospheric wave disturbance formed when stable air flow passes over a mountain or mountain ridge. Mountain waves are a form of mechanical turbulence which develop above and downwind of mountains and frequently produce severe to extreme turbulence. When sufficient moisture is present in the upstream flow, mountain waves produce cloud formations, including cap clouds, cirrocumulus standing lenticular (CCSL), altocumulus standing lenticular (ACSL), and rotor clouds. These clouds provide visual proof that mountain waves exist, however, the clouds may be absent if the air is too dry.

13. Explain the difference between an increasing headwind shear and a decreasing headwind shear. (FAA-H-8083-28)

An increasing headwind (or decreasing tailwind) shear increases indicated airspeed and thus increases performance. The airplane will tend to pitch up to regain trim airspeed. An additional consideration is that this type of shear may reduce normal deceleration during flare which could cause overrun. An increasing tailwind (or decreasing headwind) shear will decrease indicated airspeed and performance capability. Due to airspeed loss, the airplane may tend to pitch down to regain trim speed.

14. Concerning wind shear and microburst detection systems, what do the abbreviations LLWAS, TDWR, WSP and ITWS indicate in the *Chart Supplement U.S.* information for an airport? (AIM 4-3-7)

LLWAS—Low-level wind shear alert system. Provides wind shear alert and gust front information in and around an airport; does not provide microburst alerts or detect wind shear beyond the periphery of an airport.

TDWR—Terminal Doppler Weather Radar. Located 8 to 12 miles off of the airport proper and designed to look at the airspace around and over the airport to detect microbursts, gust fronts, wind shifts, and precipitation intensities.

WSP—Weather service processor. Provides the same information as TDWR at a fraction of the cost of TDWR. Accesses weather information from the existing ASR-9 radar located on or near the airport and depicts six levels of precipitation, gust fronts, and predicted storm movement.

ITWS—Integrated Terminal Weather System. Provides alerts for microbursts, wind shear, and significant thunderstorm activity, and displays wind information oriented to the threshold or departure end of the runway.

15. What is clear air turbulence (CAT)? (FAA-H-8083-28)

Clear air turbulence is defined as "sudden severe turbulence occurring in cloudless regions that causes violent buffeting of aircraft." This term is commonly applied to higher altitude turbulence associated with wind shear. The most comprehensive definition is high altitude turbulence encountered outside of convective clouds. This includes turbulence in cirrus clouds, within and in the vicinity of standing lenticular clouds and, in some cases, in clear air in the vicinity of thunderstorms.

16. What information will you provide when giving a wind shear report? (AIM 7-1-22)

The FAA has specific requirements for wind shear reports to ensure the dissemination of accurate and essential information to pilots. When providing a wind shear report, the FAA requires the inclusion of the following information:

a. *Location*—The specific location or areas affected by wind shear. This includes specifying the airport, runway(s), and/or altitude range(s) where wind shear conditions exist.

b. *Magnitude*—The magnitude or intensity of the wind shear. This includes information on the strength and direction of the wind at different altitudes, as well as any rapid or drastic changes in wind speed and direction.

c. *Altitude range*—The altitude range affected by wind shear. This includes specifying whether the wind shear is prevalent at the surface, low-level, or upper-level altitudes.

d. *Timing and duration*—The timing of the wind shear conditions, including the expected duration. This helps pilots plan their operations accordingly and take appropriate measures to mitigate the effects of wind shear.

e. *Mitigation measures*—Any recommended mitigation measures or actions that pilots should take to safely navigate wind shear. This may involve adjusting airspeed, modifying the flight path, or selecting alternate runways or airports.

f. *Additional information*—Any relevant additional information, such as the source of the wind shear, weather conditions, or associated hazards, should be provided to enhance situational awareness.

(continued)

Note: The exact requirements and reporting procedures for wind shear reports may vary depending on the specific airport or airspace regulations. Pilots should consult the appropriate FAA guidance, such as the *Aeronautical Information Manual* (AIM) or specific airport directives, to ensure compliance with the reporting standards in their particular operational environment.

Airplane
Systems

4

Some of the following questions reference the systems of a Cessna 172-RG. For accuracy, you should review your aircraft's AFM or POH. Be capable of explaining the diagrams and schematics of the various systems in your aircraft.

A. Primary Flight Controls and Trim

1. How are primary flight controls actuated on most light general aviation aircraft? (AFM/POH)

The flight control surfaces are manually actuated through use of either a rod or cable system. A control wheel actuates the ailerons and elevator, and rudder/brake pedals actuate the rudder.

2. How are trim systems actuated on most light general aviation aircraft? (AFM/POH)

On most light general aviation aircraft, trim systems are actuated using manual controls. The primary purpose of trim systems is to relieve control pressure and allow the aircraft to maintain a desired attitude or airspeed with minimal input from the pilot. Trim adjustments help balance the aerodynamic forces acting on the aircraft's control surfaces, reducing the need for constant control input by the pilot.

The most common types of trim systems found in light general aviation aircraft are:

Trim wheels—Many aircraft have a trim wheel located within easy reach of the pilot. Turning the trim wheel adjusts the position of the trim tab on the control surface, which alters the control surface's neutral position and helps maintain the desired attitude.

Trim tabs—Some aircraft have electrically or manually adjustable trim tabs on the control surfaces. The pilot can use a control in the cockpit to move the trim tab up or down, thereby adjusting the control surface's neutral position and relieving control pressure.

Electric trim—In more modern aircraft, especially those equipped with electrically operated control systems, electric trim controls are often integrated into the yoke or control column. By pressing buttons or switches on the yoke, the pilot can electrically adjust the trim settings.

Trimmer switches—In certain aircraft with sophisticated avionics systems, trim can be adjusted using trimmer switches on the instrument panel or a trim controller interface.

Regardless of the type of trim system, the purpose remains the same: to allow the pilot to make fine adjustments to the aircraft's control surfaces, ensuring stable and controlled flight without continuous manual pressure on the flight controls. Properly using trim helps reduce pilot workload and fatigue, contributing to a more comfortable and safe flying experience.

B. Wing Flaps, Leading Edge Devices, and Spoilers

1. What are flaps, and what is their function? (FAA-H-8083-25)

The wing flaps are movable panels on the inboard trailing edges of the wings. They are hinged so they may be extended downward into the flow of air beneath the wings to increase both lift and drag. Their purpose is to permit a slower airspeed and a steeper angle of descent during a landing approach. In some cases, they may also be used to shorten the takeoff distance.

2. What are the main types of flaps systems that are found on aircraft? (FAA-H-8083-25)

There are four main types of aircraft flap systems commonly used in aviation: plain flaps, split flaps, slotted flaps, and Fowler flaps.

Plain flaps—Plain flaps are the simplest type of flaps, consisting of a hinged section that extends downward from the wing's trailing edge. When deployed, they increase the wing's surface area, thus generating additional lift and drag. Plain flaps are commonly found on smaller aircraft and are effective for increasing lift at lower speeds.

Split flaps—Split flaps are characterized by their ability to split the airflow both over and under the wing when deployed. These flaps pivot downward from the lower surface of the wing, significantly increasing drag and providing extra lift. Split flaps are effective at lower speeds and are commonly found on older aircraft designs.

(continued)

Slotted flaps—Slotted flaps feature a gap (slot) between the wing and the flap surface when deployed. This design allows high-energy air from the lower surface of the wing to flow over the top of the flap, delaying airflow separation. Slotted flaps increase lift while minimizing the associated drag, making them effective for a range of flight speeds. They are commonly used on modern commercial aircraft.

Fowler flaps—Fowler flaps are the most sophisticated and versatile type of flaps. They consist of multiple sections that extend both downward and aft from the wing's trailing edge, simultaneously increasing the wing area and changing its shape. Fowler flaps can be extended rearward, increasing both lift and drag, or extended downward, increasing only lift. This flexibility allows for optimal control of an aircraft's performance during various flight phases. Fowler flaps are commonly found on large transport aircraft.

3. **State some examples of leading edge lift devices.** (FAA-H-8083-31)

Slots—A slot in the leading edge of a wing directs high-energy air from under the wing to the airflow above the wing, accelerating upper airflow. By accelerating the airflow above the wing, airflow separation will be delayed to higher angles of attack. This allows the wing to continue to develop lift at substantially higher angles of attack.

Slats—A miniature airfoil mounted on the leading edge of a wing. They may be movable or fixed. At low angles of attack, movable slats are held flush against the leading edge by positive air pressure. At high angles of attack, the slats are moved forward either by the pilot or automatically by the low pressures present at the leading edge. Slats provide the same results as slots.

4. **What are spoilers?** (FAA-H-8083-31)

Spoilers are devices located on the upper surface of a wing which are designed to reduce lift by "spoiling" the airflow above the wing. They are typically used as speed brakes to slow an airplane down, both in flight as well as on the ground immediately after touchdown.

C. Pitot / Static Flight Instruments

1. What instruments operate from the pitot/static system? (FAA-H-8083-15)

The pitot/static system operates the altimeter, vertical speed indicator, and airspeed indicator.

2. What would an alternate static system be used for? (FAA-H-8083-25)

In the event of an external static port blockage, a static pressure alternate source may be located inside the cabin of the aircraft. Typically, this will be located within reach of the pilot under the instrument panel or on a side wall and will supply static pressure from inside the cabin instead of from the external ports. Using an alternate static source located in the pressurized cabin introduces errors because the pressure inside the cabin is higher than the pressure outside the aircraft at the same altitude. As a result, the alternate static source will measure a higher pressure than the actual outside air pressure.

3. How does an altimeter work? (FAA-H-8083-15)

A sensitive altimeter is an aneroid barometer that measures the absolute pressure of the ambient air and displays it in terms of feet above a selected pressure level. The sensitive element in a sensitive altimeter is a stack of evacuated, corrugated bronze aneroid capsules. The air pressure acting on these aneroids tries to compress them against their natural springiness, which tries to expand them. The result is that their thickness changes as the air pressure changes. Stacking several aneroids increases the dimension change as the pressure varies over the usable range of the instrument.

4. A pressure altimeter is subject to what limitations?
(FAA-H-8083-15)

Non-standard pressure and temperature:

a. Temperature variations expand or contract the atmosphere and raise or lower pressure levels that the altimeter senses.

   On a warm day—The pressure level is higher than on a standard day. The altimeter indicates lower than actual altitude.

   On a cold day—The pressure level is lower than on a standard day. The altimeter indicates higher than actual altitude.

b. Changes in surface pressure also affect pressure levels at altitude.

   Higher than standard pressure—The pressure level is higher than on a standard day. The altimeter indicates lower than actual altitude.

   Lower than standard pressure—The pressure level is lower than on a standard day. The altimeter indicates higher than actual altitude.

Remember: High to low or hot to cold, look out below!

5. Define and state how you would determine the following altitudes: indicated altitude, pressure altitude, true altitude, density altitude, and absolute altitude.
(FAA-H-8083-25)

Indicated altitude—The altitude read directly from the altimeter (uncorrected) after it is set to the current altimeter setting.

Pressure altitude—The height above the standard datum plane indicated when the altimeter setting window is adjusted to 29.92. It is used for computer solutions to determine density altitude, true altitude, true airspeed.

True altitude—The true vertical distance of the aircraft above sea level. Airport, terrain, and obstacle elevations found on aeronautical charts are true altitudes.

Density altitude—Pressure altitude corrected for nonstandard temperature variations. Directly related to an aircraft's takeoff, climb, and landing performance.

Absolute altitude—The vertical distance of an aircraft above the terrain.

6. How does the airspeed indicator operate?
(FAA-H-8083-25)

The airspeed indicator is a sensitive, differential pressure gauge which measures the difference between impact pressure from the pitot head and undisturbed atmospheric pressure from the static source. The difference is registered by the airspeed pointer on the face of the instrument.

7. What are the limitations of the airspeed indicator?
(FAA-H-8083-25)

The airspeed indicator is subject to proper flow of air in the pitot/static system.

8. The airspeed indicator is subject to what errors?

Position error—Caused by the static ports sensing erroneous static pressure; slipstream flow causes disturbances at the static port, preventing actual atmospheric pressure measurement. It varies with airspeed, altitude, and configuration, and may be a plus or minus value.

Density error—Changes in altitude and temperature are not compensated for by the instrument.

Compressibility error—Caused by the packing of air into the pitot tube at high airspeeds, resulting in higher than normal indications. It is usually not a factor.

9. What are the different types of aircraft speeds?
(FAA-H-8083-25)

Indicated airspeed (IAS)—The speed of the airplane as observed on the airspeed indicator. It is the airspeed without correction for indicator, position (or installation), or compressibility errors.

Calibrated airspeed (CAS)—The airspeed indicator reading corrected for position (or installation), and instrument errors. CAS is equal to TAS at sea level in a standard atmosphere. The color-coding for various design speeds marked on airspeed indicators may be IAS or CAS.

(continued)

Equivalent airspeed (EAS)—The airspeed indicator reading corrected for position (or installation), or instrument error, and for adiabatic compressible flow for the particular altitude. EAS is equal to CAS at sea level in standard atmosphere.

True airspeed (TAS)—CAS corrected for altitude and nonstandard temperature; the speed of the airplane in relation to the air mass in which it is flying.

10. What airspeed limitations apply to the color-coded marking system of the airspeed indicator? (FAA-H-8083-25)

Color-coded marking	Indicated limitation
White arc	Flap operating range
Lower A/S limit white arc	V_{S0} (stalling speed or minimum steady flight speed in landing configuration)
Upper A/S limit white arc	V_{FE} (maximum flap extension speed)
Green arc	Normal operating range
Lower A/S limit green arc	V_{S1} (stall speed clean or specified configuration)
Upper A/S limit green arc	V_{NO} (normal operations speed or maximum structural cruise speed)
Yellow arc	Caution range (operations in smooth air only)
Red line	V_{NE} (never exceed speed; above this speed structural failure may occur)
Red radial line	V_{MC} (a speed established by the manufacturer, published in the AFM/POH, and marked on most airspeed indicators in multi-engine aircraft)
Blue radial line	V_{YSE} (best rate of climb single engine, even if it is negative)

11. **What are some examples of important airspeed limitations that are not marked on the face of the airspeed indicator, but are found on placards and in the AFM or POH?** (FAA-H-8083-25)

   a. Design maneuvering speed (V_A).

   b. Landing gear operating speed (V_{LO}).

   c. Landing gear extended speed (V_{LE}).

   d. Best angle-of-climb speed (V_X).

   e. Best rate-of-climb speed (V_Y).

   f. Maximum speed in level flight with maximum continuous power (V_H).

   g. Maximum speed at which a rejected takeoff can be initiated in the event of an emergency (V_1).

12. **How does the vertical speed indicator work?** (FAA-H-8083-15)

   The vertical speed indicator is a pressure differential instrument. Inside the instrument case is an aneroid very much like the one in an airspeed indicator. Both the inside of this aneroid and the inside of the instrument case are vented to the static system, but the case is vented through a calibrated orifice that causes the pressure inside the case to change more slowly than the pressure inside the aneroid. As the aircraft ascends, the static pressure becomes lower and the pressure inside the case compresses the aneroid, moving the pointer upward, showing a climb and indicating the number of feet per minute the aircraft is ascending.

13. **What are the limitations of the vertical speed indicator?** (FAA-H-8083-25)

   The vertical speed indicator is commonly considered a "trend" instrument. It is not accurate when sudden or abrupt changes in aircraft attitude are introduced and it will cause erroneous instrument readings as airflow fluctuates over the static port. Both rough control and turbulent air result in unreliable indications. The vertical speed indicator should be relied upon in stabilized level flight, climbs, or descents.

D. Gyroscopic Flight Instruments

1. Which instruments contain gyroscopes?
(FAA-H-8083-25)

The most commonly gyroscopically driven instruments have historically been attitude indicators and heading indicators. Some turn coordinators may also be gyroscopic. Many modern aircraft no longer have vacuum-driven gyroscopic instruments, and a pilot should know which systems are in the aircraft they will be operating.

2. What are the two fundamental properties of a gyroscope? (FAA-H-8083-25)

Rigidity in space—A gyroscope remains in a fixed position in the plane in which it is spinning.

Precession—The tilting or turning of a gyro in response to a deflective force. The reaction to this force does not occur at the point where it was applied; it occurs at a point 90° later in the direction of rotation. The rate at which the gyro precesses is inversely proportional to the speed of the rotor and proportional to the deflective force.

3. What are the various sources that may be used to power the gyroscopic instruments in an airplane?
(FAA-H-8083-25)

In some airplanes, all the gyros are vacuum, pressure, or electrically operated; in others, vacuum or pressure systems provide the power for the heading and attitude indicators, while the electrical system provides the power for the turn coordinator. Most airplanes have at least two sources of power to ensure at least one source of bank information if one power source fails.

4. How does the vacuum system operate? (FAA-H-8083-25)

Air is drawn into the vacuum system by the engine-driven vacuum pump. It first goes through a filter, which prevents foreign matter from entering the vacuum or pressure system. The air then moves through the attitude and heading indicators, where it causes the gyros to spin. A relief valve prevents the vacuum pressure, or suction, from exceeding prescribed limits. After that, the air is expelled overboard or used in other systems, such as for inflating pneumatic deicing boots.

5. How does the attitude indicator work? (FAA-H-8083-25)

The attitude indicator's gyro is mounted on a horizontal plane (a bar representing true horizon) and depends upon rigidity in space for its operation. The fixed gyro remains in a horizontal plane as the airplane is pitched or banked about its axis, indicating the attitude of the airplane relative to the true horizon.

6. Discuss the limits of an attitude indicator. (FAA-H-8083-25)

Pitch and bank limits depend upon the make and model of the instrument. Limits in the banking plane are usually from 100° to 110°, pitch limits are usually from 60° to 70°. If either limit is exceeded, the instrument will tumble or spill giving incorrect indications until reset. Some modern attitude indicators will not tumble.

7. The attitude indicator is subject to what errors? (FAA-H-8083-15)

Attitude indicators are free from most errors, but depending on the speed with which the erection system functions, there may be a slight nose-up indication during a rapid acceleration and a nose-down indication during a rapid deceleration. There is also a possibility of a small bank angle and pitch error after a 180° turn. These inherent errors are small and correct themselves within a minute or so after returning to straight-and-level flight. An attitude indicator may be subject to more error if the vacuum pump is not delivering sufficient pressure. Make sure the pressure is within the recommended range for the vacuum system installed in your aircraft.

8. How does the heading indicator operate? (FAA-H-8083-25)

It uses the principle of rigidity in space; the rotor turns in a vertical plane, and the compass card is fixed to the rotor. Since the rotor remains rigid in space, the points on the card hold the same position in space relative to the vertical plane. As the instrument case and the airplane revolve around the vertical axis, the card shows clear, accurate heading information.

9. What are the limitations of the heading indicator?
(FAA-H-8083-25)

The pitch and bank limits depend upon the make and model of the instrument. Limits in the banking plane are usually from 100° to 110°, and the pitch limits are usually from 60° to 70°. If either limit is exceeded, the instrument will tumble or spill and will give incorrect indications until realigned. A number of modern attitude indicators do not tumble. A heading indicator may be subject to more error if the vacuum pump is not delivering sufficient pressure. Make sure the pressure is within the recommended range for the vacuum system installed in your aircraft. A heading indicator receiving low pressure will typically result in precession of the heading indicator.

10. What error is the heading indicator subject to?
(FAA-H-8083-25)

Because of precession, caused chiefly by friction, the heading indicator will creep or drift from a heading to which it is set. Among other factors, the amount of drift depends upon the condition of the instrument. The heading indicator may indicate as much as 15° of error per every hour of operation.

11. How does the turn coordinator operate? (FAA-H-8083-25)

The turn part of the instrument uses precession to indicate direction and approximate rate of turn. A gyro reacts by trying to move in reaction to the force applied thus moving the needle or miniature aircraft in proportion to the rate of turn. The slip/skid indicator is a liquid-filled tube with a ball that reacts to centrifugal force and gravity.

12. What information does the turn coordinator provide?
(FAA-H-8083-25)

It shows the yaw and roll of the aircraft around the vertical and longitudinal axes. The miniature airplane indicates direction of the turn as well as rate of turn. When aligned with the turn index, it represents a standard rate of turn of 3° per second. The inclinometer of the turn coordinator indicates the coordination of aileron and rudder. The ball indicates whether the airplane is in coordinated flight or is in a slip or skid.

13. **What will the turn indicator indicate when the aircraft is in a skidding or a slipping turn?** (FAA-H-8083-25)

Skid—The ball in the tube will be to the outside of the turn; too much rate of turn for the amount of bank.

Slip—The ball in the tube will be on the inside of the turn; not enough rate of turn for the amount of bank.

E. Magnetic Compass

1. **How does the magnetic compass work?** (FAA-H-8083-25)

Magnetized needles fastened to a float assembly, around which is mounted a compass card, align themselves parallel to the earth's lines of magnetic force. The float assembly is housed in a bowl filled with acid-free white kerosene.

2. **What limitations does the magnetic compass have?** (FAA-H-8083-15)

This jewel-and-pivot type mounting allows the float freedom to rotate and tilt up to approximately 18° angle of bank. At steeper bank angles, the compass indications are erratic and unpredictable.

3. **What are the various compass errors?** (FAA-H-8083-15)

Oscillation error—Erratic movement of the compass card caused by turbulence or rough control technique.

Deviation error—Due to electrical and magnetic disturbances in the aircraft.

Variation error—Angular difference between true and magnetic north; reference isogonic lines of variation.

Dip errors:

a. *Acceleration error*—On east or west headings, while accelerating, the magnetic compass shows a turn to the north, and when decelerating, it shows a turn to the south.

   Remember: ANDS

   Accelerate

   North

   Decelerate

   South

(continued)

b. *Northerly turning error*—The compass leads in the south half of a turn, and lags in the north half of a turn.

Remember: UNOS

Undershoot

North

Overshoot

South

F. Landing Gear

1. What are some of the most common ways landing gear systems operate on light general aviation aircraft? (FAA-H-8083-25)

Most light general aviation aircraft have one of three types of landing gear operation systems. They might be electrically driven motors that actuate a gear system, electric motors that pump a hydraulic system, or even a manual gear retraction and deployment system. It is critical for a pilot to understand not only how the gear operates but also backup systems that allow for gear deployment in the event of a primary system failure. Frequently, a hand pump hydraulic option, a free-fall system, or a manually operated crank will be present to allow for a gear deployment in the event of the primary system failure.

2. How do most aircraft lock the gear in a down position? (FAA-H-8083-25)

Mechanical down locks are incorporated into the nose and main gear assembly. Understanding if the aircraft has a gear depiction light to indicate a down and locked condition for each individual gear, or if a single indicator is present that will not actuate if any one gear is not locked in place, is critical.

3. How do most aircraft lock a gear in the up position? (FAA-H-8083-25)

A gear may be locked up by a mechanical system, through the shutting off of a gear motor, or through maintaining a positive "up" position through pressure in a hydraulic system for most common light general aviation aircraft systems.

4. How is accidental gear retraction prevented on the ground? (FAA-H-8083-25)

Inadvertent gear retraction is typically prevented by a safety (squat) switch on one of the gear. Whenever this switch is compressed by the weight of the aircraft on the ground, the switch electrically prevents the operation of the landing gear system.

5. How is landing gear position typically indicated on the instrument panel? (FAA-H-8083-25)

In most light general aviation aircraft, a gear position of up or down is indicated by lights or depictions on a glass panel display. Most newer aircraft display separate indications for each individual gear. Some older aircraft only have a single up, down, or potentially in-transit or unsafe light. Indicator light(s) will illuminate green when in the down and locked position, and typically indicate amber or red when in an unsafe or in transit position. Also be sure to reference your AFM/POH to determine indications for landing gear positions.

6. What are some types of landing gear warning systems used in light general aviation aircraft? (FAA-H-8083-25)

Manifold lever switches—Most aircraft will actuate a visual or auditory indication if the manifold pressure is reduced beyond a low point threshold if the gear has not been deployed and is down and locked.

Flaps position switches—Some aircraft will actuate a visual or auditory indication if the flaps have been deployed beyond a given range if the gear has not been deployed and is down and locked.

Airspeed threshold—A few aircraft may have installed pitot tubes related to the gear system that will cause a gear to automatically drop if a minimum airspeed is reached if the gear has not been deployed to the down and locked position.

Ground/airspeed speed threshold—Some aircraft will actuate a visual or auditory indication if a minimum ground or airspeed has been reached and the gear is not in a down and locked position. Similarly, if the throttle or manifold pressure drop below a certain point and the gear is not in the down and locked position, you could receive the same visual or auditory warning.

(continued)

Laser gear advisory—A few aircraft are equipped with laser gear advisory systems. These systems detect if the aircraft is over water or land surfaces and illuminate or annunciate a gear advisory.

7. **In an aircraft with an interconnected nose wheel, how is steering accomplished on the ground?** (AFM/POH)

Aircraft with an interconnected nose wheel may have mechanical linkage or bungees from rudder pedals to the nose wheel to effect steering when the pilot applies pressure to the rudders. In larger aircraft, directional control may be controlled through dedicated steering control using a tiller or steering wheel. Differential braking may also be available to assist with further turning efforts.

8. **In an aircraft with a free-castering nose wheel, how is steering accomplished on the ground?** (AFM/POH)

In an aircraft with a free-castering nose wheel, steering on the ground is typically accomplished using differential braking and asymmetrical thrust.

In this configuration, the nose wheel is free to rotate freely without any direct steering input. Instead, the pilot relies on differential braking to control the direction of the aircraft while on the ground. By applying more braking force on one side of the aircraft compared to the other, the pilot can induce a yawing motion, causing the aircraft to turn in the desired direction. To make a turn to the left, the pilot would apply more braking pressure to the left main landing gear compared to the right. This creates a moment that pivots the aircraft around the main landing gear, resulting in a left turn. Similarly, to make a right turn, the pilot would apply more braking pressure to the right main landing gear.

Additionally, asymmetrical thrust can also assist in ground steering. By applying more power to one engine or using differential thrust if the aircraft has multiple engines, the pilot can create a yawing moment that aids in turning the aircraft.

Note: The effectiveness of ground steering using differential braking and asymmetrical thrust may vary based on factors such as aircraft design, weight distribution, runway conditions, and other operational considerations.

G. Powerplant

1. **Describe how each of the following engine gauges work: oil temperature, oil pressure, cylinder head temperature, tachometer, manifold pressure, fuel pressure.** (AFM/POH)

   Oil temperature—Electrically powered from the aircraft electrical system.

   Oil pressure—A direct-pressure oil line from the engine delivers oil at engine operating pressure to the gauge.

   Cylinder head temperature—Electrically powered from the aircraft electrical system.

   Tachometer—Engine-driven mechanically.

   Manifold pressure—Direct reading of induction air manifold pressure in inches of mercury.

   Fuel pressure—Indicates fuel pressure to the carburetor.

2. **What will the manifold pressure gauge indicate when the engine isn't running? After starting, what will it indicate? Explain.** (FAA-H-8083-25)

   When the engine isn't running, the manifold pressure gauge will indicate ambient atmospheric pressure, which is typically around 29.92 inches of mercury (inHg) at sea level under standard atmospheric conditions. This reading represents the pressure of the surrounding air and is often referred to as "pressure altitude" when the engine is not operating.

   After starting the engine and during normal operation, the manifold pressure gauge will indicate the pressure in the intake manifold, which is created by the engine's intake stroke. The manifold pressure is a measure of the air pressure inside the intake manifold relative to the surrounding atmospheric pressure. This pressure varies based on the engine's power settings and throttle position.

   For example, during idle or low-power settings, the manifold pressure will be relatively low, indicating a lower pressure in the intake manifold. During high-power settings, such as takeoff or climbing, the manifold pressure will increase, indicating a higher pressure in the intake manifold as more air is drawn into the engine.

3. **What four strokes must occur in each cylinder of a typical four-stroke engine in order for it to produce full power?** (FAA-H-8083-25)

The four strokes are:

Intake—Fuel mixture is drawn into cylinder by downward stroke.

Compression—Mixture is compressed by upward stroke.

Power—Spark ignites mixture forcing piston downward and producing power.

Exhaust—Burned gases pushed out of cylinder by upward stroke.

4. **Explain the operation of a carburetor.** (FAA-H-8083-25)

   a. Outside air first flows through an air filter, usually located at an air intake in the front part of the engine cowling.

   b. The filtered air flows into the carburetor and through a venturi, a narrow throat in the carburetor.

   c. When the air flows through the venturi, a low-pressure area is created which forces the fuel to flow through a main fuel jet located at the throat.

   d. The fuel then flows into the airstream where it is mixed with the flowing air.

   e. The fuel/air mixture is then drawn through the intake manifold and into the combustion chambers where it is ignited.

5. **Explain the function of the float in a float-type carburetor system.** (FAA-H-8083-25)

The float-type carburetor acquires its name from a float, which rests on fuel within the float chamber. A needle attached to the float opens and closes an opening at the bottom of the carburetor bowl. This meters the correct amount of fuel into the carburetor depending upon the position of the float, which is controlled by the level of fuel in the float chamber. When the level of the fuel forces the float to rise, the needle valve closes the fuel opening and shuts off the fuel flow to the carburetor. The needle valve opens again when the engine requires additional fuel. The flow of the fuel/air mixture to the combustion chambers is regulated by the throttle valve, which is controlled by the throttle in the flight deck.

6. How does the carburetor heat system work? (AFM/POH)

A carburetor heat valve, controlled by the pilot, allows unfiltered, heated air from a shroud located around an exhaust riser or muffler to be directed to the induction air manifold prior to the carburetor. Carburetor heat should be used anytime suspected or known carburetor icing conditions exist.

7. A pilot notices that when applying carburetor heat during an engine runup on the ground, an increase in RPM occurs. What does this indicate? (FAA-H-8083-25)

When a pilot notices an increase in RPM (revolutions per minute) while applying carburetor heat during an engine runup on the ground, it indicates the presence of carburetor ice.

Carburetor ice occurs when the moisture in the air combines with the fuel vapor in the carburetor, causing ice to form. This ice can block or restrict the flow of air and fuel into the engine, resulting in a decrease in engine power and a drop in RPM. To prevent this, aircraft are equipped with a carburetor heat system.

When the pilot applies carburetor heat, the system directs warm air from the engine's exhaust or another heat source to the carburetor, melting any ice that has formed and preventing further ice accumulation. However, because the application of carburetor heat introduces warm, less dense air into the engine, it can lead to a temporary increase in RPM. As the ice is melted, the flow of air and fuel into the engine improves, which can cause the engine RPM to rise temporarily until the balance of air and fuel is restored. Once the carburetor heat is applied for a sufficient time, the RPM should stabilize, and the engine should run smoothly.

Carburetor icing can occur on the ground and is especially dangerous if not noticed before a takeoff roll is initiated, as it can result in the aircraft engine not producing full takeoff power.

8. What is fuel Injection? (FAA-H-8083-25)

Fuel injectors have replaced carburetors in some airplanes. In a fuel injection system, the fuel is normally injected into the system either directly into the cylinders or just ahead of the intake valves; whereas in a carbureted system, the fuel enters the airstream at the throttle valve. There are several types of fuel injection systems in use today, and though there are variations in design, the operational methods are generally simple. Most designs incorporate an engine-driven fuel pump, fuel/air control unit, fuel manifold valve, discharge nozzles, auxiliary fuel pump, and fuel pressure/flow indicators.

9. **What are some advantages of fuel injection?** (FAA-H-8083-25)

a. Reduction in evaporative icing.
b. Better fuel flow.
c. Faster throttle response.
d. Precise control of mixture.
e. Better fuel distribution.
f. Easier cold weather starts.

10. **Are there any disadvantages associated with fuel-injected engines?** (FAA-H-8083-25)

a. Difficulty in starting a hot engine.
b. Vapor locks during ground operations on hot days.
c. Problems associated with restarting an engine that quits because of fuel starvation.

11. **What is an alternate induction air system and when is it used?** (FAA-H-8083-3)

It is a device which opens, either automatically or manually, to allow induction airflow to continue should the primary induction air opening become blocked. In the event of impact ice accumulating over normal engine air induction sources, carburetor heat (carbureted engines) or alternate air (fuel-injected engines) should be selected. On some fuel-injected engines, an alternate air source is automatically activated with blockage of the normal air source.

12. **What is the condition known as vapor lock?** (FAA-H-8083-31)

Vapor lock is a condition in which Avgas vaporizes in the fuel line or other components between the fuel tank and the carburetor. This typically occurs on warm days on aircraft with engine-driven fuel pumps that suck fuel from the tank(s). Vapor lock can be caused by excessively hot fuel, low pressure, or excessive turbulence of the fuel traveling through the fuel system. In each case, liquid fuel vaporizes prematurely and blocks the flow of liquid fuel to the carburetor. Various steps can be taken to prevent vapor lock. The most common is the use of boost pumps located in the fuel tank that force pressurized liquid fuel to the engine.

13. What does the throttle do? (FAA-H-8083-25)

The throttle allows the pilot to manually control the amount of fuel/air charge entering the cylinders. This in turn regulates the engine manifold pressure.

14. What does the mixture control do? (FAA-H-8083-25)

It regulates the fuel-to-air ratio. Most airplane engines incorporate a device called a mixture control, by which the fuel/air ratio can be controlled by the pilot during flight. The purpose of a mixture control is to prevent the mixture from becoming too rich at high altitudes, due to decreasing air density. Leaning the mixture during cross-country flights conserves fuel and provides optimum power.

15. What are turbochargers? (FAA-H-8083-25)

Higher performance aircraft typically operate at higher altitudes where air density is substantially less. The decrease in air density as altitude increases results in a decreased power output of an unsupercharged engine. By compressing the thin air by means of an air compressor, the turbocharged engine will maintain the preset power as altitude is increased. The turbocharger consists of a compressor to provide pressurized air to the engine, and a turbine driven by exhaust gases of the engine to drive the compressor.

16. What are cowl flaps? (FAA-H-8083-32)

Cowl flaps are located on the engine cowling and allow the pilot to control the operating temperature of the engine by regulating the amount of air circulating within the engine compartment. Cowl flaps may be manually or electrically activated and usually allow for a variety of flap positions.

17. When are cowl flaps used? (AFM/POH)

a. Normally the cowl flaps will be in the "open" position in the following operations:

- During starting of the engine.
- While taxiing.
- During takeoff and high-power climb operation.

The cowl flaps may be adjusted in cruise flight for the appropriate cylinder head temperature.

b. The cowl flaps should be in the "closed" position in the following operations:

- During extended let-downs.
- Anytime excessive cooling is a possibility (i.e., approach to landing, engine-out practice, etc.).

18. During the before takeoff magneto check, what are you testing when moving the ignition switch from the BOTH to LEFT, BOTH to RIGHT, and back to the BOTH position? (FAA-H-8083-25, FAA-H-8083-32)

During the before takeoff magneto check, moving the ignition switch from the BOTH to LEFT, BOTH to RIGHT, and back to the BOTH position is a standard procedure to test the operation of each magneto and ensure the engine's ignition system is functioning correctly. Here's what is being tested during each step:

BOTH to LEFT—When moving the ignition switch from BOTH to LEFT, you are selecting the left magneto only. This test checks the left magneto's ability to independently provide ignition to the engine's cylinders. The RPM drop observed during this step is typically higher than during the next step (BOTH to RIGHT), as the left magneto is connected to the non-firing spark plugs, leading to a more noticeable drop in engine RPM.

BOTH to RIGHT—Moving the ignition switch from BOTH to RIGHT selects the right magneto only. This test checks the right magneto's ability to independently provide ignition to the engine's cylinders.

Back to BOTH—Returning the ignition switch to the BOTH position reconnects both magnetos to the engine's ignition system. In this position, the engine receives ignition from both magnetos simultaneously. During this step, you should verify that the engine

RPM returns to its original setting, indicating that both magnetos are operating correctly.

During the magneto check, the RPM drop observed in each position should be within the acceptable limits specified in the aircraft's pilot's operating handbook (POH) or checklist. If the RPM drop exceeds the prescribed limits or is uneven between the left and right magnetos, it may indicate a problem with one of the magnetos or the ignition system, and further inspection or maintenance should be performed before takeoff. Properly functioning magnetos are essential for reliable engine performance during flight.

19. **While in flight in an airplane with a controllable-pitch propeller, how will the failure of a single magneto affect RPM indication in the cockpit?** (FAA-H-8083-25)

In an airplane with a controllable-pitch propeller and a single magneto failure, the RPM indication in the cockpit will be affected differently based on the specific type of magneto failure. Effects include the following:

a. *Loss of one magneto*—If one of the two magnetos fails during flight, the engine will continue to operate on the remaining magneto, but with a reduced number of firing cylinders. The RPM indication in the cockpit will likely show a decrease from the normal RPM reading. The magnitude of the RPM drop will depend on the design of the engine and the number of cylinders affected by the failed magneto.

b. *Dual ignition system design*—In most aircraft with a controllable-pitch propeller, the engine is equipped with a dual ignition system, meaning there are two separate magnetos, each providing ignition to a different set of spark plugs in the engine cylinders. If one magneto fails, the other magneto will still be operational, providing ignition to a portion of the engine's cylinders.

c. *Loss of engine power*—As a result of the single magneto failure, the engine's power output will be reduced. The actual reduction in RPM will depend on factors such as the number of cylinders affected, engine design, and altitude. The pilot should expect a noticeable decrease in engine performance and a reduction in RPM from the normal cruise RPM setting.

(continued)

d. *RPM limitations*—Pilots should refer to the aircraft's pilot's operating handbook (POH) or airplane flight manual (AFM) for specific procedures and limitations related to a single magneto failure. Some aircraft may have limitations on maximum power settings or operational restrictions when operating on a single magneto.

In the event of a magneto failure, pilots should take appropriate action as specified in the emergency procedures section of the POH or checklist. This may include troubleshooting and attempting to restore the magneto functionality or preparing for a precautionary landing if required.

H. Propeller

1. What are two main different types of fixed-pitch propellers that might be installed on an aircraft to accomplish a specific performance goal? (FAA-H-8083-25)

Two types of fixed-pitch propellers are:

Climb propeller—has a lower pitch, therefore less drag. Results in higher RPM and more horsepower being developed by the engine; increases performance during takeoffs and climbs, but decreases performance during cruising flight.

Cruise propeller—has a higher pitch, therefore more drag. Results in lower RPM and less horsepower capability; decreases performance during takeoffs and climbs, but increases efficiency during cruising flight.

2. Discuss variable-pitch propellers (constant speed). (FAA-H-8083-25)

An airplane equipped with a constant-speed propeller is capable of continuously adjusting the propeller blade angle to maintain a constant engine speed. For example, if engine RPM increases as a result of a decreased load on the engine (descent), the system automatically increases the propeller blade angle (increasing air load) until the RPM has returned to the preset speed. The propeller governor can be regulated by the pilot with a control in the cockpit, so that any desired blade angle setting (within its limits) and engine operating RPM can be obtained, thereby increasing the airplane's efficiency in various flight conditions.

3. **What does the propeller control do?** (FAA-H-8083-25)

The propeller control regulates propeller pitch and engine RPM as desired for a given flight condition. The propeller control adjusts a propeller governor which establishes and maintains the propeller speed, which in turn maintains the engine speed.

4. **When operating an aircraft with a variable pitch (constant speed) propeller, what setting would be most desirable for maximum performance during a takeoff?** (FAA-H-8083-25)

A low pitch, high RPM setting produces maximum power and thrust. The low blade angle keeps the angle of attack small and efficient with respect to the relative wind. At the same time, it allows the propeller to handle a smaller mass of air per revolution. This light load allows the engine to turn at high RPM and to convert the maximum amount of fuel into heat energy in a given time. The high RPM also creates maximum thrust because the mass of air handled per revolution is small, the number of revolutions per minute is many, the slipstream velocity is high, and the airplane speed is low.

5. **What is a propeller governor?** (FAA-H-8083-32)

The propeller governor, with the assistance of a governor pump, controls the flow of engine oil to or from a piston in the propeller hub. When the engine oil, under high pressure from the governor pump, pushes the piston forward, the propeller blades are twisted toward a high pitch/low RPM condition. When the engine oil is released from the cylinder, centrifugal force, with the assistance of an internal spring, twists the blades towards a low pitch/high RPM condition.

6. **When operating an airplane with a constant-speed propeller, which condition induces the most stress on the engine?** (FAA-H-8083-3)

Excessive manifold pressure raises the cylinder compression pressure, resulting in high stresses within the engine. Excessive pressure also produces high engine temperatures. A combination of high manifold pressure and low RPM can induce damaging detonation; however, it is a fallacy that (in non-turbocharged engines) the manifold pressure in inches of mercury should *never* exceed RPM in hundreds for cruise power settings. The cruise power charts in the AFM/POH should be consulted when selecting cruise power settings. Whatever the combinations of RPM and manifold pressure listed in these charts—they have been flight tested and approved by the airframe and powerplant engineers for the respective airframe and engine manufacturer.

7. For variable-pitch (constant speed) propellers, where does the fluid used to control the propeller condition come from? (AFM/POH, FAA-H-8083-3)

Generally, the oil pressure used for pitch changes comes directly from the engine lubricating system. When a governor is employed, engine oil is used and the oil pressure is usually boosted by a pump that is integrated with the propeller governor.

Exam Tip: Have an in-depth understanding of the constant-speed propeller on your airplane. Make a copy of the AFM/POH propeller governor diagram and have it readily available during your explanation. Be capable of explaining exactly what occurs when you move the propeller control in the cockpit.

8. If a loss of oil pressure in a constant speed propeller occurs, what effect will this have on the propeller pitch and RPM? (AFM/POH)

In the event of a loss of oil pressure in the propeller system of an aircraft equipped with a constant-speed propeller, the effect on the propeller pitch and RPM will depend on the specific type of propeller system installed on the aircraft.

Single-engine aircraft—Single-engine aircraft are typically equipped with propeller systems that will cause the propeller to default to a low-pitch, high RPM setting in the event of a loss of pressure. This allows the aircraft to still be flown at high power settings if the engine is still operating.

Multi-engine aircraft—In most multi-engine aircraft, a loss of oil pressure in the propeller system will cause the propeller to default to a high-pitch, low RPM, or even feathered position. This allows the pilot to reduce drag on the overall flight condition since there is another engine that should be operating.

I. Fuel System

1. In a high-wing aircraft, a fuel system is typically fed by what mechanism? (FAA-H-8083-25)

In most light general aviation aircraft with high wings, fuel is fed to the engine via gravity. Some aircraft will also have an engine fuel pump, and a few may even have electrical boost, priming, or emergency fuel pumps that could be used anytime fuel pressure falls below a selected value.

2. In a low-wing aircraft, a fuel system is typically fed by what mechanism? (FAA-H-8083-25)

In most light general aviation aircraft with low wings, fuel is fed to the engine through an engine-driven fuel pump. For most low-wing aircraft, an additional electrical pump of some sort is installed to serve as an emergency and/or priming pump that could be used anytime fuel pressure falls below a selected value. It should be noted that the backup electric pumps will not always provide sufficient flow to keep an engine running at full power. A pilot should consult with the AFM/POH for more information on any fuel pump limitations.

3. When an aircraft is equipped with fuel selectors that allow for specific tanks to be selected, most commonly left or right, or both positions, what would be reasons for a pilot to switch tanks? (FAA-H-8083-25)

Aircraft equipped with a "Both" fuel selector option may, in many instances, be operated drawing fuel from both tanks at the same time. An unequal fuel burn may occur if the wings are not consistently kept level during flight, due to a venting problem or a fuel flow restriction. If this happens, a pilot might need to select one or the other tank to bring the aircraft back into balance. When an aircraft is only able to draw fuel from one tank or the other at a time, a pilot should manage the fuel burn to keep the aircraft balanced during flight. While fuel tanks are commonly located near or at the center of gravity and will many times have little effect on forward or aft CG positions, lateral stability may be affected. In extreme instances, crosswind capabilities may be affected, or aileron control inputs will be needed to keep an aircraft flying level. Some modern aircraft have operational limitations set forth for maximum allowable fuel imbalances.

4. Where are fuel vents typically located for an aircraft's fuel tanks? (AFM/POH)

Many aircraft will have either vents on the wing for each tank or vented fuel caps, or in some cases will have a vent on one tank and a cross vented through a tank on the other side of the aircraft. Frequently, a vent line will have a check valve.

5. What purpose do fuel tank vents have? (FAA-H-8083-25)

As the fuel level in an aircraft fuel tank decreases, without vents a vacuum would be created within the tank which would eventually result in a decreasing fuel flow and finally engine stoppage. Fuel system venting provides a way of replacing fuel with outside air, preventing formation of a vacuum. Tanks may be vented through the filler cap or through a tube extending through the surface of the wing.

6. If an aircraft is certified to use 100LL fuel, can it be fueled with any other fuel types? (AFM/POH)

Airplane engines are designed to operate using a specific grade of fuel as recommended by the manufacturer. In some cases, supplemental type certificates are available to allow an aircraft engine to be operated with an alternate fuel source. If the proper grade of fuel is not available, it is possible, but not desirable, to use the next higher grade as a substitute. If using a higher grade fuel than that specified as a minimum grade for your engine, the engine manufacturer's instructions must be observed. This is because the higher-octane fuels normally used in higher-compression engines must ignite at higher temperatures—but not prematurely.

7. What color of dye is added to the following fuel grades: 80, 100, 100LL, Jet A? (FAA-H-8083-25, FAA-P-8740-35)

Grade / Color
80 (obsolete) = Red
100 (obsolete) = Green
100LL = Blue
Jet A = Colorless or straw

8. **What is the function of the manual primer, and how does it operate?** (AFM/POH)

The manual primer's function is to provide assistance in starting the engine. The primer draws fuel from the fuel strainer and injects it directly into the cylinder intake ports. This usually results in a quicker, more efficient engine start.

9. **What is the purpose of having fuel drain valves on an aircraft?** (FAA-H-8083-25)

Drain valves, sometimes many of them, are installed on aircraft to allow for testing of fuel quality. Finding any water or debris in fuel drained from these valves may be an indicator that engine performance may be degraded or interrupted with such contaminants.

10. **Are fuel quantity indicators required to be accurate?** (FAA-H-8083-25)

14 CFR §91.205 states that a fuel gauge indicating the quantity of fuel in each tank is required equipment. 14 CFR §23.2430 says that fuel systems must provide the flightcrew with a means to determine the total usable fuel available.

It is common folklore that a fuel gauge only needs to be accurate when it reads empty. These two FARs drive the appropriate answer to this question to the point that if the fuel gauges are not accurately indicating, the aircraft would be deemed unairworthy as it would not be meeting the requirement of providing "the flightcrew with a means to determine the total usable fuel available."

Additionally, a pilot should never just depend on the accuracy of the fuel quantity gauges. The pilot should always visually or mechanically check the fuel level in each tank to be used during the preflight inspection and compare it with the corresponding fuel quantity indication.

J. Oil System

1. Briefly describe the engine oil system. (AFM/POH)

Aircraft engine lubrication and oil for propeller governor operation is supplied from a sump on the bottom of the engine.

2. How would a pilot know the minimum and maximum oil operational ranges? (AFM/POH)

A pilot will find the maximum and minimum allowable operational oil limits in the AFM/POH for the aircraft in the limitations section. It will also typically be marked on the oil dipstick and may even be placarded on the inside of the cowling.

3. How would a pilot know the minimum and maximum oil temperatures and pressures for operational ranges? (AFM/POH)

A pilot will find the maximum and minimum allowable operational oil limits in the AFM/POH for the aircraft in the limitations section. It will be placarded as ranges of operation on the aircraft instrumentation.

4. What are two types of oil a pilot might use in the operation of a piston-powered aircraft? (FAA-H-8083-32)

Mineral oil—Also known as non-detergent oil; contains no additives. This type of oil is normally used after an engine overhaul or when an aircraft engine is new; normally used for engine break-in purposes.

Ashless dispersant—Mineral oil with additives; high antiwear properties along with multi-viscosity (ability to perform in wide range of temps). Also picks up contamination and carbon particles and keeps them suspended so that buildups and sludge do not form in the engine.

K. Electrical System

1. Describe the electrical system on this aircraft. (AFM/POH)

Electrical energy is provided by a 28-volt, direct-current system, powered by an engine-driven 60-amp alternator and a 24-volt battery.

2. What is the purpose of a battery on an aircraft that is otherwise equipped with a generator or alternator? (AFM/POH)

A battery on an aircraft is typically used for starting the aircraft. Once the aircraft is started, the battery remains the primary source of power to the electrical equipment as a stable source of voltage and is charged by an alternator or generator. Some aircraft will have multiple batteries as backup systems, and some aircraft will even have multiple alternators as backup systems. Know the electrical system on your aircraft and the failure modes. Knowing if there are primary and essential busses on the aircraft and what equipment will be affected or still work and for how long is important when determining what response times and resources you have in the event of failures or emergencies.

3. What is a bus bar? (FAA-H-8083-25)

A bus bar is used as a terminal in the aircraft electrical system to connect the main electrical system to the equipment using electricity as a source of power. This simplifies the wiring system and provides a common point from which voltage can be distributed throughout the system.

4. What aircraft systems are commonly powered by the electrical system in light general aviation aircraft?

Normally the following:
a. Radio equipment.
b. Turn coordinator.
c. Fuel gauges.
d. Pitot heat.
e. Landing light.
f. Taxi light.
g. Strobe lights.

(continued)

h. Interior lights.

i. Instrument lights.

j. Position lights.

k. Flaps (maybe).

l. Stall warning system (maybe).

m. Oil temperature gauge.

n. Cigarette lighter (maybe).

o. Starting motor.

p. Electric fuel pump.

q. Gear systems.

5. What does the ammeter indicate? (FAA-H-8083-25)

It shows if the alternator/generator is producing an adequate supply of electrical power to the system by measuring the amperes of electricity, and also indicates whether the battery is receiving an electrical charge. If the needle indicates a plus value, it means that the battery is being charged. If the needle indicates a minus value, it means that the generator or alternator output is inadequate and energy is being drawn from the battery to supply the system.

6. What function does the voltage regulator have? (FAA-H-8083-25)

A voltage regulator controls the rate of charge to the battery by stabilizing the generator or alternator electrical output. The generator/alternator voltage output is usually slightly higher than the battery voltage. For example, a 12-volt battery would be fed by a generator/alternator system of approximately 14 volts. The difference in voltage keeps the battery charged.

7. Does the aircraft have an external power source receptacle, and if so where is it located? (AFM/POH)

Yes, the receptacle is located behind a door on the left side of the fuselage aft of the baggage compartment door.

8. What type of ignition system does your airplane have? (FAA-H-8083-25)

Engine ignition is provided by two engine-driven magnetos, and two spark plugs per cylinder. The ignition system is completely independent of the aircraft electrical system. The magnetos are self-contained units supplying electrical current without using an external source of power. However, before they can produce current, the magnetos must be actuated as the engine crankshaft is rotated by some other means. To accomplish this, the aircraft battery furnishes electrical power to operate a starter which, through a series of gears, rotates the engine crankshaft. This in turn actuates the armature of the magneto to produce the sparks for ignition of the fuel in each cylinder. After the engine starts, the starter system is disengaged and the battery no longer contributes to the actual operation of the engine.

9. **What are the two main advantages of a dual ignition system?** (FAA-H-8083-25)

   a. Increased safety—in case one system fails, the engine may be operated on the other until a landing is safely made.

   b. More complete and even combustion of the mixture, and consequently improved engine performance; i.e., the fuel/air mixture will be ignited on each side of the combustion chamber and burn toward the center.

L. Environmental System

1. **What are the two main types of heater systems commonly found on general aviation aircraft?** (FAA-H-8083-25)

   Fresh air heaters—Fresh air heaters that pass air over an exhaust shroud into the cabin through ducts are a type of combustion heater commonly used in general aviation aircraft. As the fresh air flows over the hot exhaust shroud, it absorbs the heat from the engine exhaust, significantly increasing its temperature. The heated air is then distributed into the aircraft cabin through a network of ducts. These ducts are strategically placed to ensure proper circulation of warm air throughout the cabin.

   Combustion heaters—Combustion heaters, also known as fuel-burning heaters, utilize a combustion process to generate heat. These heaters typically burn aviation fuel, such as Jet-A or avgas, to produce heat that is then distributed throughout the aircraft cabin. Combustion heaters are often equipped with a heat exchanger, which transfers the heat from the combustion chamber to the cabin air. Air circulation fans help distribute the heated air throughout the cabin, providing warmth to occupants. Combustion heaters are commonly found in many piston-engine aircraft and smaller turboprop aircraft.

2. **What are the main aeromedical risks associated with cabin heater systems in general aviation aircraft?** (FAA-H-8083-25)

Cabin heater systems in general aviation aircraft, while providing comfort and warmth, can pose certain aeromedical risks. The main risks associated with cabin heater systems include:

Carbon monoxide (CO) poisoning—CO is a colorless and odorless gas produced by incomplete combustion of fuels, such as aviation fuel or other hydrocarbons used in the heater system. If there is a leak or malfunction in the heater system, CO can enter the aircraft cabin, leading to CO poisoning. Inhaling high levels of CO can cause symptoms ranging from headaches, dizziness, and nausea to more severe consequences, including loss of consciousness or death. A common cause for carbon monoxide in a cabin is cracked tubing or exhaust shrouds that allow the gas into the cabin.

Oxygen depletion—Another risk associated with cabin heaters is the potential for oxygen depletion. Some combustion-based heater systems consume oxygen during the combustion process. In an inadequately ventilated or sealed cabin, excessive use of a combustion heater can lead to a reduction in the available oxygen levels. This can result in hypoxia, which is a condition characterized by an insufficient supply of oxygen to the body's tissues and organs. Hypoxia can impair cognitive function, decrease alertness, and potentially lead to a loss of consciousness.

3. **What are the three main components of aircraft oxygen systems?** (FAA-H-8083-25)

   a. A storage system (containers).
   b. A delivery system.
   c. Mask or nasal cannula.

4. **What are several types of oxygen systems in use?** (FAA-H-8083-25, FAA-H-8083-31)

Systems are often characterized by the type of regulator used to dispense the oxygen:

   a. Diluter-demand.
   b. Pressure-demand.
   c. Continuous-flow.
   d. Electrical pulse-demand.

5. Can any kind of oxygen be used for aviator's breathing oxygen? (FAA-H-8083-31)

No, oxygen used for medical purposes or welding normally should not be used because it may contain too much water. The excess water could condense and freeze in the oxygen lines when flying at high altitudes. Specifications for aviator's breathing oxygen are 99.5 percent pure oxygen with not more than two milliliters of water per liter of oxygen.

6. How does a continuous-flow oxygen system operate? (FAA-H-8083-25)

Continuous-flow oxygen systems are usually provided for passengers. The passenger mask typically has a reservoir bag that collects oxygen from the continuous-flow oxygen system during the time when the mask user is exhaling. The oxygen collected in the bag allows a higher inspiratory flow rate during the inhalation cycle, which reduces the amount of air dilution. Ambient air is added to the supplied oxygen during inhalation after the reservoir bag oxygen supply is depleted. The exhaled air is released to the cabin.

7. How does a pressure-demand oxygen system operate? (FAA-H-8083-25)

Pressure-demand oxygen systems are similar to diluter demand oxygen equipment, except that oxygen is supplied to the mask under pressure at cabin altitudes above 34,000 feet. Pressure-demand regulators create airtight and oxygen-tight seals, but they also provide a positive pressure application of oxygen to the mask face piece that allows the user's lungs to be pressurized with oxygen; this makes them safe at altitudes above 40,000 feet. Some systems may have a pressure-demand mask with the regulator attached directly to the mask, rather than mounted on the instrument panel or other area within the flight deck.

8. **Explain how a diluter-demand oxygen system operates.** (FAA-H-8083-25)

   Diluter-demand oxygen systems supply oxygen only when the user inhales through the mask. An automix lever allows the regulators to automatically mix cabin air and oxygen or supply 100 percent oxygen, depending on the altitude. The demand mask provides a tight seal over the face to prevent dilution with outside air and can be used safely up to 40,000 feet.

9. **Explain the operation of an electrical pulse-demand oxygen system.** (FAA-H-8083-25)

   Portable electrical pulse-demand oxygen systems deliver oxygen by detecting an individual's inhalation effort and provide oxygen flow during the initial portion of inhalation. Pulse-demand systems do not waste oxygen during the breathing cycle because oxygen is only delivered during inhalation. Most systems incorporate an internal barometer that automatically compensates for changes in altitude by increasing the amount of oxygen delivered for each pulse as altitude is increased.

10. **What is a pressurized aircraft?** (FAA-H-8083-25)

    In a pressurized aircraft, the cabin, flight compartment, and baggage compartments are incorporated into a sealed unit which is capable of containing air under a pressure higher than outside atmospheric pressure. On aircraft powered by turbine engines, bleed air from the engine compressor section is used to pressurize the cabin, and piston-powered aircraft may use air supplied from each engine turbocharger through a sonic venturi (flow limiter). Air is released from the fuselage by a device called an outflow valve. Since the superchargers provide a constant inflow of air to the pressurized area, the outflow valve, by regulating the air exit, is the major controlling element in the pressurization system.

11. **What operational advantages are there in flying pressurized aircraft?** (FAA-H-8083-25)

    A cabin pressurization system performs several functions:

    a. It allows an aircraft to fly higher which can result in better fuel economy, higher speeds, and the capability to avoid bad weather and turbulence.

b. It will typically maintain a cabin pressure altitude of 8,000 feet at the maximum designed cruising altitude of the airplane.

c. It prevents rapid changes of cabin altitude which may be uncomfortable or injurious to passengers and crew.

d. It permits a reasonably fast exchange of air from inside to outside of the cabin. This is necessary to eliminate odors and to remove stale air.

12. Describe a typical cabin pressure control system. (FAA-H-8083-25)

The cabin pressure control system provides cabin pressure regulation, pressure relief, vacuum relief, and the means for selecting the desired cabin altitude in the isobaric and differential range. In addition, dumping of the cabin pressure is a function of the pressure control system. A cabin pressure regulator, an outflow valve, and a safety valve are used to accomplish these functions.

13. What are the components of a cabin pressure control system? (FAA-H-8083-25)

a. *Cabin pressure regulator*—Controls cabin pressure to a selected value in the isobaric range and limits cabin pressure to a preset differential value in the differential range.

b. *Cabin air pressure safety valve*—A combination pressure relief, vacuum relief, and dump valve.

- Pressure relief valve: prevents cabin pressure from exceeding a predetermined differential pressure above ambient pressure.

- Vacuum relief valve: prevents ambient pressure from exceeding cabin pressure by allowing external air to enter the cabin when the ambient pressure exceeds cabin pressure.

- Dump valve: actuated by a cockpit control which will cause the cabin air to be dumped to the atmosphere.

c. *Instrumentation*—Several instruments used in conjunction with the pressurization controller are:

- Cabin differential pressure gauge: Indicates difference between inside and outside pressure; should be monitored to ensure that the cabin does not exceed maximum allowable differential pressure.

(continued)

- Cabin altimeter: This is a check on system performance. Sometimes differential pressure and cabin altimeter combined into one:
- Cabin rate-of-climb: Indicates cabin rate-of-climb or descent.

M. Deicing and Anti-Icing

1. What is the difference between a deice system and an anti-ice system? (FAA-H-8083-31)

A deice system is used to eliminate ice that has already formed. An anti-ice system is used to prevent the formation of ice.

2. What types of systems are used in the prevention and elimination of airframe ice? (FAA-H-8083-31)

Pneumatic—A deice type of system; consists of inflatable boots attached to the leading edges of the wings and tail surfaces. Compressed air from the pressure side of the engine vacuum pump is cycled through ducts or tubes in the boots causing the boots to inflate. Most systems also incorporate a timer.

Hot air—An anti-ice type system; commonly found on turboprop and turbojet aircraft. Hot air is directed from the engine (compressor) to the leading edges of the wings.

Electrical—Electrical deicing systems in general aviation aircraft use embedded heating elements or wires on critical surfaces like wings, tailplanes, and propellers. Activating the system sends an electrical current through the elements, generating heat to prevent or remove ice buildup. Temperature sensors monitor surface temperatures for optimal deicing. Power is supplied through the aircraft's electrical system or dedicated sources such as batteries.

Fluid—Liquid deicing systems are used in general aviation aircraft to remove ice and prevent its formation. A liquid deicing system typically involves spraying a specialized deicing fluid onto critical surfaces such as wings, tailplanes, and propellers. This fluid contains anti-icing agents that prevent ice buildup and facilitate ice removal. The deicing fluid is stored in dedicated tanks and distributed through a network of tubing and nozzles. Pilots activate the system to spray the fluid onto the surfaces before or during flight. The fluid coats the surfaces and is intended to provide a protective layer to prevent further ice formation or accumulation.

3. **What types of systems are used in the prevention and elimination of propeller ice?** (FAA-H-8083-31)

Electrically heated boots—Consist of heating elements incorporated into the boots which are bonded to the propeller. The ice buildup on the propeller is heated from below and then thrown off by centrifugal force.

Fluid system—Consists of an electrically driven pump which, when activated, supplies a fluid, such as alcohol, to a device in the propeller spinner which distributes the fluid along the propeller assisted by centrifugal force.

4. **What types of systems are used in the prevention and elimination of windshield ice?** (FAA-H-8083-31)

Fluid system—A liquid fluid system, typically driven by an electric pump, can be activated to spray deicing fluid onto the windshield (or other surfaces) of the aircraft to prevent formation of ice. A best practice is to deploy this fluid before ice accumulates and begins to coat surfaces. It is intended to be most effective at stopping ice from bonding to surfaces, not removing it once it has built up.

Electrical system—Heating elements are embedded in the windshield or in a device attached to the windshield which when activated, prevents the formation of ice.

N. Avionics

1. **What function does the avionics power switch have?** (AFM/POH)

The avionics power switch controls power from the primary bus to the avionics bus. The circuit is protected by a combination power switch/circuit breaker. Aircraft avionics are isolated from electrical power when the switch is in the "Off" position. Also, if an overload should occur in the system, the avionics power switch will move to the "Off" position, causing an interruption of power to all aircraft avionics.

2. What are static dischargers? (FAA-H-8083-31)

Static dischargers are installed on aircraft to reduce radio receiver interference caused by corona discharge, which is emitted from the aircraft as a result of precipitation static. Static dischargers, normally mounted on the trailing edges of the control surfaces, wing tips, and vertical stabilizer, discharge the precipitation static at points a critical length away from the wing and tail extremities where there is little or no coupling of the static into the radio antenna.

3. Within what frequency band does the following type of navigational and communication equipment installed on board most aircraft operate? (AIM)

VOR receiver (VHF band): 108.0 to 117.95 MHz
Communication transceivers (VHF band): 118.0 to 136.975 MHz
DME receiver (UHF band): 960 MHz to 1215 MHz
ADF receiver (LF to MF band): 190 to 530 kHz
ILS Localizer: 108.1 to 111.95 MHz (odd tenths)

Exam Tip: Expect to be questioned on the antenna locations for all installed equipment, such as VHF communication radios, transponder/DME, VOR/localizer/glideslope receivers, GPS equipment, and ELT transmitter.

4. Describe the function of the following avionics equipment acronyms: AHRS, ADC, PFD, MFD, FD, FMS, TAWS. (FAA-H-8083-16)

AHRS—attitude and heading reference system. Composed of three-axis sensors that provide heading, attitude, and yaw information for aircraft. AHRS are designed to replace traditional mechanical gyroscopic flight instruments and provide superior reliability and accuracy.

ADC—air data computer. An aircraft computer that receives and processes pitot pressure, static pressure, and temperature to calculate very precise altitude, indicated airspeed, true airspeed, vertical speed, and air temperature.

PFD—primary flight display. A display that provides increased situational awareness to the pilot by replacing the traditional six instruments with an easy-to-scan display that shows the horizon, airspeed, altitude, vertical speed, trend, trim, rate-of-turn, and more.

MFD—multi-function display. A cockpit display capable of presenting information (navigation data, moving maps, terrain awareness, etc.) to the pilot in configurable ways; often used in concert with the PFD.

FD—flight director. An electronic flight computer that analyzes the navigation selections, signals, and aircraft parameters. It presents steering instructions on the flight display as command bars or crossbars for the pilot to position the nose of the aircraft over or follow.

FMS—flight management system. A computer system containing a database for programming of routes, approaches, and departures that can supply navigation data to the flight director/autopilot from various sources, and can calculate flight data such as fuel consumption, time remaining, possible range, and other values.

TAWS—terrain awareness and warning system. Uses the aircraft's GPS navigation signal and altimetry systems to compare the position and trajectory of the aircraft against a more detailed terrain and obstacle database. This database attempts to detail every obstruction that could pose a threat to an aircraft in flight.

5. What is the function of a magnetometer?
(FAA-H-8083-16)

A magnetometer is a device that measures the strength of the earth's magnetic field to determine aircraft heading; it provides this information digitally to the AHRS, which then sends it to the PFD.

6. If a failure of one of the displays (PFD or MFD) occurs in an aircraft with an electronic flight display, what will happen to the remaining operative display?
(FAA-H-8083-16)

In the event of a display failure, some systems offer a reversion capability to display the primary flight instruments and engine instruments on the remaining operative display.

Exam Tip: Be prepared to answer questions about any and all equipment installed in the aircraft during both the oral and flight portions of the practical test. For example, if your aircraft has an autopilot, have an in-depth knowledge of its operation, even if you rarely use it.

7. Describe the ADS-B system. (AIM 4-5-7)

The Automatic Dependent Surveillance-Broadcast (ADS-B) system is composed of aircraft avionics and a ground infrastructure. Onboard avionics determine the position of the aircraft by using the GNSS and transmit its position along with additional information about the aircraft to ground stations for use by ATC and other ADS-B services. This information is automatically transmitted at a rate of approximately once per second. ADS-B is:

Automatic—because the system automatically broadcasts aircraft position with no external interrogation required.

Dependent—because the system depends on GPS for position information.

Surveillance—because the system provides surveillance information to ATC.

Broadcast—because the system is always broadcasting.

8. What are the two types of ADS-B equipment?
(AC 90-114, AIM 4-5-7)

ADS-B Out automatically broadcasts aircraft's GPS position, altitude, velocity, and other information to ATC ground-based surveillance stations as well as directly to other aircraft. ADS-B-Out is required in all airspace where transponders are required.

ADS-B In is the receipt, processing, and display of ADS-B transmissions. ADS-B In capability is necessary to receive ADS-B traffic and broadcast services (e.g., FIS-B and TIS-B).

Emergency
Procedures

5

A. Spin Recovery

1. What is a spin? (AC 61-67)

A spin in a small airplane or glider is a controlled (recoverable) or uncontrolled (possibly unrecoverable) maneuver in which the airplane or glider descends in a helical path while flying at an angle of attack (AOA) greater than the critical AOA. Spins result from aggravated stalls in either a slip or a skid. If a stall does not occur, a spin cannot occur. In a stall, one wing will often drop before the other and the nose will yaw in the direction of the low wing.

2. Describe several flight situations where an unintentional spin may occur. (AC 61-67)

A stall/spin situation can occur in any phase of flight but is most likely to occur in the following situations:

a. *Engine failure on takeoff during climbout*—Pilot tries to stretch glide to landing area by increasing back pressure or makes an uncoordinated turn back to departure runway at a relatively low airspeed.

b. *Crossed-controlled turn from base to final (slipping or skidding turn)*—Pilot overshoots final (possibly due to a crosswind) and makes an uncoordinated turn at a low airspeed.

c. *Engine failure on approach to landing*—Pilot tries to stretch glide to runway by increasing back pressure.

d. *Go-around with excessive nose-up trim*—Pilot applies power with full flaps and nose-up trim combined with uncoordinated use of rudder.

e. *Go-around with improper flap retraction*—Pilot applies power and retracts flaps rapidly resulting in a rapid sink rate followed by an instinctive increase in back pressure.

3. What is the recommended procedure for recovery from a spin? (FAA-H-8083-3)

In the absence of the manufacturer's recommended spin recovery procedures and techniques, the following spin recovery procedures are recommended.

a. Reduce the power (throttle) to idle.

b. Position the ailerons to neutral.

c. Apply full opposite rudder against the rotation.

d. Apply a positive and brisk, straightforward movement of the elevator control forward of the neutral position to break the stall.

e. After spin rotation stops, neutralize the rudder.

f. Begin applying back-elevator pressure to raise the nose to level flight.

Remember: PARE

Power—Reduce to idle.

Ailerons—Position to neutral.

Rudder—Apply full opposite against rotation.

Elevator—Apply positive, forward of neutral, movement to break stall.

4. **What does an aft center of gravity do to an airoraft's spin characteristics?** (FAA-H-8083-25)

Recovery from a stall in any aircraft becomes progressively more difficult as its center of gravity moves aft. This is particularly important in spin recovery, as there is a point in rearward loading of any airplane at which a flat spin will develop. A flat spin is one in which centrifugal force acting through a center of gravity located well to the rear, will pull the tail of the airplane out away from the axis of the spin, making it impossible to get the nose down and recover.

5. **What does an aft center of gravity do to an aircraft's probability of encountering a stall?** (FAA-H-8083-25)

An aft center of gravity (CG) in an aircraft can have significant effects on its flight characteristics and increase its probability of encountering a stall. An aft CG means that the aircraft's center of mass is located closer to the tail or rearward of the specified range.

An aircraft with an aft CG tends to be less stable, especially in pitch. It becomes more difficult to control and has a greater tendency to pitch nose-down, requiring constant attention from the pilot to maintain stable flight. With an aft CG, the control surfaces, such as the elevator, have less effectiveness in controlling the aircraft's pitch. The reduced control authority can make it challenging to maintain the desired pitch attitude and control inputs. While stability is compromised, an aft CG can enhance maneuverability. The aircraft becomes more responsive to control inputs and has a greater ability to perform maneuvers such as steep turns.

An aft CG position shifts the aircraft's neutral point rearward, reducing the margin before the wing reaches its critical angle of attack. This makes the wing more prone to stalling, resulting in a loss of lift and potential loss of control. An aft center of gravity increases the angle of attack and increases the probability that an aircraft may encounter a stall. When the center of gravity moves aft, it becomes progressively more difficult to recover from a spin, potentially becoming unrecoverable if the center of gravity moves too far aft for control inputs to decrease the angle of attack and break the stalled condition.

6. **What does a forward center of gravity do to an aircraft's probability of encountering a stall?** (FAA-H-8083-25)

A forward center of gravity (CG) in an aircraft can have significant effects on its flight characteristics and increase the probability of encountering a stall. A forward CG means that the aircraft's center of mass is located closer to the nose or forward of the specified range.

An aircraft with a forward CG tends to be more stable, especially in pitch. It is less likely to pitch up abruptly and has a greater resistance to changes in pitch, providing a more stable and predictable flight.

With a forward CG, the maneuverability of the aircraft may be compromised. It may have a reduced ability to perform certain maneuvers, such as rapid changes in pitch or steep turns.

A forward CG can also increase the probability of encountering a stall. A forward CG position shifts the aircraft's neutral point forward, making it easier for the wing to reach its critical angle of attack. This increases the likelihood of the wing stalling, where it loses lift abruptly.

7. **What is the greatest potential danger during takeoff for an aircraft loaded with a forward center of gravity?** (FAA-H-8083-25)

   An aircraft that is loaded with a center of gravity too far forward may encounter a condition where sufficient control input is not available to rotate and climb out on takeoff. In a worst-case scenario, an aircraft might break ground but be unable to climb out of ground effect and complete the takeoff.

8. **What load factor is present in a spin?** (FAA-H-8083-25)

   The load factor during a spin will vary with the spin characteristics of each airplane but is usually found to be slightly above the 1G load of level flight. There are two reasons this is true:

   a. The airspeed in a spin is very low (usually within 2 knots of the unaccelerated stalling speed); and

   b. The airplane pivots, rather than turns, while it is in a spin.

B. Emergency Checklist

1. Discuss the use of an emergency checklist.

In the event of an in-flight emergency, the pilot should be sufficiently familiar with emergency procedures to take immediate action instinctively to prevent more serious situations from occurring. However, as soon as circumstances permit, the emergency checklist should be reviewed to ensure that all required items have been checked. Additionally, before takeoff, a pilot should be sure that the emergency checklist will be readily accessible in flight if needed.

2. What is the best place for a pilot to determine emergency procedures for various conditions that might be encountered? (AFM/POH)

Section 4 of most FAA-approved AFM/POH documents describe emergency procedures for which the manufacturer has provided information for a pilot. This is the best location to find checklists and handling procedures for emergencies that a pilot might encounter.

3. **Some aircraft come with a pilot's operating handbook and others come with an airplane flight manual. Why do they have different names, and is there a difference between them?** (AFM/POH)

   While both POH and AFM are generally used to mean the same thing, they do have some specific differences.

   An AFM is meant and built specific to make and model, or by serial number. In fact, while other aircraft of the same make/model can have very similar AFMs, each AFM is usually tailored for a specific aircraft. Not only is it FAA/regulatory approved, but it contains specific instructions that pilots comply with to operate the aircraft safely.

   A POH contains similar FAA/regulatory approved information and should indicate certain sections of the documents are approved. The same make and model of aircraft generally use and refer to the same POH. Mostly used in general aviation, the POH is also known as the standardized AFM, following the same exact format.

   The other two types of documents you may encounter are an owner's manual (which usually goes along with a thinner AFM and provides some of the information found in the newer-style POH) and a pilot information manual (PIM), which is a generic version of the POH that many pilots buy so they can study the procedures without removing the regulatory document from the aircraft.

   Light aircraft manufactured after March 1, 1979, must carry an FAA-approved airplane flight manual (AFM). An AFM is issued for a specific airplane, and it's not valid for any other, even if it's the same make and model. However, a POH is still required to be in the plane.

4. **What are the primary sections that the FAA requires to be included in an airplane flight manual?** (AFM/POH)

   The FAA requires certain sections to be included in an airplane flight manual (AFM) to ensure compliance with regulatory standards. These required sections typically cover crucial information necessary for the safe operation of the aircraft. The FAA-mandated sections of an AFM generally include the following:

Section 1: General Information—This section provides an overview of the AFM and includes information such as document revision status, distribution control, record of revisions, and any applicable limitations or warnings.

Section 2: Limitations—This section outlines the aircraft's operating limitations and restrictions. It includes details on weight and balance limits, airspeed limitations, load limits, and any other specific operational restrictions.

Section 3: Emergency Procedures—This section covers procedures to be followed in emergency situations, such as engine failures, fires, electrical failures, or other critical events. It includes step-by-step guidance on actions to be taken to ensure the safety of the aircraft and its occupants.

Section 4: Normal Procedures—This section contains step-by-step instructions for normal aircraft operations, including checklists, starting procedures, normal takeoff and landing procedures, and general handling procedures.

Section 5: Performance—The performance section provides performance charts and data for various phases of flight, including takeoff, climb, cruise, descent, and landing. It includes information on fuel consumption, climb rates, range, endurance, and other performance-related parameters.

Section 6: Weight and Balance—This section contains information on the aircraft's weight and balance limitations, including the allowable loading limits and calculations for determining the center of gravity (CG) range.

Section 7: Systems Description—This section provides detailed descriptions and explanations of the aircraft's systems, such as electrical, hydraulic, fuel, and avionics systems. It includes information on the operation, limitations, and procedures related to each system.

Section 8: Handling, Service, and Maintenance—This section describes the maintenance and inspections recommended by the manufacturer and the regulations, preventive maintenance allowed to be completed by certificated pilots, and procedures for aircraft ground handling and storage.

(continued)

Section 9: Supplements—This section contains information necessary to safely operate the aircraft when equipped with operational systems and equipment.

These sections, among others, are typically required by the FAA to be included in the AFM for an aircraft. The content and organization of the AFM may vary based on the specific aircraft model, its complexity, and other regulatory requirements. Some older aircraft were certificated under different standards and may have flight manuals that do not contain all of these areas.

C. Partial Power Loss

1. What procedures should be followed concerning a partial loss of power in flight? (AFM/POH)

If a partial loss of power occurs, the first priority is to establish and maintain a suitable airspeed (best glide airspeed if necessary).

Then, select an emergency landing area and remain within gliding distance. As time allows, attempt to determine the cause and correct it. Complete the following checklist:

a. Check the carburetor heat.
b. Check the amount of fuel in each tank and switch fuel tanks if necessary.
c. Check the fuel selector valve's current position.
d. Check the mixture control.
e. Check that the primer control is all the way in and locked.
f. Check the operation of the magnetos in all three positions: both, left, or right.

D. Engine Failure

1. In the event of a partial or complete engine power loss on takeoff during the takeoff run, what procedure is recommended? (AFM/POH)

If an engine failure occurs during the takeoff run, the following checklist should be completed:

a. Retard the throttle to idle.
b. Apply pressure to the brakes.
c. Retract the wing flaps.

d. Set the mixture control to "Idle Cut-off."
e. Turn the ignition switch to "Off."
f. Turn the master switch to "Off."

2. **In the event of a partial or complete engine power loss on takeoff after rotation in a small GA aircraft, what procedure is recommended?** (FAA-H-8083-3)

    If a pilot experiences an engine failure on takeoff after rotation, with sufficient runway remaining, the pilot should retard throttle and land. In most cases, this would be advisable even if it meant rolling off the end of the runway.

3. **If a pilot experiences a partial or complete power loss after liftoff without sufficient runway remaining to land, what is the best procedure?** (FAA-H-8083-3)

    A pilot in a partial or complete power loss who has not attained sufficient altitude to turn back to the airport is advised to not turn more than 45 degrees to either side while establishing a best climb airspeed or best glide if all power has been lost. If a climb or maintaining altitude is possible, a turnback may be possible. If not, the pilot should select a field directly ahead or slightly to either side to complete an emergency off-field landing.

4. **What is the recommended procedure to be followed for an engine failure while en route?** (AFM/POH)

    If an engine power loss, either partial or complete, is experienced during an enroute portion of flight, the pilot's first priority is to establish best-glide airspeed. The pilot should then select an emergency landing area and remain within gliding distance. As time permits, they can then address potential solutions to the cause of the failure. These solutions could first focus on fuel supply (either switching tanks or using a supplemental fuel pump) or determining if a magneto has failed. The pilot should then utilize the emergency engine out checklist for the aircraft if sufficient altitude and time is available. An airstart procedure may be attempted at this point.

5. **How will a pilot know what speed to establish as a best glide in the event of a partial or full power loss?** (AFM/POH)

A pilot can determine the best glide speed in the event of a partial or full power loss by referring to the aircraft's pilot's operating handbook (POH) or airplane flight manual. These documents provide the recommended best glide speed for the specific aircraft model.

The best glide speed, also known as the glide ratio speed or minimum sink speed, is the airspeed at which the aircraft achieves the greatest horizontal distance covered per unit of altitude lost during a glide. It is the speed that provides the most efficient glide performance.

The POH or AFM typically includes a performance section that provides a table or graph indicating the best glide speed. The speed is often specified in knots or indicated airspeed (IAS) and may vary depending on the aircraft's weight, configuration, and other factors.

In the absence of the POH or AFM, pilots can use a general rule of thumb to approximate the best glide speed. Typically, it is around the speed for best angle of climb (V_X) or best rate of climb (V_Y), but this can vary between aircraft models.

6. **After experiencing an engine failure immediately after takeoff (before reaching safe maneuvering altitude), why is it usually inadvisable to attempt a landing on the runway you have just departed from?** (FAA-H-8083-3)

The ability to make a 180° turn does not necessarily mean that the departure runway can be reached in a power-off glide; this depends on the wind, the distance traveled during the climb, the height reached, and the glide distance of the airplane without power. The pilot should also remember that a turn back to the departure runway will in fact require more than a 180° change in direction.

7. **Explain the approximate altitude loss and factors to consider when maneuvering an airplane that has just taken off, experienced an engine failure at 300 feet AGL, and is attempting to turn back to the departure runway.** (FAA-P-8740-44)

The turn back to the runway will require approximately 270° (180° to get turned around, 45° to get pointed at the runway, and 45° for final alignment with the runway). Using a standard rate turn of 3° per second, it will take approximately 90 seconds to make the turn. If the airplane descends at approximately 500 fpm, it will have descended approximately 750 feet, placing it 450 feet below the runway. Other factors to consider:

a. The initial reaction time of 4 seconds and corresponding loss of airspeed and altitude.

b. The downwind turn must be made immediately, which increases the ground speed and rushes the pilot even more in the performance and planning of the procedure.

c. The apparent increase in ground speed could mislead the pilot into attempting to prematurely slow the airplane down, resulting in a possible stall.

d. The pilot will tend to use steeper bank angles than required for a standard rate turn, resulting in an increase in load factor, stall speed, and rate of descent.

e. The airplane will lose considerable altitude during the turn and might still be in a bank when the ground is contacted.

E. Emergency Landing

1. **If an engine failure has occurred while en route and a forced landing is imminent, what procedures should be followed?** (AFM/POH)

a. Establish an airspeed of 75 KIAS.

b. Begin a scan for an appropriate field for landing using the following order of preference:
   • Paved airport.
   • Unpaved airport.
   • Paved road with no obstacles.

(continued)

- Unpaved road with no obstacles.
- Grass field.
- Plowed field.
- Lakes or ponds.
- Trees or other structures.

c. Attempt an engine restart.

d. Set your transponder to "7700."

e. Transmit a "mayday" message on either the frequency in use or 121.5.

f. Begin to spiral down over the approach end of the selected landing site.

g. On your final approach complete the forced landing checklist.

2. **If a forced landing is imminent in a retractable gear aircraft, should the landing gear be left up or put down and locked?** (AFM/POH)

There can't be a hard and fast rule concerning the position of a retractable landing gear at touchdown. In rugged terrain and trees, or during impacts at high sink rate, an extended gear would definitely have a protective effect on the cockpit/cabin area. But weigh this advantage against the possible side effects of a collapsing gear, such as a ruptured fuel tank. As always, the manufacturer's recommendations as outlined in the AFM/POH should be followed. When a normal touchdown is assured, and ample stopping distance is available, a gear-up landing on level-but-soft terrain, or across a plowed field, may result in less airplane damage than a gear-down landing.

3. **If an engine failure has occurred while over water, and you are beyond power-off gliding distance to land, what procedures should be followed?** (AFM/POH)

a. Set your transponder to "7700" and broadcast a "mayday" message on the frequency in use or 121.5 MHz. If you are already on a frequency with ATC, remain in contact with them on that frequency as long as possible.

b. Make sure all heavy objects are secured or, if possible, jettison them.

c. Select landing gear up.

d. Set flaps to 20–30°.

e. Set power (if available) so as to establish a 300 fpm (or lower if possible) descent rate and establish a touchdown speed close to stall speed.

f. Approach and land parallel to heavy sea swells when in light winds, and approach and land into the wind when high winds and heavy seas exist.

g. Establish a glide speed for final touchdown close to stall speed but do not allow the aircraft to stall prior to impact. Remain in control of the aircraft through touchdown.

h. Open all cabin doors prior to touchdown. Consider the flaps position. In some aircraft, putting flaps down may block the ability to open a door fully after impact.

i. Initiate your touchdown in a level flight attitude.

j. Just prior to touchdown, protect body with life vests, clothing, etc.

k. After touchdown, begin evacuation of the airplane. Open the windows to equalize pressure if the doors do not open easily.

l. Inflate life vests and raft if available.

4. **In the event of an emergency requiring a forced landing, what information should be included in the emergency briefing to the passengers?** (FAA-H-8083-3)

In the event of an emergency requiring a forced landing, the pilot should provide a clear and concise emergency briefing to the passengers to ensure their safety and preparedness. The briefing should include the following information:

a. *Remain calm*—The pilot should emphasize the importance of remaining calm and following instructions to increase the chances of a safe outcome.

b. *Brace for impact*—Passengers should be instructed on the proper brace position to assume during the landing to minimize the risk of injury.

c. *Use seatbelts*—Reinforce the importance of keeping seatbelts securely fastened throughout the flight, as they provide significant protection during an emergency landing.

(continued)

d. *Location of emergency exits*—Point out the location of emergency exits and how to operate them in case an evacuation becomes necessary.

e. *Inflation of life vests*—If the aircraft is equipped with life vests, explain how to inflate them, where they are located, and when to use them.

f. *Follow crew instructions*—Passengers should be informed to listen carefully to any instructions provided by the flight crew during the emergency.

g. *Silence electronics*—Instruct passengers to turn off electronic devices to avoid interference with communication and navigation equipment.

h. *Brace for landing*—As the aircraft approaches the forced landing, instruct passengers to assume the brace position and secure any loose items.

i. *After landing*—After a successful landing, passengers should be told to stay seated and await further instructions from the flight crew.

j. *Evacuation procedures*—If evacuation is necessary, provide guidance on how to exit the aircraft safely and where to assemble once outside.

k. *Avoid hazards*—Instruct passengers to stay away from any hazardous materials or conditions that may be present after the landing.

The emergency briefing should be delivered in a calm and reassuring manner. The pilot should use clear and simple language to ensure that all passengers understand the procedures. The briefing is an essential part of emergency preparedness, as it provides passengers with critical information to enhance their safety during an emergency situation.

5. During an emergency landing, you realize that you have misjudged the glidepath and will undershoot the forced landing area. What procedures should be used for an undershoot? (FAA-H-8083-3)

If during an emergency landing, you realize that you have misjudged the glidepath and will undershoot the intended forced landing area, there are several procedures you can use to attempt to reach the desired landing spot or find an alternative safe landing area:

a. *Increase glide performance*—Reduce drag and increase glide performance by retracting any unnecessary landing gear or flaps (if applicable) to extend the glide distance.

b. *Select an alternate landing area*—Identify an alternative suitable landing area if available ahead of the aircraft that can be reached safely.

At all times, a speed at or greater than best glide should be maintained until the intended landing field can be reached.

6. During an emergency landing, you realize that you have misjudged the glidepath and will overshoot the forced landing area. What procedures should be used for an overshoot? (FAA-H-8083-3)

If during an emergency landing, you realize that you have misjudged the glidepath and will overshoot the intended forced landing area, there are several procedures you can use to attempt to reach the desired landing spot or find an alternative safe landing area:

a. *Decrease glide performance*—Increase drag and decrease glide performance by deploying any drag tools such as gear, flaps, speed, or speed brakes (if applicable) to decrease the glide distance.

b. *Slip the aircraft*—Utilizing a slip can maximize descent angle over distance by decreasing glide and increasing drag.

c. *Select an alternate landing area*—Identify an alternative suitable landing area if available ahead of the aircraft that can be reached safely.

7. **What effect does the wind have on an emergency approach and landing procedure?** (FAA-H-8083-3)

The wind can have significant effects on an emergency approach and landing procedure, and pilots must consider these factors to execute a safe and controlled landing. Some of the key effects of wind during an emergency landing are:

a. *Ground speed and drift*—The wind affects the ground speed of the aircraft. A headwind reduces the ground speed, making it easier to control the aircraft's descent rate and providing more time to plan and execute the landing. Conversely, a tailwind increases the ground speed, which can make the approach faster and reduce the available landing distance. Crosswinds can cause the aircraft to drift laterally during the approach, requiring additional correction to maintain alignment with the desired landing area.

b. *Glide distance*—Headwinds decrease the aircraft's glide distance, as the aircraft ground speed will be slower and the aircraft will cover less distance. Conversely, a tailwind increases the glide distance, potentially increasing the available landing options. In an emergency landing situation, a tailwind can be beneficial as it provides a larger area for potential landing sites.

c. *Touchdown speed*—Wind affects the aircraft's touchdown speed. A headwind reduces the ground speed at touchdown, resulting in a lower touchdown speed and shorter landing rollout. On the other hand, a tailwind increases the touchdown speed and may require more runway to come to a stop.

d. *Approach angle*—The wind affects the angle of descent during the approach. A headwind steepens the descent angle, while a tailwind shallows it. Pilots must adjust the approach angle to ensure a safe descent and landing flare.

e. *Drift correction*—Crosswinds during the approach can cause the aircraft to drift off the desired flight path. Pilots need to apply appropriate control inputs, such as crabbing or using a slip, to maintain alignment with the chosen landing area and prevent lateral drift.

f. *Turbulence*—Wind can cause turbulence, especially near the ground or in turbulent conditions. Pilots must be prepared to encounter turbulence during the landing phase and be ready to manage it to maintain control.

In an emergency landing situation, pilots should carefully assess the wind conditions and choose the most suitable landing area based on wind direction and strength. They should also make appropriate adjustments during the approach and landing to ensure a safe and controlled touchdown.

F. Engine Roughness or Overheat

1. What is detonation? (FAA-H-8083-25)

Detonation is an uncontrolled, explosive ignition of the fuel/ air mixture within the cylinder's combustion chamber. It causes excessive temperatures and pressures which, if not corrected, can quickly lead to failure of the piston, cylinder, or valves. In less severe cases, detonation causes engine overheating, roughness, or loss of power. It is characterized by high cylinder head temperatures, and is most likely to occur when operating at high power settings.

2. What are some of the most common operational causes of detonation? (FAA-H-8083-25, AFM/POH)

a. Using a lower fuel grade than that specified by the aircraft manufacturer.

b. Operating with extremely high manifold pressures in conjunction with low RPM.

c. Operating the engine at high power settings with an excessively lean mixture.

d. Extended ground operations or steep climbs where cylinder cooling is reduced.

3. What action should be taken if detonation is suspected? (FAA-H-8083-25, AFM/POH)

Detonation may be avoided by following these basic guidelines during the various phases of ground and flight operations:

a. Make sure the proper grade of fuel is being used.

b. While on the ground, keep the cowl flaps (if available) in the full-open position.

(continued)

c. During takeoff and initial climb, use an enriched fuel mixture, as well as a shallower climb angle to increase cylinder cooling.

d. Avoid extended, high power, steep climbs.

e. Develop habit of monitoring engine instruments to verify proper operation.

4. What is preignition? (FAA-H-8083-25, AFM/POH)

Preignition occurs when the fuel/air mixture ignites prior to the engine's normal ignition event. Premature burning is usually caused by a residual hot spot in the combustion chamber, often created by a small carbon deposit on a spark plug, a cracked spark plug insulator, or other damage in the cylinder that causes a part to heat sufficiently to ignite the fuel/air charge. Preignition causes the engine to lose power, and produces high operating temperature. As with detonation, preignition may also cause severe engine damage, because the expanding gases exert excessive pressure on the piston while still on its compression stroke.

5. What actions should be taken if preignition is suspected? (FAA-H-8083-25)

Detonation and preignition often occur simultaneously and one may cause the other. Since either condition causes high engine temperature accompanied by a decrease in engine performance, it is often difficult to distinguish between the two. Using the recommended grade of fuel, and operating the engine within its proper temperature, pressure, and RPM ranges, reduces the chance of detonation or preignition.

6. If the engine begins to run rough when flying through heavy rain, what action should be taken? (AFM/POH)

During flight through heavy rain, it is possible for the induction air filter to become water saturated. This situation will reduce the amount of available air to the carburetor resulting in an excessively rich mixture and a corresponding loss of power. Carburetor heat may be used as an alternate source of air in such a situation.

7. **Are there any special considerations necessary when using the auxiliary pump after an engine-driven fuel pump failure?** (AFM/POH)

In a high-wing, single-engine aircraft, which has sustained an engine-driven fuel pump failure, gravity flow will provide sufficient fuel flow for level or descending flight. If the failure occurs while in a climb or the fuel pressure falls below 0.5 psi, the auxiliary fuel pump should be used.

8. **What operating procedure could be used to minimize spark plug fouling?** (AFM/POH)

Engine roughness may occur due to fouling of the spark plug electrodes. This condition may occur on the ground or in the air and is usually the result of an excessively rich mixture setting which causes unburned carbon and lead deposits to collect on the spark plug electrodes. A pilot may alleviate this problem to some degree by always using the recommended lean setting for the given condition.

G. Loss of Oil Pressure

1. **During a cross-country flight you notice that the oil pressure is low, but the oil temperature is normal. What is the problem and what action should be taken?** (AFM/POH)

A low oil pressure in flight could be the result of any one of several problems, the most common being that of insufficient oil. If the oil temperature continues to remain normal, a clogged oil pressure relief valve or an oil pressure gauge malfunction could be the culprit. In any case, a landing at the nearest airport is advisable to check for the cause of the trouble.

2. **If a loss of oil pressure occurs accompanied by a rising oil temperature, what is indicated?** (AFM/POH)

The oil required for cooling has been lost, and an engine failure is imminent. The throttle should be reduced, and a suitable landing area should be established as soon as possible. Use minimum power to reach the emergency landing area.

H. Smoke and Fire

1. What procedure should be followed if an engine fire develops on the ground during starting? (AFM/POH)

Continue to attempt an engine start as a start will cause flames and excess fuel to be sucked back through the carburetor.

a. *If the engine starts:*
- Increase the power to a higher RPM for a few moments; and
- Shut down the engine and inspect it.

b. *If the engine does not start:*
- Set the throttle to the "Full" position.
- Set the mixture control to "Idle cutoff."
- Continue to try an engine start in an attempt to put out the fire by vacuum.

c. *If the fire continues:*
- Obtain fire extinguisher and/or fire personnel assistance
- Turn the master switch to "Off."
- Turn the ignition switch to "Off."
- Set the fuel selector to "Off."
- Extinguish the fire using extinguisher.

Evacuate the aircraft and obtain a fire extinguisher and/or fire personnel assistance.

2. What procedure should be followed if an engine fire develops in flight? (AFM/POH)

In the event of an engine fire in flight, the following procedure should be used:

a. Set the mixture control to "Idle cutoff."

b. Set the fuel selector valve to "Off."

c. Turn the master switch to "Off."

d. Set the cabin heat and air vents to "Off;" leave the overhead vents "On."

e. Establish an airspeed of 105 KIAS and increase the descent, if necessary, to find an airspeed that will provide for an incombustible mixture.

f. Execute a forced landing procedures checklist.

3. What procedure should be followed if an electrical fire develops inside the aircraft? (AFM/POH)

If an electrical fire is suspected (burning odor), the pilot should initially try to identify the possible source by checking all circuit breakers, avionics and instruments. If the problem is not detected and the odor or smoke continues, the following checklist should be completed:

a. Turn the master switch to "Off."

b. Set the avionics power switch to "Off."

c. Set all other switches to "Off" except the ignition switch.

d. Close all air/heat vents as well as any other air vents.

e. Use fire extinguisher.

4. What troubleshooting procedure should be followed in determining the cause of an electrical fire that is not readily apparent? (AFM/POH)

If the electrical fire is out and electrical power is necessary for continued flight, the following may be performed:

a. Turn the master switch "On."

b. Check all the circuit breakers for their status; *do not reset.*

c. Check that all radio switches are "Off."

d. Turn avionics power switch "On."

e. Cautiously turn radio and electrical switches "On" one at a time with a short delay after each until short circuit is isolated.

5. What procedure should be followed if a cabin fire develops in flight? (AFM/POH)

Typically cabin fires are electrical in nature and identifying and disabling the faulty circuit is the first priority. However, careless smoking by passengers has also been a significant cause of cabin fires. The following checklist should be completed:

a. Turn the master switch to "Off."

b. Close all air/heat vents.

c. Use a fire extinguisher if available.

d. Land as soon as possible.

6. What procedure should be followed if a wing fire develops in flight? (AFM/POH)

If a wing fire develops in flight, the following checklist should be completed:

a. Set the navigation light switch to "Off."

b. Set the strobe light switch to "Off."

c. Set the pitot heat switch to "Off."

Initiate a sideslip maneuver to avoid flames from getting to the fuel tank and cabin area, then land as soon as possible.

I. Icing

1. What are the two main categories of aircraft icing? (AC 91-74)

Aircraft icing in flight is usually classified as being either structural icing or induction icing. Structural icing refers to the ice that forms on aircraft surfaces and components, and induction icing refers to ice in the engine's induction system.

2. Name the three types of structural ice that may occur in flight. (FAA-H-8083-28)

Clear Icing, or glaze ice, is a glossy, clear, or translucent ice formed by the relatively slow freezing of large, supercooled water droplets. Clear icing conditions exist more often in an environment with warmer temperatures, higher liquid water contents, and larger droplets. It forms when only a small portion of the drop freezes immediately while the remaining unfrozen portion flows or smears over the aircraft surface and gradually freezes.

Rime icing is a rough, milky, and opaque ice formed by the instantaneous freezing of small, supercooled water droplets after they strike the aircraft. Rime icing formation favors colder temperatures, lower liquid water content, and small droplets. It grows when droplets rapidly freeze upon striking an aircraft. The rapid freezing traps air and forms a porous, brittle, opaque, and milky-colored ice.

Mixed icing is a mixture of clear ice and rime ice. It forms as an airplane collects both rime and clear ice due to small-scale variations in liquid water content, temperature, and droplet sizes. Mixed ice appears as layers of relatively clear and opaque ice when examined from the side. Mixed icing poses a similar hazard to an aircraft as clear ice. It may form horns or other shapes that disrupt airflow and cause handling and performance problems.

Note: In general, rime icing tends to occur at temperatures colder than −15°C, clear icing when the temperature is warmer than −10°C, and mixed ice at temperatures in-between. This is only general guidance. The type of icing will vary depending on the liquid water content, droplet size, and aircraft-specific variables.

3. What is necessary for structural icing to occur?
(FAA-H-8083-28)

The aircraft must be flying through visible water such as rain or cloud droplets; temperature must be at the point where moisture strikes the aircraft at 0°C or colder.

4. Describe the types of icing found in stratiform clouds, and the types found in cumuliform clouds.
(FAA-H-8083-28)

Stratiform clouds—Both rime icing and mixed icing are found in stratiform clouds. Icing in middle and low-level stratiform clouds is confined, on average, to a layer between 3,000 and 4,000 feet thick. A change in altitude of only a few thousand feet may take the aircraft out of icing conditions, even if it remains in clouds. The main hazard lies in the great horizontal extent of stratiform cloud layers.

(continued)

Cumuliform Clouds—Icing is usually clear or mixed with rime in the upper levels. The icing layer is smaller horizontally but greater vertically than in stratiform clouds. Icing is more variable in cumuliform clouds because the factors conducive to icing depend on the particular cloud's stage of development. Icing intensities may range from a trace in small cumulus to severe in a large towering cumulus or cumulonimbus, especially in the upper portion of the cloud where the updraft is concentrated and supercooled large drops (SLDs) are plentiful.

5. **During your preflight planning, what type of meteorological information should you be aware of with respect to icing?** (AC 91-74)

  a. *Location of fronts*—The front's location, type, speed, and direction of movement.

  b. *Cloud layers*—The location of cloud bases and tops; this is valuable when determining if you will be able to climb above icing layers or descend beneath those layers into warmer air; reference PIREPS and area forecasts.

  c. *Freezing level(s)*—Important when determining how to avoid icing and how to exit icing conditions if accidentally encountered.

  d. *Air temperature and pressure*—Icing tends to be found in low-pressure areas and at temperatures at or around freezing.

6. **What is the definition of the term *freezing level* and how can you determine where that level is?** (FAA-H-8083-28)

The freezing level is the lowest altitude in the atmosphere over a given location at which the air temperature reaches 0°C. It is possible to have multiple freezing layers when a temperature inversion occurs above the defined freezing level. A pilot can use current icing products (CIP) and forecast icing products (FIP), as well as the freezing level graphics chart to determine the approximate freezing level. Other potential sources of icing information are: GFA, PIREPs, AIRMETs, SIGMETs, surface analysis charts, low-level significant weather charts, and winds and temperatures aloft (for air temperature at altitude).

7. **What action is recommended if you inadvertently encounter icing conditions?** (FAA-H-8083-28)

You should leave the area of visible moisture. This might mean descending to an altitude below the cloud bases, climbing to an altitude above the cloud tops, or turning to a different course. If unable to leave the area of visible moisture, the pilot must move to an altitude where the temperature is above freezing. If you're going to climb, do so quickly; procrastination may leave you with too much ice. If you're going to descend, you must know the temperature of the air and the type of terrain below.

Exam Tip: Know what your plan will be if you accidentally encounter in-flight icing. Be able to explain how you will determine the potential for icing during preflight planning. Include the weather products will you use on the ground and in flight to determine potential areas of icing (GFA, CIP, FIP, prognostic charts, winds aloft forecast, etc.).

8. **If you encounter in-flight icing, and ATC asks you to report your conditions, what are the official reportable icing values that you are expected to use?** (AIM 7-1-19)

Trace, light, moderate, and severe.

9. **If icing has been inadvertently encountered, how would your landing approach procedure be different?** (AFM/POH, AC 91-74)

The following guidelines may be used when flying an airplane which has accumulated ice:

a. Maintain more power during the approach than normal.

b. Maintain a higher airspeed than normal.

c. Expect a higher stall speed than normal.

d. Expect a longer landing roll than normal.

e. A "no flaps" approach is recommended.

f. Maintain a consistently higher altitude than normal.

g. Avoid a missed approach (get it right the first time).

10. **Which type of precipitation will produce the most hazardous icing conditions?**

    Freezing rain produces the most hazardous icing conditions.

11. **Do stall warning horn systems have any protection from icing?** (AFM/POH)

    The answer to this question will depend on the specific systems of the aircraft. While many aircraft do not have heated stall vents, some may be equipped with heated stall warning vanes, sensor units, or heating elements on the leading edge of the wing. Usually, the system is activated by the same switch as the pitot heat if equipped.

12. **What causes carburetor icing and what are the first indications of its presence?** (FAA-H-8083-25)

    The vaporization of fuel, combined with the expansion of air as it passes through the carburetor, causes a sudden cooling of the mixture. The temperature of the air passing through the carburetor may drop as much as 60°F within a fraction of a second. Water vapor is squeezed out by this cooling, and, if the temperature in the carburetor reaches 32°F or below, the moisture will be deposited as frost or ice inside the carburetor.

    For airplanes with a fixed pitch propeller, the first indication of carburetor icing is a loss of RPM. For airplanes with controllable-pitch (constant speed) propellers, the first indication is usually a drop in manifold pressure.

13. **What conditions are favorable for carburetor icing?** (FAA-H-8083-25)

    Carburetor ice is most likely to occur when temperatures are below 70°F (21°C) and the relative humidity is above 80 percent. However, due to the sudden cooling that takes place in the carburetor, icing can occur even with temperatures as high as 100°F (38°C) and humidity as low as 50 percent. This temperature drop can be as much as 60 to 70°F. Therefore, at an outside air temperature of 100°F, a temperature drop of 70°F results in an air temperature in the carburetor of 30°F. Generally, higher humidity at mid-range temperatures will result in greater probability of carburetor icing occurrence.

14. **If an airplane has anti-icing and/or deicing equipment installed, can it be flown into icing conditions?** (FAA-H-8083-3)

    The presence of anti-icing and deicing equipment does not necessarily mean that an airplane is approved for flight in icing conditions. The AFM/POH, placards, and manufacturer should be consulted for specific determination of approvals and limitations. For an aircraft to be operated into known icing conditions, it will be certificated as capable of "flight into known icing (FIKI)."

15. **A pilot flying an aircraft certificated for flight in known icing (FIKI) should be aware of a phenomenon known as roll upset. What is roll upset?** (FAA-H-8083-28, FAA-H-8083-15)

    Roll upset is an uncommanded and uncontrolled roll phenomenon associated with severe in-flight icing.

    It can occur without the usual symptoms of ice accumulation or a perceived aerodynamic stall.

    Pilots flying certificated FIKI aircraft should be aware that severe icing is a condition outside of the aircraft's certification icing envelope. The roll upset that occurs may be caused by airflow separation (aerodynamic stall), which induces self-deflection of the ailerons and loss of or degraded roll handling characteristics. The aileron deflection may be caused by ice accumulating in a sensitive area of the wing aft of the deicing boots.

16. **If an aircraft is equipped with icing equipment or FIKI certified, does that mean it can handle all icing conditions?** (AFM/POH)

    No, the fact that an aircraft is equipped with anti-icing or deicing equipment or is FIKI (flight into known icing) certified does not mean it can handle all icing conditions. FIKI certification signifies that an aircraft has been tested and approved to operate in specific known icing conditions as defined by the certification standards.

    The specific icing conditions that an aircraft is certified for can vary depending on factors such as the aircraft's design, anti-ice or deice systems, and the certification requirements in the jurisdiction where the certification was obtained.

    (continued)

FIKI certification typically means that the aircraft has systems and features in place to mitigate or remove ice accumulation on critical surfaces such as wings, tailplanes, and propellers. These systems may include anti-ice or deice mechanisms, such as heated surfaces or pneumatic boots, that help prevent ice from forming or remove ice that has accumulated. However, it's important to note that FIKI certification does not guarantee immunity from all icing conditions. It is essential for pilots to be aware of the limitations of their aircraft's FIKI certification, understand the operational procedures, and exercise caution when encountering icing conditions beyond the aircraft's certified capabilities.

Pilots should always consult the aircraft's documentation, including the AFM or POH, to fully understand the aircraft's anti-icing or de-icing capabilities and limitations for safe and effective operations in icing conditions.

17. What is the recommended recovery procedure for a roll upset? (AC 91-74)

a. Reduce the angle of attack by increasing airspeed. If in a turn, roll wings level.

b. Set appropriate power and monitor the airspeed and angle of attack. A controlled descent is a vastly better alternative than an uncontrolled descent.

c. If flaps are extended, do not retract them unless it can be determined that the upper surface of the airfoil is clear of ice, because retracting the flaps will increase the AOA at a given airspeed.

d. Verify that wing ice protection is functioning normally by visual observation of the left and right wing.

18. Are fuel-injected engines subject to induction system failures? (FAA-H-8083-25)

Yes, fuel-injected engines are still subject to induction system icing. While fuel injection systems provide certain advantages over carbureted engines, such as improved fuel efficiency and reliability, they do not completely eliminate the risk of induction system icing.

Induction system icing occurs when moisture in the air condenses and freezes on the surfaces of the induction system components. This can include the throttle body, fuel injector nozzles, intake manifold, and other parts of the induction system. As ice accumulates, it can restrict airflow, disrupt the air-fuel mixture, and potentially lead to a loss of engine power or rough engine operation.

In fuel-injected engines, the fuel is injected directly into the combustion chamber or intake port rather than being mixed with air in a carburetor. While this can reduce the risk of icing in certain areas of the induction system, some components may still be susceptible to icing, especially in certain atmospheric conditions.

To address the risk of induction system icing in fuel-injected engines, some aircraft are equipped with anti-icing systems, such as electrically heated induction air filters or alternate air sources. These systems help prevent ice formation or can provide a source of warmer air to melt ice and restore proper engine performance.

J. Pressurization

1. What is meant by decompression? (FAA-H-8083-25)

Decompression is the inability of the aircraft's pressurization system to maintain the designed aircraft cabin pressure. For example, an aircraft is flying at an altitude of 29,000 feet but the aircraft cabin is pressurized to an altitude equivalent to 8,000 feet. If decompression occurs, the cabin pressure may become equivalent to that of the aircraft's altitude of 29,000 feet. The rate at which this occurs determines the severity of decompression.

2. What are the three types of decompression?
(FAA-H-8083-25, AC 61-107)

Explosive decompression—Cabin pressure decreases faster than the lungs can decompress. Most authorities consider any kind of decompression which occurs in less than ½ second as explosive and potentially dangerous. This type of decompression could only be caused by structural damage, material failure, or by a door popping open.

(continued)

Rapid decompression—A change in cabin pressure where the lungs decompress faster than the cabin. Rapid decompression decreases the period of useful consciousness because oxygen in the lungs is exhaled rapidly. The pilot's effective performance time is reduced by one-third to one-fourth its normal time.

Gradual or slow decompression—Can be the most dangerous and occurs when the cabin pressure decreases at a rate so slow that it may not be detected by the flight crew. If not corrected, the insidious effects of hypoxia take effect and eventually result in crew incapacitation. Possible causes of a slow decompression include cracked windows, pressure seal leaks, and pressurization system component failures. Automatic visual and aural warning systems generally provide an indication of a slow decompression.

3. **What are the dangers of decompression?**
   (FAA-H-8083-25)
   a. Hypoxia.
   b. At higher altitudes, being tossed or blown out of the airplane.
   c. Evolved gas decompression sickness (the bends).
   d. Exposure to wind blast and extreme cold.

K. Emergency Descent

1. **When would an emergency descent procedure be necessary?** (FAA-H-8083-3)

   An emergency descent is a maneuver for descending as rapidly as possible, within the structural limitations of the airplane, to a lower altitude or to the ground for an emergency landing. The need for this maneuver may result from an uncontrollable fire, a sudden loss of cabin pressurization, or any other situation demanding an immediate and rapid descent.

2. **What procedure should be followed in establishing an emergency descent?** (FAA-H-8083-3)

   Generally the maneuver should be configured as recommended by the manufacturer. Except when prohibited by the manufacturer, the following procedure may be used:
   a. Reduce power to idle.
   b. Place propeller control in low pitch (high RPM)—acts as an aerodynamic brake.

c. Configure the aircraft with respect to the POH/AFM with gear and flap positions as directed. Some aircraft may call for full flaps and gear down, while others may not. In absence of a described procedure from the POH/AFM, a pilot may choose a "clean" or a "dirty" configuration.

d. Establish a 30° to 45° bank for the purposes of clearing the area below.

e. Allow the aircraft to accelerate to either maximum allowable gear or flaps operating speed, whichever is lower if the descent will be conducted with the flaps and gear down, or to a maximum normal operating speed if the descent will be done in a clean configuration.

f. Execute a level off upon reaching a sufficient descent altitude or upon establishing a transition to an emergency landing.

3. What standards are you expected to maintain when demonstrating an emergency descent? (FAA-S-ACS-7)

You will demonstrate the ability to:

a. Clear the area.

b. Establish and maintain the appropriate airspeed and configuration for the scenario specified by the evaluator and as covered in the POH/AFM for the emergency descent.

c. Demonstrate orientation, division of attention, and proper planning.

d. Use a bank angle between 30° and 45° to maintain positive load factors during the descent.

e. Maintain appropriate airspeed +0/-10 knots, and level off at specified altitude, +/-100 feet.

f. Complete the appropriate checklist.

L. Pitot/Static System and Associated Flight Instruments

1. **What instruments are affected when the pitot tube freezes?** (FAA-H-8083-25)

   a. *Pitot tube blocked and associated drain hole remains clear*—Airspeed decreases to zero; altimeter and vertical speed read normal.

   b. *Pitot tube and drain hole blocked*—Airspeed indicator acts as an altimeter; reads high in climb and low in descent. Altimeter and vertical speed read normal.

2. **What instruments are affected when the static port freezes?** (FAA-H-8083-25)

   Airspeed indicator—Accurate at the altitude frozen as long as the static pressure in the indicator and the system equals outside pressure. If the aircraft descends, the airspeed indicator would read high (outside static pressure greater than that trapped). If the aircraft climbs, the airspeed indicator will read low.

   Altimeter—Indicates the altitude at which the system was blocked.

   Vertical speed—Indicates level flight.

3. **What protections from icing are commonly in place for a pitot system?** (FAA-H-8083-25)

   Most light general aviation aircraft, especially those certificated for IFR flight operations, are equipped with a pitot tube heating system.

4. **What corrective action is needed if the pitot tube freezes? If the static port freezes?** (FAA-H-8083-25)

   Pitot tube—Turn pitot heat on.

   Static port—Use alternate air if available, or break the face of a static instrument (either the VSI or ASI).

5. **What indications should you expect while using alternate air?** (FAA-H-8083-15)

In many unpressurized aircraft equipped with a pitot-static tube, an alternate source of static pressure is provided for emergency use. If the alternate source is vented inside the airplane, where static pressure is usually lower than outside, selection of the alternate static source may result in the following indications:

Altimeter—will indicate higher than the actual altitude

Airspeed—will indicate greater than the actual airspeed

Vertical speed—will indicate a momentary climb then stabilize if altitude is held constant

Note: Always consult the AFM/POH to determine the amount of error.

6. **What flight instrument indications would you see if both the pitot static tube and static port became blocked for some reason?** (FAA-H-8083-15)

If both the pitot static tube and static port become blocked, several key flight instruments will be affected, potentially leading to unreliable or incorrect indications. This condition is commonly referred to as a "total loss of pitot-static instruments" or "pitot-static blockage." The affected flight instruments include:

a. *Airspeed indicator*—With the pitot tube blocked, the airspeed indicator will freeze at its current reading and will not show any changes in airspeed, even if the aircraft is accelerating or decelerating.

b. *Altimeter*—The static port blockage will cause the altimeter to freeze at its current altitude reading. As the aircraft climbs or descends, the altimeter will not reflect any changes in altitude.

c. *Vertical speed indicator (VSI)*—The VSI, which relies on static pressure, will also freeze at its current rate of climb or descent. It will not show any changes in vertical speed.

M. Vacuum System and Associated Flight Instruments

1. **What instruments may be relied upon in the event of a complete vacuum system failure while operating in instrument meteorological conditions?** (AFM/POH)

   Turn and slip/turn coordinator—bank information.

   Magnetic compass—bank information.

   Airspeed—pitch information.

   Altimeter—pitch information.

   Vertical speed indicator—pitch information.

2. **In a traditional vacuum pump equipped aircraft, what instruments are affected by the vacuum pump?** (FAA-H-8083-25)

   In most conventional light general aviation aircraft, the vacuum system powers the heading indicator and the attitude indicator.

3. **Is there a backup system available if the engine-driven vacuum pump were to fail?** (AFM/POH)

   Some general aviation aircraft may be equipped with a backup vacuum system. This system may be electrically driven or could be an engine-driven vacuum pump running in parallel to the primary pump.

N. Electrical

1. **What recommended procedure should be used in resetting a tripped circuit breaker?** (FAA-H-8083-30, AC 120-80)

   A tripped circuit breaker should not be reset in flight unless doing so is consistent with procedures specified in an approved AFM, or unless, in the judgment of the PIC, resetting the breaker is necessary for safe completion of the flight. Repeated resetting of a circuit breaker can lead to circuit or component damage, or worse, the possibility of a fire or explosion. A generally accepted practice if a breaker is allowed to be reset is to not reset it more than one time.

2. Interpret the following ammeter indications. (AFM/POH)

  a. Ammeter indicates a right deflection (positive).

  After starting—The power from the battery used for starting is being replenished by the alternator. Or, if a full-scale charge is indicated for more than 1 minute, the starter is still engaged and a shutdown is indicated.

  During flight—A faulty voltage regulator is causing the alternator to overcharge the battery.

  b. Ammeter indicates a left deflection (negative).

  After starting—Normal during start. Other times indicates the alternator is not functioning or an overload condition has occurred in the system. The battery is not receiving a charge.

  During flight—The alternator is not functioning or an overload has occurred in the system. The battery is not receiving a charge.

3. What action should be taken if the ammeter indicates a continuous discharge (left needle) while in flight? (AFM/POH)

The alternator has quit producing a charge, so the master switch and the alternator circuit breaker should be checked and reset if necessary. If this does not correct the problem, the following should be accomplished:

  a. The alternator should be turned off; pull the circuit breaker (field circuit will continue to draw power from the battery).

  b. All electrical equipment not essential to flight should be turned off (the battery is now the only source of electrical power).

  c. The flight should be terminated and a landing made as soon as possible.

4. What action should be taken if the ammeter indicates a continuous charge (right needle) while in flight (more than two needle widths)? (AFM/POH)

If a continuous excessive rate of charge were allowed for any extended period of time, the battery would overheat and evaporate the electrolyte at an excessive rate. A possible explosion of the battery could result. Also, electronic components in the electrical system would be adversely affected by higher than normal voltage. Protection is provided by an overvoltage sensor which will shut the alternator down if an excessive voltage is detected. If this should occur the following should be done:

a. The alternator should be turned off; pull the circuit breaker (the field circuit will continue to draw power from the battery).

b. All electrical equipment not essential to flight should be turned off (the battery is now the only source of electrical power).

c. The flight should be terminated and a landing made as soon as possible.

5. If the low-voltage warning light illuminates, what has occurred? (AFM/POH)

Illumination of the low-voltage light along with a discharge indication on the ammeter can occur during low RPM conditions with a full electrical load on the system. This event usually occurs on the ground with low RPMs while taxiing. Another possibility is the alternator has been shutdown; the airplane is equipped with a combination alternator/regulator high-low voltage control unit which, when an over-voltage condition occurs, will shut down the alternator and illuminate the warning light. The battery is now supplying all current to the electrical system. The ammeter will indicate a discharge. A pilot should be aware of what the battery may charge, if load shedding is advised at this point, and if an alternate backup system is in place. In some aircraft, a secondary emergency battery may be present that could power limited resources. Many modern aircraft have a primary and an essential bus that power different equipment. The pilot should be aware of the systems available and what the manufacturer indicates will be powered in different scenarios.

6. Describe several methods for disconnecting a malfunctioning autopilot? (FAA-H-8083-16)

Disconnecting a malfunctioning autopilot is essential for regaining manual control of the aircraft. The specific methods for disconnecting the autopilot may vary depending on the aircraft's make and model, but here are several common methods that pilots can use:

a. *Autopilot disconnect button*—Most modern aircraft are equipped with an autopilot disconnect button on the control yoke or control column. Pressing this button will immediately disengage the autopilot and return control to the pilot.

b. *Manual override switch*—Some aircraft have a manual override switch specifically designed to disengage the autopilot. This switch can be a physical toggle or a guarded button located on the instrument panel.

c. *Control column override*—In certain aircraft, applying significant force on the control column or yoke in any direction can disengage the autopilot. This function is designed as a safety feature to allow the pilot to quickly regain control if needed.

d. *Flight director override*—If the autopilot is coupled to a flight director system, simply deselecting the flight director mode will disconnect the autopilot.

e. *Circuit breaker*—In extreme cases where other methods fail, some aircraft have circuit breakers that can be pulled to deactivate the autopilot system. However, pilots should exercise caution with this method, as it may also affect other systems connected to the same circuit.

O. Landing Gear

1. In an aircraft equipped with a retractable landing gear, if the gear is selected down and a positive down indication is not given, what action is recommended? (FAA-H-8083-3)

In systems that are electrically actuated, either electric hydraulic systems or electric motor systems, a pilot should first make sure the master switch is set to on, then check that all circuit breakers related to the gear system are in and not tripped. In many systems, a pilot could check an indicator bulb by swapping it with another bulb in the display to see if a bulb has failed. At this point, if the problem has not been resolved, the pilot should proceed to the emergency gear extension checklist for the aircraft as given in the AFM/POH.

2. **What is the recommended procedure a pilot should use if a landing gear fails to retract after takeoff?** (AFM/POH)

A best practice is to check to make sure that the master switch is on, that no circuit breakers related to the gear system have popped, and that the gear selector switch is in the fully up position. If this does not work, a pilot is recommended to put the gear back in the down position and ensure that a full down and locked position indication is present. Best practices at this point would have a pilot not attempt to retract the gear again and divert to where maintenance can address the concern while operating the aircraft within manufacturer-provided gear down limitations.

3. **What procedure is recommended for a pilot during landing if they believe that the gear is down and locked but do not have an indication that corresponds with that belief?** (FAA-H-8083-3)

A pilot who has proceeded through an emergency gear extension checklist after not receiving a down and locked indication may have other methods of determining if a gear is likely down and locked. If a light indication is not illuminated, but a pilot has attempted to verify gear position through backup systems such as a manifold pressure switch, a mirror that may show the gear position, or even flying over a tower for a person on the ground to visually check the gear position, the pilot may be led to the belief that the gear is down but not properly indicating. In this case, the pilot should complete the normal before-landing checklist and conduct a normal approach with full flaps at a minimum controllable airspeed for touchdown. During touchdown, the pilot should establish a tail-low landing and use minimum braking. A pilot may elect to taxi clear of the runway at this point, but a best practice is to bring the aircraft to a stop as soon as in a safe location to have the gear inspected before additional taxiing or towing of the aircraft is conducted.

4. **How should a pilot configure an aircraft and its approach for landing if the gear system is not able to be deployed to a down and locked position?** (FAA-H-8083-3)

A pilot who is unable to establish a locked down gear position should prepare for a gear-up landing. Many manufacturers have recommended procedures outlined for this in the AFM/POH. In general, a pilot should complete a normal before landing checklist and approach with full flaps. A tail-low landing is recommended. It is also commonly recommended that shortly before touchdown the pilot reduce mixture on the aircraft to stop the engine, turn the magnetos off, and potentially even turn off the fuel selector and electrical master switch. This can minimize the potential for fire during the landing slide and if any structural damage occurs.

5. **What is the recommended procedure in dealing with a flat main landing gear tire?** (AFM/POH)

   a. Establish a normal approach configuration with full flaps.

   b. Touch down with the good tire first on that side of the runway and keep the aircraft off of the flat tire for as long as possible.

   c. Use braking on the good wheel as required to maintain directional control.

6. **What is a best practice to follow if a nose gear is unsafe or the tire is flat?** (FAA-H-8083-3)

   A pilot who suspects or confirms a nose gear is flat or unsafe should complete the normal before landing checklist and plan for a landing where the nose gear may collapse. Best practices in this situation would have a pilot shift weight to the rear by moving passengers and/or baggage if possible. The pilot should have all doors unlatched and maximum flaps deployed (unless they would encumber the opening of the door). The pilot should touch down on the main gear and keep the nose off as long as possible. After committing to the landing, it is recommended that the pilot turn off the avionics and aircraft master switches. The mixture prior to touchdown should be reduced to "idle-cutoff," and the magnetos should be set to "Off." The fuel selector should additionally be set to the "Off" position. After touchdown, when the aircraft has stopped moving, the aircraft should be evacuated as soon as possible.

7. **Why should taxiing on a slush, snow, or ice covered taxiway in a retractable gear airplane be avoided?** (FAA-H-8083-28)

During thawing conditions, mud and slush can be thrown into wheel wells during taxiing and takeoff. If it then freezes during flight, this mud and slush could create landing gear operational problems. The practice of recycling the gear after a takeoff can be used as a preventive procedure. However, the safest procedure is to avoid these surface conditions with retractable gear aircraft.

P. Wing Flaps (Asymmetrical Position)

1. **What is an asymmetrical flap emergency?** (FAA-H-8083-3)

An asymmetric split flap situation is one in which one flap deploys or retracts while the other remains in position. The problem is indicated by a pronounced roll toward the wing with the least flap deflection when wing flaps are extended or retracted.

2. **What procedure should be followed in an asymmetrical flap emergency?** (FAA-H-8083-3)

The roll encountered in a split flap situation is countered with opposite aileron. The yaw caused by the additional drag created by the extended flap will require substantial opposite rudder, resulting in a cross-control condition. Almost full aileron may be required to maintain a wings-level attitude, especially at the reduced airspeed necessary for approach and landing. The approach to landing with a split flap condition should be flown at a higher than normal airspeed. The pilot should not risk an asymmetric stall and subsequent loss of control by flaring excessively. The airplane should be flown onto the runway so that the touchdown occurs at an airspeed consistent with a safe margin above flaps-up stall speed.

Q. Inoperative Elevator

1. **What procedure should be followed if a loss of elevator or stabilator authority occurs?** (AFM/POH)

    a. Extend the landing gear.

    b. Lower flaps by 10°.

    c. Set trim for level flight.

    d. Using throttle and elevator trim control, establish an airspeed of 70 knots.

    Do not change the established trim setting. Maintain control of the glide angle by adjusting power. At the landing flare, the elevator trim should be adjusted to full noseup and the power reduced. At the moment of touchdown, close the throttle.

2. **What procedure should you use if the trim control on your aircraft has become inoperative, resulting in excessive control pressures in flight?** (AFM/POH)

    If the trim control on an aircraft becomes inoperative, resulting in excessive control pressures during flight, the situation can become challenging for the pilot to maintain control of the aircraft. Here are the recommended procedures to handle this situation:

    a. *Identify the issue*—First, the pilot must quickly identify that the trim control has become inoperative. Excessive control pressures and difficulty in maintaining straight-and-level flight are signs that the trim system is not functioning properly.

    b. *Verify the trim position*—Ensure that the trim is indeed stuck or inoperative and not inadvertently set in an extreme position, causing the control difficulties.

    c. *Use manual trim*—Many aircraft have a manual trim option available. Check the aircraft's pilot's operating handbook (POH) or flight manual for instructions on how to operate the manual trim system. Manually trimming the aircraft can help alleviate excessive control pressures.

    d. *Adjust airspeed*—If the aircraft is experiencing excessive control pressures, adjusting airspeed can help relieve some of the pressure. Slowing down the aircraft may reduce the aerodynamic forces on the control surfaces, making it easier to maintain control.

    (continued)

e. *Use coordinated flight*—Properly coordinate the flight using rudder and aileron inputs to minimize adverse yaw and maintain coordinated flight. This will help in reducing the amount of control pressure required to keep the aircraft level.

f. *Reduce bank angle*—Avoid steep turns or excessive bank angles, as they can increase control pressures and make it more challenging to control the aircraft.

g. *Communicate and request assistance*—If the situation becomes overwhelming or uncontrollable, communicate the problem to air traffic control (ATC) or other nearby aircraft. Request assistance and inform ATC of your intentions and emergency status if necessary.

h. *Plan for landing*—As soon as practical, start planning for a landing at the nearest suitable airport or landing area. Consider the need for emergency services and inform them of your situation and intentions.

R. Inadvertent Door Opening

1. What procedure should be followed if a cabin door accidentally opens in flight? (AFM/POH)

Many modern aircraft have manufacturer-recommended procedures for an inadvertent door opening during flight. In absence of such procedures, and in a general best practice, a pilot should reduce speed to at or below maneuvering speed. The most important action at this point is to maintain control of the aircraft and make flying the aircraft the first priority. In some aircraft, a door may be able to be closed during flight, but in many it will not be possible. If a pilot has a passenger or co-pilot who can attempt to close the door, they may attempt this. If not, a pilot is typically encouraged to divert to the nearest airport while flying a normal pattern and approach to a landing and then deal with the open door on the ground. In some aircraft, the effect of an open door will create pressures that require a pilot to counteract the airflow created by an open door.

2. **What procedure should be followed if a baggage door opens in flight?** (AFM/POH)

Baggage compartments tend to be located in the aft section of the airplane and under no circumstances should the pilot allow anyone to attempt to close the doors while in flight. By design, the baggage compartment door will tend to remain closed during flight due to airflow pressure. The pilot should divert to a nearest suitable airport and handle an open baggage door condition on the ground after the aircraft has been stopped and shut down.

S. Emergency Equipment and Survival Gear

1. **What two factors should be considered in choosing the type of survival equipment to carry for a flight over an uninhabited area?** (AIM 6-2-6)

   a. The type of climate.
   b. The type of terrain.

2. **What additional equipment is required if an aircraft is operated for hire over water and beyond power-off gliding distance from shore?** (14 CFR 91.205)

If an aircraft is operated for hire over water and beyond power-off gliding distance from shore, approved flotation gear readily available to each occupant and at least one pyrotechnic signaling device are required. "For hire" is commonly misunderstood here. An aircraft that is being operated in private carriage with a pilot who is being paid to fly it, acting commercially, is not constrained to the same over-water limitations as an aircraft operated commercially, such as a Part 135 approved operation or other similar commercial activities. While it may be allowed for a pilot to operate beyond gliding distance of land (which can commonly occur in and around the Great Lakes), a best practice is to have suitable flotation devices for pilot and passengers if the operation takes them beyond gliding distance.

3. **What are some things that are part of an aircraft that might be used to aid in survival if necessary?**

   a. The compass will keep you going in one direction.

   b. Gasoline will help make a fire.

   c. Oil can be used for smoke signals.

   d. Seat upholstery may be used to wrap around feet or hands.

   e. Wiring may be used for tie strings.

   f. The battery may be used to ignite fuel.

   g. The aircraft body may be used as a shelter for protection from the elements.

4. **What are some considerations for pilots regarding fire extinguishers in aircraft?** (FAA-H-8083-25)

   Fire extinguishers in general aviation aircraft have limitations and considerations that pilots should be aware of. These limitations may vary based on the type and size of the aircraft, but here are some common points to consider:

   a. *Type of extinguisher*—The type of fire extinguisher installed in the aircraft should be appropriate for the types of fires commonly encountered in aviation, such as Class A (ordinary combustibles like paper, wood, and cloth) and Class B (flammable liquids like fuel and oil) fires.

   b. *Expiration date*—Fire extinguishers have a limited shelf life, typically indicated by an expiration date or a recommended service interval. It is essential to regularly inspect and maintain the extinguisher to ensure it is within its valid service life.

   c. *Mounting and accessibility*—Fire extinguishers must be properly mounted and easily accessible to the pilot and crew. They should not obstruct any critical flight controls or impede access to exits.

   d. *Weight and balance*—Adding a fire extinguisher to the aircraft may affect the weight and balance. Pilots should ensure that the addition of the extinguisher does not exceed the aircraft's maximum weight limitations or shift the center of gravity beyond acceptable limits.

   e. *Training and familiarity*—It is essential for pilots and crew to receive training on how to use the fire extinguisher properly.

They should be familiar with the extinguisher's operation, the types of fires it can handle, and the appropriate techniques for effective firefighting.

f. *Fire types*—Fire extinguishers have limitations based on the types of fires they can effectively control. While they are useful for small, contained fires, they may not be sufficient for larger or rapidly spreading fires.

g. *Secondary response*—Fire extinguishers should be considered a first line of defense for small fires. In the event of a larger or uncontrollable fire, pilots should prioritize safe flight and emergency procedures, including landing as soon as possible and evacuating the aircraft if necessary.

Always adhere to the aircraft manufacturer's recommendations, regulatory requirements, and any specific limitations specified in the aircraft's AFM or POH. Regular maintenance and inspection of the fire extinguisher are vital to ensure its reliability in case of an emergency.

5. When may a pilot test an ELT on an aircraft? (AIM 6-2-4)

The Federal Aviation Regulations provide specific guidelines for testing an emergency locator transmitter (ELT) on an aircraft. According to 14 CFR §91.207, an ELT should be tested as follows:

a. *Testing during maintenance*—An ELT can be tested on the ground during the aircraft's maintenance checks as long as it is done in accordance with the manufacturer's instructions. This maintenance testing should not be done more than 12 calendar months after the last test.

b. *3-minute test*—A pilot can test the ELT in flight for up to 3 minutes (or less) during the first 5 minutes after the hour. This test must be conducted at least every 12 calendar months.

Exception: For aircraft that are operated under Part 91 and equipped with a 121.5 MHz ELT, the 3-hour test is not required after January 1, 2009. However, these aircraft must still comply with the annual maintenance testing requirement.

Note: When testing the ELT in flight, the pilot should follow certain precautions to avoid causing false distress alerts. These precautions may include notifying the appropriate air traffic control facility before the test and ensuring the ELT is properly secured or muted during the test.

Performance
and Limitations

6

A. Atmospheric Conditions

1. How is aircraft performance significantly affected as air becomes less dense? (FAA-H-8083-25)

As air becomes less dense, it reduces:

a. Power because the engine takes in less air.
b. Thrust because the propeller is less efficient in thin air.
c. Lift because thin air exerts less force on airfoils.

2. What is the standard atmosphere at sea level? (FAA-H-8083-25)

Standard atmosphere at sea level includes a surface temperature of 59°F or 15°C, and a surface pressure of 29.92 inHg or 1013.2 millibars.

3. What are standard atmosphere temperature and pressure lapse rates? (FAA-H-8083-25)

A standard temperature lapse rate is one in which the temperature decreases at the rate of approximately 3.5°F or 2°C per 1,000 feet up to 36,000 feet. Above this point, the temperature is considered constant up to 80,000 feet. A standard pressure lapse rate is one in which pressure decreases at a rate of approximately 1 inHg per 1,000 feet of altitude gain to 10,000 feet.

4. Define the term *pressure altitude*. (FAA-H-8083-25)

Pressure altitude is the height above a standard datum plane (SDP). An altimeter is a sensitive barometer calibrated to indicate altitude in the standard atmosphere. If the altimeter is set for 29.92 inHg SDP, the altitude indicated is the pressure altitude—the altitude in the standard atmosphere corresponding to the sensed pressure.

5. Why is pressure altitude important? (FAA-H-8083-25)

Pressure altitude is important as a basis for determining airplane performance as well as for assigning flight levels to airplanes operating above 18,000 feet.

6. What are three methods of determining pressure altitude? (FAA-H-8083-25)

Pressure altitude can be determined by these methods:

a. By setting the barometric scale of the altimeter to 29.92 and reading the indicated altitude.

b. By applying a correction factor to the indicated altitude according to the reported altimeter setting.

c. By using a flight computer.

7. Define the term *density altitude*. (FAA-H-8083-25)

Density altitude is pressure altitude corrected for nonstandard temperature. It is the altitude in the standard atmosphere corresponding to a particular value of air density.

8. How does air density affect aircraft performance? (FAA-H-8083-25)

As the density of the air increases (lower density altitude), airplane performance increases and conversely, as air density decreases (higher density altitude), airplane performance decreases. A decrease in air density means a high density altitude; an increase in air density means a lower density altitude.

9. How is density altitude determined? (FAA-H-8083-25)

First find pressure altitude and then correct it for nonstandard temperature variations. Because density varies directly with pressure, and inversely with temperature, a given pressure altitude may exist for a wide range of temperatures. However, a known density occurs for any one temperature and pressure altitude. Regardless of the actual altitude at which the airplane is operating, it will perform as though it were operating at an altitude equal to the existing density altitude.

10. What factors affect air density? (FAA-H-8083-25)

Air density is affected by changes in altitude, temperature, and humidity. High density altitude refers to thin air while low density altitude refers to dense air. The conditions that result in a high density altitude are high elevations, low atmospheric pressures, high temperatures, high humidity, or some combination of these factors. Lower elevations, high atmospheric pressure, low temperatures, and low humidity are more indicative of low density altitude.

11. What effect does atmospheric pressure have on air density? (FAA-H-8083-25)

Air density is directly proportional to pressure. If the pressure is doubled, the density is doubled, and if the pressure is lowered, so is the density. This statement is true only at a constant temperature.

12. What effect does temperature have on air density? (FAA-H-8083-25)

Increasing the temperature of a substance decreases its density. Conversely, decreasing the temperature increases the density. Thus, the density of air varies inversely with temperature. This statement is true only at a constant pressure.

13. Since temperature and pressure decrease with altitude, how will air density be affected overall? (FAA-H-8083-25)

The decrease in temperature and pressure have conflicting effects on density as you go up in altitude, but the fairly rapid drop in pressure with increasing altitude is usually the dominating factor. Hence, the density is likely to decrease with altitude gain.

14. What effect does humidity have on air density? (FAA-H-8083-25)

Water vapor is lighter than air, so moist air is lighter than dry air. As the water content of the air increases, the air becomes less dense, increasing density altitude and decreasing performance. It is lightest or least dense when it contains the maximum amount of water vapor. Humidity alone is usually not considered an important factor in calculating density altitude and airplane performance, but it does contribute.

15. What is the definition of *relative humidity*?
(FAA-H-8083-25)

Relative humidity refers to the amount of water vapor in the atmosphere, and is expressed as a percentage of the maximum amount of water vapor the air can hold. This amount varies with the temperature—warm air can hold more water vapor and colder air can hold less.

16. What effect does landing at high-elevation airports have on ground speed with comparable conditions relative to temperature, wind and airplane weight? (FAA-H-8083-25)

Even if you use the same indicated airspeed appropriate for sea level operations, true airspeed is faster, resulting in a faster ground speed (with a given wind condition) throughout the approach, touchdown, and landing roll. This means greater distance to clear obstacles during the approach, a longer ground roll, and consequently the need for a longer runway. All of these factors should be taken into consideration when landing at high-elevation fields, particularly if the field is short.

17. While performing a preflight inspection on your aircraft for an early-morning departure, you notice frost has formed on the top of both wings. How will this affect the aircraft on departure? (FAA-H-8083-25)

Frost on an aircraft's surfaces can have a significant impact on its performance and flight characteristics. Here are some ways in which frost affects aircraft performance:

a. *Increased weight*—Frost adds weight to the aircraft, which can affect the aircraft's maximum takeoff weight and reduce its payload capacity. It may also increase the stall speed slightly due to the added weight.

b. *Aerodynamic drag*—Frost creates a rough and uneven surface on the wings, fuselage, and control surfaces, increasing aerodynamic drag. This results in decreased lift and increased drag, which can lead to reduced climb performance and increased fuel consumption.

c. *Reduced lift*—The rough surface caused by frost disrupts smooth airflow over the wings, reducing lift generation. As a result, the aircraft may require higher airspeeds to achieve the necessary lift for takeoff or landing, increasing the takeoff and landing distances.

d. *Altered center of gravity (CG)*—The distribution of frost on the aircraft can alter its center of gravity, potentially affecting its stability and control during flight. Pilots must ensure that the aircraft's CG remains within the allowable limits.

e. *Impaired control*—Frost on control surfaces, such as ailerons, elevators, and rudder, can affect their ability to respond to pilot inputs smoothly and precisely. This may result in reduced control authority and potentially affect the aircraft's maneuverability.

f. *Icing hazard*—Frost can also create an icing hazard during flight. If the aircraft encounters clouds or precipitation, the frost can quickly turn into ice, further degrading the aircraft's performance and potentially leading to hazardous conditions.

Given these performance impacts, it is essential for pilots and ground crews to thoroughly remove all frost from an aircraft before flight.

B. Aircraft Performance

1. What are some of the main elements of aircraft performance? (FAA-H-8083-25)

a. Takeoff and landing distance.
b. Rate-of-climb.
c. Ceiling.
d. Payload.
e. Range.
f. Speed.
g. Maneuverability.
h. Stability.
i. Fuel economy.

2. What is the relationship of lift, weight, thrust, and drag in steady, unaccelerated, level flight? (FAA-H-8083-25)

For the airplane to remain in steady, level flight, equilibrium must be obtained by a lift equal to the airplane weight and powerplant thrust equal to the airplane drag.

3. **What are the two types of drag?** (FAA-H-8083-25)

   Total drag may be divided into two parts: the wing drag (induced), and drag from everything but the wings (parasite).

4. **Define *induced drag*.** (FAA-H-8083-25)

   Induced drag is the part of total drag created by the production of lift. Induced drag increases with a decrease in airspeed. The lower the airspeed, the greater the angle of attack required to produce lift equal to the airplane's weight, and therefore the greater the induced drag.

5. **Define *parasite drag*.** (FAA-H-8083-25)

   Parasite drag is drag caused by the friction of air moving over the aircraft structure; its amount varies directly with the airspeed. It is the drag that is not associated with the production of lift and includes the displacement of the air by the aircraft, turbulence generated in the airstream, or a hindrance of air moving over the surface of the aircraft and airfoil. There are three types of parasite drag: form drag, interference drag, and skin friction drag.

6. **How much will drag increase as airplane speed increases?** (FAA-H-8083-25)

   If an airplane in a steady flight condition at 100 knots is then accelerated to 200 knots, the parasite drag becomes four times as great, but the power required to overcome that drag is eight times the original value. Conversely, when the airplane is operated in steady, level flight at twice as great a speed, the induced drag is one-fourth the original value, and the power required to overcome that drag is only one-half the original value.

7. **Climb performance is a result of using the aircraft's potential energy provided by one, or a combination of two, factors. What are those two factors?** (FAA-H-8083-25)

   a. Use of excess power above that required for level flight. An aircraft equipped with an engine capable of 200 horsepower (at a given altitude) but using 130 horsepower to sustain level flight (at a given airspeed) has 70 excess horsepower available for climbing.

   (continued)

b. Use of the aircraft's kinetic energy. An aircraft can trade off its kinetic energy and increase its potential energy by reducing its airspeed. The reduction in airspeed will increase the aircraft's potential energy, making the aircraft climb.

8. Define the term *service ceiling*. (FAA-H-8083-25)

Service ceiling is the maximum density altitude where the best rate-of-climb airspeed will produce a 100 feet-per-minute climb at maximum weight while in a clean configuration with maximum continuous power.

9. Will an aircraft always be capable of climbing to and maintaining its service ceiling? (FAA-H-8083-25)

No. Depending on the density altitude, an airplane may not be able to reach it published service ceiling on any given day.

10. What is the definition of *absolute ceiling*? (FAA-H-8083-25)

Absolute ceiling is the altitude at which a climb is no longer possible.

11. The values for V_X and V_Y will be equal at what altitude? (FAA-H-8083-25)

The values for V_X (best angle of climb) and V_Y (best rate of climb) will be equal at the altitude known as the *absolute ceiling* or *service ceiling* of the aircraft. The absolute ceiling is the altitude at which the aircraft can no longer climb at a positive rate. At this altitude, the aircraft's rate of climb diminishes to zero, and further ascent is not possible while maintaining level flight.

At the absolute ceiling, the aircraft is unable to sustain a climb at either V_X or V_Y speeds. Both V_X and V_Y represent specific airspeeds optimized for climb performance. V_X is the airspeed that provides the greatest altitude gain per unit of horizontal distance covered, while V_Y is the airspeed that provides the greatest altitude gain per unit of time.

Below the absolute ceiling, V_X and V_Y will have different values, with V_X typically being slower than V_Y. V_X is used for clearing obstacles during takeoff and initial climb, while V_Y is used for achieving the highest rate of climb during normal climb operations.

Note: The absolute ceiling can vary depending on factors such as aircraft weight, atmospheric conditions, and other performance-related parameters specific to the aircraft model. Pilots should consult the aircraft's documentation, such as the AFM or POH, to obtain accurate and precise information regarding the absolute ceiling and the associated climb speeds.

12. What happens to V_X and V_Y as altitude is increased? (FAA-H-8083-25)

As altitude is increased, the values for V_X (best angle of climb) and V_Y (best rate of climb) typically increase. The reason for this increase is primarily due to the decrease in air density with increasing altitude. As the air density decreases, the aircraft's wings generate less lift, and the engine produces less thrust. Consequently, the aircraft's performance capabilities are affected.

For V_X, which is the airspeed that provides the greatest altitude gain per unit of horizontal distance covered, the speed will generally increase with altitude. This is because a higher ground speed is required to cover the same horizontal distance as the air density decreases. V_X allows the aircraft to clear obstacles during takeoff and initial climb with the steepest climb angle.

Similarly, V_Y, which is the airspeed that provides the greatest altitude gain per unit of time, will also increase with altitude. As the air density decreases, the aircraft's climb rate decreases. To maintain the highest climb rate, the aircraft must fly at a higher airspeed.

13. What is meant by the terms *power loading* and *wing loading*? (FAA-H-8083-25)

Power loading is expressed in pounds per horsepower and is obtained by dividing the total weight of the airplane by the rated horsepower of the engine. It is a significant factor in the airplane's takeoff and climb capabilities.

Wing loading is expressed in pounds per square foot and is obtained by dividing the total weight of the airplane in pounds by the wing area (including ailerons) in square feet. It is the airplane's wing loading that determines the landing speed.

14. Does the horizontal stabilizer provide lift? How does it affect longitudinal stability? (FAA-H-8083-25)

The horizontal stabilizer of an aircraft does provide lift, but its primary role is to contribute to the longitudinal stability of the aircraft rather than to generate significant lift for flight. The horizontal stabilizer, often located at the tail of the aircraft, generates a downward force known as negative lift or negative lift component. This negative lift acts in opposition to the lift generated by the wings. The purpose of this negative lift is to balance the moments and forces acting on the aircraft and contribute to its longitudinal stability. The horizontal stabilizer's negative lift helps maintain the desired pitch attitude and stability during flight. By producing a downward force, it counteracts the tendency of the aircraft's nose to pitch upward. This counteracting force contributes to the aircraft's overall stability, allowing for smoother and more controlled flight.

Additionally, the horizontal stabilizer often houses the elevator, which is a movable control surface attached to its trailing edge. The elevator controls the aircraft's pitch and allows the pilot to adjust the aircraft's attitude and change the vertical direction of flight.

While the horizontal stabilizer does provide a small amount of lift, its primary function is to contribute to the aircraft's longitudinal stability and control rather than to sustain flight itself. The wings are the main lift-generating surfaces of the aircraft.

15. Define the terms *maximum range* and *maximum endurance*. (FAA-H-8083-25)

Maximum range is the maximum distance an airplane can fly for a given fuel supply and is obtained at the maximum lift/drag ratio (L/D_{MAX}). For a given airplane configuration, the maximum lift/drag ratio occurs at a particular angle of attack and lift coefficient, and is unaffected by weight or altitude.

Maximum endurance is the maximum amount of time an airplane can fly for a given fuel supply and is obtained at the point of minimum power required since this would require the lowest fuel flow to keep the airplane in steady, level flight.

16. In the event of an engine failure, what airspeed should you use to achieve the most distance forward for each foot of altitude lost? (FAA-H-8083-3)

The best glide speed is the one at which the airplane will travel the greatest forward distance for a given loss of altitude in still air. This speed corresponds to an angle of attack resulting in the least drag on the airplane and giving the best lift-to-drag ratio (L/D_{MAX}).

17. What is ground effect? (FAA-H-8083-25)

Ground effect occurs due to the interference of the ground surface with the flow pattern about the airplane in flight, when the airplane is flown at approximately one wingspan above the surface. Especially with low-wing aircraft, it is most significant when the airplane is maintaining a constant attitude at low airspeed and low altitude. For example: during landing flare before touchdown, and during takeoff when the airplane lifts off and accelerates to climb speed. A wing in ground effect has a reduction in upwash, downwash, and tip vortices. With reduced tip vortices, induced drag is reduced. When the wing is at a height equal to one-fourth the span, the reduction in induced drag is about 25 percent, and when the wing is at a height equal to one-tenth the span, this reduction is about 50 percent.

18. What major problems can be caused by ground effect? (FAA-H-8083-25)

During landing—At a height of approximately one-tenth of a wing span above the surface, drag may be 50 percent less than when the airplane is operating out of ground effect. Therefore, any excess speed during the landing phase may result in a significant float distance. In such cases, if care is not exercised, the pilot may run out of runway and options at the same time.

During takeoff—Due to the reduced drag in ground effect, the aircraft may seem capable of takeoff well below the recommended speed. However, as the airplane rises out of ground effect with a deficiency of speed, the greater induced drag may result in very marginal climb performance, or the inability of the airplane to fly at all. In extreme conditions such as high gross weight and high density altitude, the airplane may become airborne initially with a deficiency of speed and then settle back to the runway.

19. What is flight in the region of normal command?
(FAA-H-8083-25)

It means that while holding a constant altitude, a higher airspeed requires a higher power setting, and a lower airspeed requires a lower power setting. The majority of all airplane flying (climb, cruise, and maneuvers) is conducted in the region of normal command.

20. What is flight in the region of reversed command?
(FAA-H-8083-25)

It means that a higher airspeed requires a lower power setting, and a lower airspeed requires a higher power setting to hold altitude. It does not imply that a decrease in power will produce lower airspeed. The region of reversed command is encountered in the low-speed phases of flight. Flight speeds below the speed for maximum endurance (lowest point on the power curve) require higher power settings with a decrease in airspeed. Because the need to increase the required power setting with decreased speed is contrary to the "normal command" of flight, flight speeds between minimum required power setting (speed) and the stall speed (or minimum control speed) is termed the *region of reversed command*. In the region of reversed command, a decrease in airspeed must be accompanied by an increased power setting in order to maintain steady flight.

21. What are examples of where an airplane would be operating in the region of reversed command?
(FAA-H-8083-25)

a. An airplane performing a low airspeed, high-pitch attitude, powered approach for a short-field landing.

b. A soft-field takeoff and climb where the pilot attempts to climb out of ground effect without first attaining normal climb pitch attitude and airspeed, is an example of inadvertently operating in the region of reversed command at a dangerously low altitude.

22. **Explain how runway surface and gradient affect performance.** (FAA-H-8083-25)

   a. *Runway surface*—Any surface that is not hard and smooth will increase the ground roll during takeoff. This is due to the inability of the tires to smoothly roll along the runway. Although muddy and wet surface conditions can reduce friction between the runway and the tires, they can also act as obstructions and reduce the landing distance.

   b. *Braking effectiveness*—The amount of power that is applied to the brakes without skidding the tires is referred to as braking effectiveness. Ensure that runways are adequate in length for takeoff acceleration and landing deceleration when less than ideal surface conditions are being reported, as it affects braking ability.

   c. *Runway gradient or slope*—A positive gradient indicates that the runway height increases, and a negative gradient indicates that the runway decreases in height. An upsloping runway impedes acceleration and results in a longer ground run during takeoff. However, landing on an upsloping runway typically reduces the landing roll. A downsloping runway aids in acceleration on takeoff resulting in shorter takeoff distances. The opposite is true when landing, as landing on a downsloping runway increases landing distances.

23. **What factors affect the performance of an aircraft during takeoffs and landings?** (FAA-H-8083-25)

   a. Air density (density altitude).
   b. Surface wind.
   c. Runway surface.
   d. Upslope or downslope of runway.
   e. Weight.
   f. Powerplant thrust.

24. What effect does wind have on aircraft performance? (FAA-H-8083-25)

Takeoff—The effect of a headwind is that it allows the aircraft to reach the lift-off speed at a lower ground speed, which will increase airplane performance by shortening the takeoff distance and increasing the angle of climb. The effect of a tailwind is that the aircraft will need to achieve greater ground speed to get to lift-off speed. This decreases aircraft performance by increasing takeoff distance and reducing the angle of climb.

Landing—The effect of wind on landing distance is identical to its effect on takeoff distance. A headwind will lower ground speed and increase airplane performance by steepening the approach angle and reducing the landing distance. A tailwind will increase ground speed and decrease performance by decreasing the approach angle and increasing the landing distance.

Cruise flight—Winds aloft have a somewhat opposite effect on airplane performance. A headwind will decrease performance by reducing ground speed, which in turn increases the fuel requirement for the flight. A tailwind will increase performance by increasing the ground speed, which in turn reduces the fuel requirement for the flight.

25. How does weight affect takeoff and landing performance? (FAA-H-8083-25)

Increased gross weight can produce these effects:

a. Higher liftoff and landing speed required.

b. Greater mass to accelerate or decelerate (slow acceleration/ deceleration).

c. Increased retarding force (drag and ground friction).

d. Longer takeoff and ground roll.

The effect of gross weight on landing distance is that the airplane will require a greater speed to support the airplane at the landing angle of attack and lift coefficient resulting in an increased landing distance.

26. What effect does an increase in density altitude have on takeoff and landing performance? (FAA-H-8083-25)

An increase in density altitude results in:

a. Increased takeoff distance (greater takeoff TAS required).

b. Reduced rate of climb (decreased thrust and reduced acceleration).

c. Increased true airspeed on approach and landing (same IAS).

d. Increased landing roll distance.

An increase in density altitude (decrease in air density) will increase the landing speed but will not alter the net retarding force. Thus, the airplane will land at the same indicated airspeed as normal but because of reduced air density the true airspeed will be greater. This will result in a longer minimum landing distance.

27. Planning for a rejected takeoff is essential to the safety of every flight. What calculation must be made prior to every takeoff? (FAA-H-8083-3)

Prior to takeoff, the pilot should have in mind a point along the runway at which the airplane should be airborne. If that point is reached and the airplane is not airborne, immediate action should be taken to discontinue the takeoff. If properly planned and executed, the airplane can be stopped on the remaining runway without using extraordinary measures, such as excessive braking that may result in loss of directional control, airplane damage, and/ or personal injury.

28. Why does the manufacturer provide various manifold pressure/prop settings for a given power output?

The various power MAP/RPM combinations are provided so the pilot has a choice between operating the aircraft at best efficiency (minimum fuel flow) or operating at best power/speed condition. An aircraft engine operated at higher RPMs will produce more friction and, as a result, use more fuel. On the other hand, an aircraft operating at higher and higher altitudes will not be able to continue to produce the same constant power output due to a drop in manifold pressure. The only way to compensate for this is by operating the engine at a higher RPM.

29. What does the term *75 percent brake horsepower* **mean?** (FAA-H-8083-25)

Brake horsepower (BHP) is the power delivered at the propeller shaft (main drive or main output) of an aircraft engine. 75 percent BHP means you are delivering 75 percent of the normally rated power or maximum continuous power available at sea level on a standard day to the propeller shaft.

30. Explain how 75 percent BHP can be obtained from your engine. (FAA-H-8083-25)

Set the throttle (manifold pressure) and propeller (RPM) to the recommended values found in the cruise performance chart of your POH.

31. When would a pilot lean a normally aspirated direct-drive engine? (FAA-P-8740-13)

a. Lean anytime the power setting is 75 percent or less at any altitude.

b. At high-altitude airports, lean for taxi, takeoff, traffic pattern entry and landing.

c. When the density altitude is high (hot, high, humid).

d. For landings at airports below 5,000 feet density altitude, adjust the mixture for descent, but only as required.

e. Always consult the POH for proper leaning procedures.

32. What are the different methods available for leaning aircraft engines? (FAA-P-8740-13)

Tachometer method—For best economy operation, the mixture is first leaned from full rich to maximum power (peak RPM), then the leaning process is slowly continued until the engine starts to run rough. Then, enrich the mixture sufficiently to obtain a smoothly firing engine.

Fuel flowmeter method—Aircraft equipped with fuel flowmeters require that you lean the mixture to the published (POH) or marked fuel flow to achieve the correct mixture.

Exhaust gas temperature method—Lean the mixture slowly to establish peak EGT then enrich the mixture by 50° rich (cooler) of peak EGT. This will provide the recommended lean condition for the established power setting.

33. Define the following airplane performance speeds: V_{SO}, V_{SI}, V_Y, V_X, V_{LE}, V_{LO}, V_{FE}, V_A, V_{NO}, V_{NE}. (FAA-H-8083-25)

V_{SO}—The calibrated power-off stalling speed or the minimum steady flight speed at which the airplane is controllable in the landing configuration.

V_{SI}—The calibrated power-off stalling speed or the minimum steady flight speed at which the airplane is controllable in a specified configuration.

V_Y—The calibrated airspeed at which the airplane will obtain the maximum increase in altitude per unit of time. This best rate-of-climb speed normally decreases slightly with altitude.

V_X—The calibrated airspeed at which the airplane will obtain the highest altitude in a given horizontal distance. This best angle-of-climb speed normally increases slightly with altitude.

V_{LE}—The maximum calibrated airspeed at which the airplane can be safely flown with the landing gear extended. This is a problem involving stability and controllability.

V_{LO}—The maximum calibrated airspeed at which the landing gear can be safely extended or retracted. This is a problem involving the air loads imposed on the operating mechanism during extension or retraction of the gear.

V_{FE}—The highest calibrated airspeed permissible with the wing flaps in a prescribed extended position. This is because of the air loads imposed on the structure of the flaps.

V_A—The calibrated design maneuvering airspeed. This is the maximum speed at which the limit load can be imposed (either by gusts or full deflection of the control surfaces) without causing structural damage. Operating at or below maneuvering speed does not provide structural protection against multiple full control inputs in one axis or full control inputs in more than one axis at the same time.

V_{NO}—The maximum calibrated airspeed for normal operation or the maximum structural cruising speed. This is the speed at which exceeding the limit load factor may cause permanent deformation of the airplane structure.

V_{NE}—The calibrated airspeed which should *never* be exceeded. If flight is attempted above this speed, structural damage or structural failure may result.

34. **Define *endurance* and *range*.** (FAA-H-8083-25)

Endurance and range are two important performance parameters used to describe the capabilities of an aircraft.

Endurance refers to the amount of time an aircraft can remain in flight on a given amount of fuel. It represents the ability of an aircraft to sustain flight and is typically measured in hours or minutes. Endurance depends on factors such as fuel consumption rate, fuel capacity, and engine efficiency. A higher endurance value indicates that the aircraft can stay in the air for a longer duration before needing to refuel. Endurance is particularly important for missions involving extended loitering or surveillance, where longer flight times are desired.

Range refers to the maximum distance an aircraft can travel without refueling. It represents the aircraft's ability to cover a specific distance in a single flight. Range depends on factors such as fuel capacity, fuel consumption rate, and the aircraft's aerodynamic efficiency. It is typically measured in nautical miles or statute miles. A longer range indicates that the aircraft can fly greater distances without the need for refueling stops. Range is crucial for missions that require traveling long distances, such as cross-country flights or intercontinental travel.

Both endurance and range are important considerations for flight planning and operational efficiency. They are influenced by various factors, including the aircraft's design, engine performance, fuel capacity, and payload.

35. **Explain the difference between the best glide speed and minimum sink speed.** (FAA-H-8083-3)

Best glide speed—The speed and configuration that provides the greatest forward distance for a given loss of altitude. In most airplanes, best glide airspeed will be roughly halfway between V_X (best angle of climb speed) and V_Y (best rate of climb speed).

Minimum sink speed—Used to maximize the time that the airplane remains in flight. Use of the minimum sink speed will result in the airplane losing altitude at the lowest rate. It is important that pilots realize that flight at the minimum sink airspeed results in less distance traveled and is useful in flight situations where time in flight is more important than distance flown (i.e., more time to fix problem, ditching at sea, etc.). Minimum sink speed is not an often published airspeed but is generally a few knots less than best glide speed.

36. **How would a pilot determine how far their aircraft could glide at the best glide speed in the event of an engine failure?** (AFM/POH)

Most AFM/POH documents produce a glide chart or offer a glide ratio. By referring to this data, a pilot could calculate glide over distance for height above ground. For example, if an aircraft can glide 1.5 nautical miles per 1,000 feet of altitude, then at 5,000 feet AGL, it could glide 7.5 miles. [(5,000 ÷ 1,000) × 1.5]

37. **What are three ways a pilot can control lift during flight?** (FAA-H-8083-25)

There are three primary ways to control lift during flight:

a. *Angle of attack (AOA)*—The angle of attack refers to the angle between the aircraft's wing chord line and the oncoming airflow. By changing the AOA, the pilot can control the amount of lift generated by the wings. Increasing the AOA increases lift, while decreasing the AOA reduces lift. The AOA is controlled by adjusting the aircraft's pitch attitude using the elevators.

b. *Airspeed*—Airspeed directly affects the lift generated by the wings. As airspeed increases, the wings generate more lift, and as airspeed decreases, the lift decreases. The pilot can control lift by adjusting the throttle or power settings to increase or decrease the airspeed. Changing the airspeed affects the flow of air over the wings, thereby altering lift.

c. *Wing flaps*—Wing flaps are adjustable surfaces on the trailing edge of the wings that can be extended or retracted. By deploying flaps, the effective camber of the wing increases, which generates more lift at lower airspeeds. Flaps allow the aircraft to maintain lift at slower speeds during takeoff and landing. The pilot can control lift by selecting the appropriate flap configuration for the desired phase of flight.

By manipulating the angle of attack, airspeed, and wing flaps, pilots can effectively control lift during various flight conditions, ensuring safe and efficient operation of the aircraft.

38. The takeoff and landing data published for any aircraft is based on what conditions? (FAA-H-8083-25, AFM/POH)

The takeoff and landing data published for an aircraft is typically based on specific standard conditions defined by aviation regulatory authorities. These conditions provide a standardized reference for aircraft performance calculations and allow for consistent comparison across different aircraft models. The commonly used standard conditions include:

a. *Standard atmospheric conditions*—The data is based on the assumption of a standard atmosphere, which includes standard temperature, pressure, and density at various altitudes. The standard temperature is 15°C at sea level, with a lapse rate of −2°C per 1,000 feet of altitude.

b. *Sea level operations*—Takeoff and landing data is generally provided for sea level operations, assuming the aircraft is at or near sea level. This ensures consistent performance calculations for airports located at different elevations.

c. *Dry runway surface*—The data is typically generated considering a dry runway surface with good braking action. It assumes no additional factors such as wet or contaminated runways that may affect the aircraft's performance during takeoff and landing.

d. *Maximum takeoff weight*—The published data is based on the aircraft operating at its maximum takeoff weight, which is the highest authorized weight for safe takeoff.

Note: Actual operating conditions may differ from the standard conditions. Factors such as altitude, temperature, runway conditions, aircraft weight, and specific aircraft configurations can influence the actual performance of the aircraft. Therefore, pilots should consult the aircraft's documentation, such as the AFM or POH, to obtain the most accurate and up-to-date performance data for their specific operating conditions.

39. Performance chart data is based upon what type of runway surface? (FAA-H-8083-25)

Performance chart data for aircraft is typically based on a dry runway surface. Dry runway conditions are considered the standard reference for performance calculations.

Dry runway surfaces provide optimal traction and braking action, allowing the aircraft to achieve its maximum performance capabilities during takeoff and landing. Performance charts, such as takeoff distance, landing distance, and climb performance charts, are generated based on the assumption of dry runway conditions.

It's important to note that actual runway conditions can vary significantly from the dry runway standard. Factors such as wet, contaminated, icy, or snow-covered runways can have a substantial impact on aircraft performance. These factors can affect the aircraft's acceleration, braking effectiveness, and overall handling characteristics.

Some aircraft do publish performance data for non-paved runways, contaminated surfaces (water, snow, or potentially ice) and other conditions. Unless data is published for these conditions, a pilot should add additional margins to any takeoff or landing considerations.

40. During landing, will there be any difference in elevator control effectiveness as the airplane enters ground effect? (FAA-H-8083-25)

There can be a difference in elevator control effectiveness as the airplane enters ground effect during landing. Ground effect is the phenomenon that occurs when an aircraft is flying close to the ground, typically within one wingspan or less. As the aircraft enters ground effect, there is a reduction in the downwash on the horizontal stabilizer caused by the interaction of the wing's airflow with the ground. The reduced downwash on the horizontal stabilizer means there is less airflow impacting the elevator, which can lead to a diminished response to elevator inputs. The elevator control may feel less responsive or have a reduced effect on the aircraft's pitch attitude during this phase of flight.

Additionally, ground effect can also lead to a slight increase in lift, which may further affect the aircraft's handling characteristics. The increased lift can cause the aircraft to float or maintain a slightly higher altitude than expected during the landing flare.

Pilots must be aware of the changes in elevator control effectiveness during landing in ground effect. They should anticipate the potential decrease in elevator response and make appropriate adjustments to maintain precise control of the aircraft's pitch attitude and landing flare. Experience and familiarity with the aircraft's handling in ground effect will help pilots effectively manage the landing phase and achieve smooth and controlled touchdowns.

C. Aircraft Performance Charts Exercises

The following questions are valuable for you to review and answer for the specific aircraft you are using during training or for your practical test, using the aircraft's AFM/POH.

1. Ensure that you know the following basic information about your specific aircraft before taking a flight check or review.

   a. What is the normal climb-out speed?

   b. What is the best rate-of-climb speed?

   c. What is the best angle-of-climb speed?

   d. What is the maximum flap extension speed?

   e. What is the maximum gear extension speed?

   f. What is the maximum gear retraction speed?

   g. What is the stall speed in the normal landing configuration?

   h. What is the stall speed in the clean configuration?

   i. What is the normal approach-to-land speed?

   j. What is the maneuvering speed?

   k. What is the red-line speed?

   l. What speed will give you the best glide ratio?

   m. What is the maximum window-open speed?

   n. What is the maximum allowable crosswind component for the aircraft?

   o. What takeoff distance is required if a takeoff were made from a sea level pressure altitude?

2. Takeoff and landing distance charts
   a. Given the following conditions:
      Pressure altitude = 4,000 feet
      Temperature = 40°F
      Runway = Hard surfaced
      Weight = Maximum takeoff weight
      Wind = 10 knot headwind
      i. What is the distance for a normal takeoff ground roll?
      ii. What is the distance to clear a 50-foot obstacle?

   b. Given the following conditions:
      Pressure altitude = 2,000 feet
      Temperature = 25°C
      Runway = Hard surfaced
      Weight = Maximum landing weight
      Wind = Calm
      i. What is the normal landing distance?
      ii. What is the minimum landing distance over a 50-foot obstacle?

3. Time, fuel, and distance-to-climb chart
   a. Given the following conditions:
      Climb = 2,000 feet to 7,000 feet pressure altitude
      Temperature = Standard
      Airspeed = Best rate-of-climb
      Wind speed = Calm
      i. How much time is required for the climb?
      ii. How much fuel is required for the climb?
      iii. What distance will be covered during the climb?

4. Maximum rate-of-climb chart
   a. Given the following conditions:
      Pressure altitude = 4,000 feet
      Outside air temperature = 0°C
      i. What is the best rate-of-climb airspeed?
      ii. What is the best rate-of-climb in feet per minute?

5. Cruise performance chart

a. Given the following conditions:

Pressure altitude = 6,000 feet
Engine RPM = 2,400
MAP = 22 inches
Temperature = Standard

i. What will the true airspeed be?

ii. What will the fuel consumption rate be?

iii. What will the percent brake horsepower be?

b. Given the following conditions:

Density altitude at cruising altitude = 4,000 feet
Temperature = Standard

i. What percentage of brake horsepower will be required to produce the maximum true airspeed?

ii. What will the required power setting be?

6. Maximum range/endurance chart

a. Given the following conditions:

Density altitude = 8,000 feet
Temperature = Standard
Weight = Maximum gross
Wind = Calm
Power = 75%
BHP fuel = Full tanks (standard) 45 minute reserve

i. What true airspeed can be expected?

ii. What maximum range will be achieved?

b. Using the data from the previous question, how long can the aircraft fly in hours?

7. How accurate should you consider the predictions of performance charts to be?

Flight tests from which performance data was obtained were flown with a new, clean airplane, correctly rigged and loaded, with an engine capable of delivering its full rated power. This data would have been tested by a skilled and experienced test pilot. You can only expect performance numbers equal to those published if your airplane is in an equivalent condition and your skills match those of the test pilot. Best practices would have a pilot build more conservative personal minimums into any performance calculations.

D. Aircraft Performance Computation Exercises

1. **Determine the approximate CAS you should use to obtain 180 knots TAS with a pressure altitude of 8,000 feet and a temperature of +4°C.**

   158 knots.

2. **At speeds below 200 knots (where compressibility is not a factor), how is true airspeed computed?**

   True airspeed can be found by correcting calibrated airspeed for pressure altitude and temperature.

3. **Compute the density altitude for the following conditions:**

   Temperature = 20°C
   Field Elevation = 4,000 feet
   Altimeter setting = 29.98

   The density altitude is 5,424 feet.

4. **Compute the standard temperature at 9,000 feet.**

   The standard temperature at sea level is 15°C. The average lapse rate is 2° per 1,000 feet. Compute standard temperature by multiplying the altitude by 2 and then subtracting that number from 15. Based on this information,

   $$15° - (2° \times 9 = 18°) = -3°C$$

   The standard temperature at 9,000 feet is $-3°C$.

5. **A descent is planned from 8,500 feet MSL when 20 NM from your destination airport. If ground speed is 150 knots and you desire to be at 4,500 feet MSL when over the airport, what should the rate of descent be?**

   - Change in altitude = 4,000 feet
   - Calculate time to go 20 NM at 150 knots (8 minutes)
   - 4,000 feet ÷ 8 minutes = 500 fpm

6. **A descent is planned from 11,500 feet MSL to arrive at 7,000 feet MSL, 5 SM from a VORTAC. With a ground speed of 160 mph and a rate of descent of 600 fpm, at what distance from the VORTAC should the descent be started?**

   - Change in altitude = 4,500 feet
   - Rate of descent = 600 fpm
   - Time to descend = 4,500 ÷ 600 = 7.5 minutes
   - Ground speed in miles per minute = 160 ÷ 60 = 2.67 miles per minute
   - 7.5 × 2.67 = 20 miles + 5 miles = 25 miles out

7. **If fuel consumption is 15.3 gph and ground speed is 167 knots, how much fuel is required for an aircraft to travel 620 NM?**

   - 620 nautical miles ÷ 167 knots = 221 minutes or 3 hours and 41 minutes
   - 15.3 gph × 3 hrs. 41 min. = 57 gallons of fuel used

8. **If the ground speed is 215 knots, how far will the aircraft travel in 3 minutes?**

   - 215 knots ÷ 60 = 3.58 NM per minute
   - 3.58 NM per minute × 3 minutes = 10.75 NM

E. Weight and Balance

1. **Are you required to perform a weight and balance calculation before each flight? Explain.** (14 CFR 91.9, 91.103)

   While a pilot is not required to complete a paper or digital weight and balance calculation prior to each flight unless required by operational certificate requirements, they are required to ensure operation within operational limitations of the aircraft. While many pilots may become very familiar with specific loading operations for their aircraft and whether they will be in compliance, if there is any question of whether they will be within operational limitations, it is encouraged that the pilot complete the calculations with the specific loading considerations.

2. **What performance characteristics will be adversely affected when an aircraft has been overloaded?** (FAA-H-8083-25)

   a. Higher takeoff speed.
   b. Longer takeoff run.
   c. Reduced rate and angle of climb.
   d. Lower maximum altitude.
   e. Shorter range.
   f. Reduced cruising speed.
   g. Reduced maneuverability.
   h. Higher stalling speed.
   i. Higher approach and landing speed.
   j. Longer landing roll.
   k. Excessive weight on the nosewheel.

3. **If the weight and balance of an aircraft has changed due to the addition or removal of fixed equipment in the aircraft, what responsibility does the owner or operator have?** (FAA-H-8083-25)

   The owner or operator of the aircraft should ensure that maintenance personnel make appropriate entries in the aircraft records when repairs or modifications have been accomplished. Weight changes must be accounted for and proper notations made in weight and balance records. The appropriate form for these changes is FAA Form 337, "Major Repairs and Alterations."

4. **Define** *center of gravity* **(CG).** (FAA-H-8083-1)

The CG is the point about which an aircraft would balance if it were possible to support the aircraft at that point. It is the mass center of the aircraft, or the theoretical point at which the entire weight of the aircraft is assumed to be concentrated. The CG must be within specific limits for safe flight.

5. **What effect does a forward center of gravity have on an aircraft's flight characteristics?** (FAA-H-8083-25)

Higher stall speed—Stalling angle of attack reached at a higher speed due to increased wing loading.

Slower cruise speed—Increased drag, greater angle of attack required to maintain altitude.

More stable—The center of gravity is further forward from the center of pressure, which increases longitudinal stability.

Greater back elevator pressure required—Longer takeoff roll, higher approach speeds and problems with the landing flare.

6. **What effect does an aft center of gravity have on an aircraft's flight characteristics?** (FAA-H-8083-25)

Lower stall speed—Less wing loading.

Higher cruise speed—Reduced drag, smaller angle of attack required to maintain altitude.

Less stable—Stall and spin recovery more difficult; when angle of attack is increased it tends to result in additional increased angle of attack.

7. **During the enroute phase of flight, the CG moves aft due to fuel burn or a passenger moving. What effect will this have on various performance factors such as airspeed, stall speed, and range?** (FAA-H-8083-25)

As the center of gravity (CG) moves aft during the enroute phase of flight due to fuel burn or a passenger moving, it can have several effects on various performance factors:

a. *Airspeed*—With an aft CG, the aircraft's stability can be reduced, and it may become more sensitive to pitch changes. As a result, maintaining a desired airspeed may require more forward pressure on the controls. The aircraft may also have a tendency to pitch up more easily, potentially leading to an increase in airspeed if not properly controlled.

b. *Stall speed*—An aft CG typically increases the aircraft's stall speed. This means that the aircraft will require a higher indicated airspeed to maintain lift and avoid stalling. The increased stall speed is due to a decreased margin between the wing's angle of attack and its critical angle of attack. Pilots must be aware of the higher stall speed and adjust their approach and landing speeds accordingly.

c. *Range*—An aft CG can affect the aircraft's range, especially in terms of fuel efficiency. As the CG moves aft, it can cause an increase in aerodynamic drag, resulting in higher fuel consumption. The increased drag can reduce the aircraft's range, meaning it will be able to cover a shorter distance with the available fuel.

It's important for pilots to monitor and manage the CG during flight. If the CG moves aft beyond the aircraft's specified limits, it can adversely impact stability, control, and overall performance.

8. Will the center of gravity be forward or aft of the center of pressure? (FAA-H-8083-25)

Forward. The designers determine how far the center of pressure (CP) will travel. It is important to understand that an aircraft's weight is concentrated at the CG and the aerodynamic forces of lift occur at the CP. When the CG is forward of the CP, there is a natural tendency for the aircraft to want to pitch nose down. If the CP is forward of the CG, a nose up pitching moment is created. Therefore, designers fix the aft limit of the CG forward of the CP for the corresponding flight speed in order to retain flight equilibrium.

9. **Define the following:** (FAA-H-8083-25)
   • **Arm**
   • **Basic empty weight (GAMA)**
   • **Center of gravity**
   • **Center of gravity limits**
   • **Center of gravity range**
   • **Datum**
   • **Floor load limit**
   • **Fuel load**
   • **Licensed empty weight**
   • **Maximum landing weight**
   • **Maximum ramp weight**
   • **Maximum takeoff weight**
   • **Maximum weight**
   • **Maximum zero fuel weight (GAMA)**
   • **Mean aerodynamic chord**
   • **Moment**
   • **Moment index**
   • **Payload (GAMA)**
   • **Standard empty weight (GAMA)**
   • **Station**
   • **Useful load**

Arm—The horizontal distance in inches from the reference datum line to the center of gravity of an item.

Basic empty weight (GAMA)—The standard empty weight plus optional and special equipment that has been installed.

Center of gravity—The point about which an aircraft would balance if it were possible to suspend it at that point, expressed in inches from datum.

Center of gravity limits—The specified forward and aft or lateral points beyond which the CG must not be located during takeoff, flight or landing.

Center of gravity range—The distance between the forward and aft CG limits indicated on pertinent aircraft specifications.

Datum—An imaginary vertical plane or line from which all measurements of arm are taken. It is established by the manufacturer.

Floor load limit—The maximum weight the floor can sustain per square inch/foot as provided by the manufacturer.

Fuel load—The expendable part of the load of the aircraft. It includes only usable fuel, not fuel required to fill the lines or that which remains trapped in the tank sumps.

Licensed empty weight—The empty weight that consists of the airframe, engine(s), unusable fuel, and undrainable oil plus standard and optional equipment as specified in the equipment list. Some manufacturers used this term prior to GAMA standardization.

Maximum landing weight—The maximum weight at which the aircraft may normally be landed. The maximum landing weight may be limited to a lesser weight when runway length or atmospheric conditions are adverse.

Maximum ramp weight—The total weight of a loaded aircraft, and includes all fuel. It is greater than the takeoff weight due to the fuel that will be burned during the taxi and runup operations. Ramp weight may also be referred to as taxi weight.

Maximum takeoff weight—The maximum allowable weight at the start of the takeoff run. Some aircraft are approved for loading to a greater weight (ramp or taxi) only to allow for fuel burnoff during ground operation. The takeoff weight for a particular flight may be limited to a lesser weight when runway length, atmospheric conditions, or other variables are adverse.

Maximum weight—The maximum authorized weight of the aircraft and all of its equipment as specified in the TCDS for the aircraft.

Maximum zero fuel weight (GAMA)—The maximum weight, exclusive of usable fuel.

Mean aerodynamic chord (MAC)—The average distance from the leading edge to the trailing edge of the wing. The MAC is specified for the aircraft by determining the average chord of an imaginary wing which has the same aerodynamic characteristics as the actual wing.

Moment—The product of the weight of an item multiplied by its arm. Moments are expressed in pound-inches.

(continued)

Moment index—A moment divided by a constant such as 100, 1,000, or 10,000. The purpose of using a moment index is to simplify weight and balance computations of large aircraft where heavy items and long arms result in large, unmanageable numbers.

Payload (GAMA)—The weight of occupants, cargo, and baggage.

Standard empty weight (GAMA)—The airframe, engines, and all items of operating equipment that have fixed locations and are permanently installed in the airplane; including fixed ballast, hydraulic fluid, unusable fuel, and full engine oil.

Station—A location in the aircraft which is identified by a number designating its distance in inches from the datum. The datum is, therefore, identified as station zero. The station and arm are usually identical. An item located at station +50 would have an arm of 50 inches.

Useful load—The weight of the pilot, copilot, passengers, baggage, usable fuel and drainable oil. It is the empty weight subtracted from the maximum allowable takeoff weight. The term applies to general aviation aircraft only.

10. **What basic equation is used in all weight and balance problems to find the center of gravity location of an airplane and/or its components?** (FAA-H-8083-25)

Weight × Arm = Moment

By rearrangement of this equation into the following forms, with any two known values, the third value can be found:

Weight = Moment ÷ Arm.
Arm = Moment ÷ Weight.
CG = Moment ÷ Weight.

11. **What basic equation is used to determine center of gravity?** (FAA-H-8083-25)

Center of gravity is determined by dividing total moments by total weight.

12. **Explain the term *percent of mean aerodynamic chord* (MAC).** (FAA-H-8083-1)

Expression of the CG relative to the MAC is a common practice in larger aircraft. The CG position is expressed as a percent MAC (percent of mean aerodynamic chord), and the CG limits are expressed in the same manner. Normally, an aircraft will have acceptable flight characteristics if the CG is located somewhere near the 25 percent average chord point. This means the CG is located one-fourth of the total distance back from the leading edge of the average wing section.

13. **If the weight of an aircraft is within takeoff limits but the CG limit has been exceeded, what actions can the pilot take to correct the situation?** (FAA-H-8083-25)

The most satisfactory solution to this type of problem is to shift baggage, passengers, or both in an effort to make the aircraft CG fall within limits.

14. **When a shift in weight is required, what standardized and simple calculations can be made to determine the new CG?** (FAA-H-8083-25)

A typical problem may involve calculation of a new CG for an aircraft which has shifted cargo due to the CG being out of limits.

Given:
Aircraft total weight = 6,680 pounds
CG = Station 80.0
CG limits = Station 70-78

Find: What is the location of the CG if 200 pounds is shifted from the aft compartment at station 150 to the forward at station 30?

Solution:

   a. $\dfrac{Weight\ shifted \times distance\ moved}{Aircraft\ gross\ weight} = CG\ change$

   b. $\dfrac{200 \times 120}{6,680} = 3.6$ inches forward

   c. Old CG   80.0 inches
      minus change   −3.6
      New CG   76.4 inches

This same formula may be used to calculate how much weight must be shifted when you know how far you want to move the CG to come within limits.

15. If the weight of an aircraft changes due to the addition or removal of cargo or passengers before flight, what formula may be used to calculate new CG? (FAA-H-8083-25)

A typical problem may involve the calculation of a new CG for an aircraft which, when loaded and ready for flight, receives some additional cargo or passengers just before departure time.

Given:
Aircraft total weight = 6,860 pounds
CG = Station 80.0

Find: What is the location of the CG if 140 pounds of baggage is added to station 150?

Solution:
a. Use the added weight formula:

$$\frac{\textit{Added weight (or removed)}}{\textit{New total weight}} = \frac{\textit{CG change}}{\textit{Distance between weight \& old CG}}$$

$$\frac{140}{6,860 + 140} = \frac{\textit{CG change}}{150 - 80}$$

$$\frac{140}{7,000} = \frac{\textit{CG change}}{70}$$

CG change = 1.4 inches aft

b. Add the CG change to the old CG:

New CG = 80.0 in. + 1.4 in. = 81.4 in.

By using "old total weight and new CG," this same formula may be used to find out how much weight to add or remove, when it is known how far you want to move the CG to come within limits.

Exam Tip: Expect the evaluator to provide a scenario that requires you to recalculate your weight and balance numbers due to a last minute addition or subtraction of a passenger, bags, or fuel.

16. What simple and fundamental weight check can be made by all pilots before flight? (FAA-H-8083-25)

A useful load check can be made to determine if the useful load limit has been exceeded. This check may be a mental calculation if the pilot is familiar with the aircraft's limits and knows that unusually heavy loads are not aboard. The pilot needs to know the useful load limit of the particular aircraft. This information may be found in the latest weight and balance report, in a logbook, or on a Major Repair and Alteration Form located in the aircraft. If the useful load limit is not stated directly, simply subtract the empty weight from the maximum takeoff weight.

17. What factors would contribute to a change in center of gravity location during flight?

The operator's flight manual should show procedures which fully account for variations in CG travel during flight caused by variables such as the movement of passengers and the effect of the CG travel due to fuel used.

18. If actual weights for weight and balance computations are unknown, what weights may be assumed for weight and balance computations? (FAA-H-8083-25)

Crew and passengers = 190 lb each
Gasoline = 6 lb/U.S. gal
Oil = 7.5 lb/U.S. gal
Water = 8.35 lb/U.S. gal

Note: These weights are not to be used in lieu of actual weights, if available.

19. How is the CG affected during flight as fuel is used? (FAA-H-8083-25)

As fuel is burned during flight, the weight of the fuel tanks will change and as a result the CG will change. Most aircraft, however, are designed with the fuel tanks positioned close to the CG; therefore, the consumption of fuel does not affect the CG to any great extent. Also, the lateral balance can be upset by uneven fuel loading or burn-off. The position of the lateral CG is not normally computed for an airplane, but the pilot must be aware of the adverse effects that will result from a laterally unbalanced condition.

20. How will an increase or decrease in weight affect maneuvering speed? (FAA-H-8083-25)

An increase or decrease in weight will have an impact on the maneuvering speed of an aircraft. Maneuvering speed, also known as V_A or design maneuvering speed, is the maximum speed at which abrupt control inputs, such as full deflection of the control surfaces, can be applied without risking structural damage to the aircraft. It is the speed at which the aircraft can safely maneuver within its design limits.

When the weight of the aircraft increases, the maneuvering speed will also increase. This is because a heavier aircraft will require more lift to counteract the increased weight. As a result, the wings need to produce more lift, which requires a higher airspeed.

Conversely, when the weight of the aircraft decreases, the maneuvering speed will decrease. With a lighter weight, the aircraft requires less lift, allowing for a lower airspeed at which maneuvering can be safely conducted.

Cross-Country
Flight Planning
and Procedures **7**

A. Flight Plan

Be prepared to exhibit knowledge of the elements related to cross-country flight planning by presenting and explaining a pre-planned VFR cross-country flight, as previously assigned by the examiner. On the day of the test, the final flight plan shall include real-time weather to the first fuel stop. Computations shall be based on maximum allowable passenger, baggage and/or cargo loads.

The examiner will ask you to discuss the following:

1. Weather products required for preflight planning, current and forecast weather for departure, enroute, and arrival phases of flight.

a. Aviation routine weather reports—METARs, SPECIs.

b. Aircraft observations—PIREPS, AIREPs.

c. Radar (NEXRAD) and satellite observations (AWC, NWS).

d. Surface analysis charts.

e. Ceiling and visibility analysis (CVA), weather depiction chart.

f. Upper air analysis—constant pressure analysis, skew-T diagram.

g. SIGMETs, AIRMETs, G-AIRMETs.

h. Center Weather Advisories (CWA).

i. Convective outlooks (AC).

j. Graphical Forecasts for Aviation (GFA).

k. Terminal aerodrome forecasts (TAF).

l. Winds and temperatures aloft (FB).

m. Current and forecast icing products (CIP/FIP) and freezing level graphics.

n. Short-range prognostic charts.

o. Significant weather forecast (SIGWX).

2. Route selection including:

a. Selection of easily identifiable en route checkpoints.

b. Selection of most favorable altitudes considering weather conditions and equipment capabilities.

c. Selection of alternate airport.

3. Appropriate sectional charts:
a. Use of appropriate and current aeronautical charts.
b. Properly identify airspace, obstructions, and terrain features.
c. Selection of appropriate navigation system/facilities and communication frequencies.

4. Current information on facilities and procedures:
a. NOTAMs relative to airport, runway, and taxiway closures.
b. Special Notices.
c. Services available at destination.
d. Airport conditions including lighting, obstructions, and other notations in the *Chart Supplement U.S.*

5. Navigation log:
a. Measurement of course (true and magnetic).
b. Distances between checkpoints and total.
c. How true airspeed was obtained.
d. Estimated ground speed.
e. Total time en route.
f. Amount of fuel required and how it was obtained.
g. Simulate filing a VFR flight plan.

6. Weight and balance:
a. Calculations for planned trip.
b. Determine computed weight and center of gravity are within the airplane's operating limitations and if the weight and center of gravity will remain within limits during all phases of flight.

B. Navigation

1. What is an RMI? (P/CG)
RMI is an abbreviation for radio magnetic indicator. It is an aircraft navigational instrument coupled with a gyro compass or similar compass that indicates the direction of a selected NAVAID (NDB or VOR) and indicates bearing with respect to the heading of the aircraft.

2. **What is an HSI?** (FAA-H-8083-15)

   The horizontal situation indicator (HSI) is a flight navigation instrument that combines the heading indicator with a CDI, in order to provide the pilot with better situational awareness of location with respect to the courseline.

3. **What is RNAV?** (FAA-H-8083-15)

   Area navigation (RNAV) equipment includes VOR/DME, LORAN, GPS, and inertial navigation systems (INS). RNAV equipment is capable of computing the aircraft position, actual track, ground speed, and then presenting meaningful information to the pilot in the form of distance, cross-track error, and time estimates relative to the selected track or WP. The aircraft's POH/AFM should always be consulted to determine the type of equipment installed, the operations that are approved, and the details of equipment use.

4. **What is DME?** (AIM 1-1-7)

   Equipment (airborne and ground) used to measure, in nautical miles, the slant range distance of an aircraft from the DME navigational aid. Aircraft equipped with DME are provided with distance and ground speed information when receiving a VORTAC or TACAN facility. Operating frequency range of a DME according to ICAO Annex 10 is from 960 MHz to 1215 MHz.

5. **What is the effective range distance for DME?** (AIM 1-1-7)

   Operating on the line-of-sight principle, DME furnishes distance information with a very high degree of accuracy. Reliable signals may be received at distances up to 199 NM at line-of-sight altitude with an accuracy of better than ½ mile or 3 percent of the distance, whichever is greater. Distance information received from DME equipment is SLANT RANGE distance and not actual horizontal distance.

6. **Give a brief description of GPS.** (AIM 1-1-17)

   The Global Positioning System (GPS) is a space-based radio navigation system used to determine precise position anywhere in the world. The 24-satellite constellation is designed to ensure at least five satellites are always visible to a user worldwide. A minimum of four satellites is necessary for receivers to establish an accurate three-dimensional position.

7. **Can handheld GPS receivers and GPS systems certified for VFR operations be used for IFR operations?** (AIM 1-1-17)

No, for the following reasons:

a. *RAIM capability*—VFR GPS panel-mount receivers and hand-held units have no RAIM alerting capability. Loss of the required number of satellites in view, or the detection of a position error, cannot be displayed to the pilot by such receivers.

b. *Database currency*—In many receivers, an updatable database is used for navigation fixes, airports, and instrument procedures. These databases must be maintained to the current update for IFR operation, but no such requirement exists for VFR use.

c. *Antenna location*—In many VFR installations of GPS receivers, antenna location is more a matter of convenience than performance. In IFR installations, care is exercised to ensure that an adequate clear view is provided for the antenna to see satellites. If an alternate location is used, some portion of the aircraft may block the view of the antenna, causing a greater opportunity to lose navigation.

Note: VFR and handheld GPS systems are not authorized for IFR navigation, instrument approaches, or as a principal instrument flight reference. During IFR operations they may be considered only as an aid to situational awareness.

8. **Required preflight preparations for an IFR flight using GPS for navigation should include a review of what information?** (FAA-H-8083-15)

a. GPS is properly installed and certified for the operation.

b. Verify that the databases (navigation, terrain, obstacle, etc.) have not expired.

c. GPS and WAAS NOTAMs.

d. GPS RAIM availability for non-WAAS receivers.

(continued)

e. Review the operational status of ground-based NAVAIDs and related aircraft equipment (e.g., 30-day VOR check) appropriate to the route of flight, terminal operations, instrument approaches at the destination, and alternate airports at ETA.

f. Determine that the GPS receiver operation manual or airplane flight manual supplement is on board and available for use.

9. **Are navigational databases required to be updated for VFR flight? What about for IFR flight?** (FAA-H-8083-15, AIM 1-1-17, AC 90-100)

Databases must be updated for IFR operations and should be updated for all other operations. However, there is no requirement for databases to be updated for VFR navigation. It is not recommended to use a moving map with an outdated database in and around critical airspace. Databases are updated every 28 days and are available from various commercial vendors. For IFR operations, all approach procedures to be flown must be retrievable from the current airborne navigation database.

10. **Who can update the navigation database of installed avionics in an airplane?** (14 CFR 43.3)

The navigation database of installed avionics in an airplane can typically be updated by authorized personnel, which may include:

a. *Avionics technicians*—Licensed avionics technicians or avionics maintenance professionals are often responsible for updating and maintaining avionics systems, including the navigation database. They have the necessary expertise and training to perform these tasks safely and accurately.

b. *Aircraft maintenance personnel*—Aircraft maintenance personnel with appropriate training and authorization may also be capable of updating the navigation database. These individuals can include certified mechanics or technicians who have received specific training on the avionics systems installed in the aircraft.

c. *Pilots*—In some cases, pilots may have the ability to update certain aspects of the navigation database, depending on the avionics system and the permissions granted by the aircraft owner or operator. This is more common in modern, user-friendly avionics systems that allow pilots to download and install updates directly.

It is important to note that updating the navigation database requires adherence to specific procedures and guidelines provided by the avionics manufacturer or the aircraft's type certificate holder. Errors during the database update process can lead to inaccurate navigation information, compromising the safety of flight operations.

11. Within which frequency band does the VOR equipment operate? (AIM 1-1-3)

VHF band: 108.00 through 117.95 MHz.

12. What are the different methods for checking the accuracy of VOR equipment? (14 CFR 91.171)

a. VOT check; ±4°
b. Ground checkpoint; ±4°
c. Airborne checkpoint; ±6°
d. Dual VOR check; 4° between each other.
e. Select a radial over a known ground point; ±6°

A repair station can use a radiated test signal, but only the technician performing the test can make an entry in the logbook.

13. What records must be kept concerning VOR checks? (14 CFR 91.171)

Each person making a VOR check shall enter the date, place, and bearing error and sign the aircraft log or other reliable record.

14. Where can a pilot find the location of the nearest VOT testing stations? (AIM 1-1-4)

Locations of airborne check points, ground check points and VOTs are published in the *Chart Supplement U.S.*

15. How may the course sensitivity be checked on a VOR receiver? (FAA-H-8083-15)

In addition to receiver tolerance checks required by regulations, course sensitivity may be checked by recording the number of degrees of change in the course selected as you rotate the OBS to move the CDI from center to the last dot on either side. The course selected should not exceed 10° or 12° either side.

16. What situation would result in reverse sensing of a VOR receiver? (FAA-H-8083-25)

Reverse sensing of a VOR (VHF omnidirectional range) receiver can occur when the aircraft is flying in an intercept angle that is greater than 90 degrees from the selected VOR radial.

Normally, when an aircraft intercepts and tracks a VOR radial, the VOR receiver displays the needle deflection relative to the aircraft's heading indicator or course deviation indicator (CDI). The needle indicates the direction and magnitude of the deviation from the selected radial, allowing the pilot to make corrections and stay on course.

However, reverse sensing occurs when the pilot mistakenly selects an intercept angle greater than 90 degrees. In this situation, the needle on the VOR receiver behaves opposite to the expected indications. Instead of deflecting toward the radial, it deflects away from it. For example, if the desired radial is to the left of the aircraft's heading, the needle will deflect to the right, leading to reverse sensing.

17. How can a pilot determine if a VOR or VORTAC has been taken out of service for maintenance? (AIM 1-1-11)

During periods of routine or emergency maintenance, coded identification (or code and voice, where applicable) is removed from certain FAA NAVAIDs. Removal of identification serves as a warning to pilots that the facility is officially off the air for tune-up or repair and may be unreliable even though intermittent or constant signals are received.

18. **If a diversion to an alternate airport becomes necessary due to an emergency, what procedure should be used?** (FAA-H-8083-25)

    a. Consider relative distance to all suitable alternates.

    b. Select the one most appropriate for the emergency at hand.

    c. Determine magnetic course to alternate and divert immediately.

    d. Wind correction, actual distance and estimated time/fuel can then be computed while en route to alternate.

19. **How can the course to an alternate be computed quickly?** (FAA-H-8083-25)

    Courses to alternates can be quickly measured by using a straight edge and the compass roses shown at VOR stations on the chart. VOR radials and airway courses (already oriented to magnetic direction) printed on the chart can be used to approximate magnetic bearings during VFR flights. Use the radial of a nearby VOR or airway that most closely parallels the course to the station. Distances can be determined by placing a finger at the appropriate place on a straight edge of a piece of paper and then measuring the approximate distance on the mileage scale at the bottom of the chart.

20. **What information is provided by a maximum elevation figure on a sectional chart?** (USRGD)

    The maximum elevation figure (MEF) represents the highest elevation, including terrain and other vertical obstacles (towers, trees, etc.), within a quadrant. MEF figures are depicted in thousands and rounded to the nearest hundred feet above mean sea level. The last two digits of the number are not shown. The chart legend also provides the highest terrain elevation for the entire chart.

21. **On IFR enroute charts, what does the "MON" designator displayed above the airport name indicate?** (USRGD, AIM 1-1-3)

MON indicates that the airport is part of the VOR Minimum Operational Network (MON). The intent of the MON designation is to alert pilots of airports that have retained ILS and VOR instrument approach procedures in the event of a GPS outage. The VOR MON includes the minimum number of geographically situated VORs in the contiguous United States necessary to provide coverage at and above 5,000 feet AGL.

C. Airport and Traffic Pattern Operations

1. **What recommended entry and departure procedures should be used at airports without an operating control tower?** (AIM 4-3-3, AC 90-66)

When entering a traffic pattern, enter the pattern in level flight, abeam the midpoint of the runway at pattern altitude. Maintain pattern altitude until abeam the approach end of the landing runway on the downwind leg. Complete the turn to final at least ¼ mile from the runway. When departing a traffic pattern, continue straight out, or exit with a 45° turn (to the left when in a left-hand traffic pattern; to the right when in a right-hand traffic pattern) beyond the departure end of the runway, after reaching pattern altitude.

Note: If remaining in the traffic pattern, commence turn to crosswind leg beyond the departure end of the runway within 300 feet of pattern altitude.

2. **What are the recommended traffic advisory practices at airports *without* an operating control tower?** (AIM 4-1-9)

Pilots of inbound traffic should monitor and communicate as appropriate on the designated CTAF from 10 miles to landing. Pilots of departing aircraft should monitor/communicate on the appropriate frequency from start-up, during taxi, and until 10 miles from the airport unless federal regulations or local procedures require otherwise.

3. **A large or turbine-powered aircraft is required to enter Class D airspace at what altitude?** (14 CFR 91.129)

A large or turbine-powered airplane shall, unless otherwise required by the applicable distance-from-clouds criteria, enter the traffic pattern at an altitude of at least 1,500 feet above the elevation of the airport and maintain at least 1,500 feet until further descent is required for a safe landing.

4. **If operating into an airport without an operating control tower which is located within the Class D airspace of an airport with an operating control tower, is it always necessary to communicate with the tower?** (14 CFR 91.129)

Yes, operations to or from an airport in Class D airspace (airport traffic area) require communication with the tower even when operating to/from a satellite airport.

5. **When conducting flight operations into an airport with an operating control tower, when should initial contact be established?** (AIM 4-3-2)

When operating at an airport where traffic control is being exercised by a control tower, pilots are required to maintain two-way radio contact with the tower while operating within Class B, Class C, and Class D surface areas unless the tower authorizes otherwise. Initial call-up should be made about 15 miles from the airport.

6. **When departing a Class D surface area, what communication procedures are recommended?** (AIM 4-3-2)

Unless there is good reason to leave the tower frequency before exiting the Class B, Class C, and Class D surface areas, it is good operating practice to remain on the tower frequency for the purpose of receiving traffic information. In the interest of reducing tower frequency congestion, pilots are reminded that it is not necessary to request permission to leave the tower frequency once outside of Class B, Class C, and Class D surface areas.

7. **You discover that both the transmitter and receiver in your aircraft have become inoperative. What procedures should be used when attempting to enter a traffic pattern and land at a tower controlled airport?** (AIM 4-2-13, 6-4-2)

   a. Remain outside or above Class D surface area.

   b. Determine direction and flow of traffic.

   c. Join the traffic pattern and wait for light gun signals.

   d. Daytime, acknowledge by rocking wings. Nighttime, acknowledge by flashing landing light or navigation lights.

   Note: When an aircraft with a coded radar beacon transponder experiences a loss of two-way radio capability, the pilot should adjust the transponder to reply on Mode A/3, Code 7600. The pilot should understand that the aircraft may not be in an area of radar coverage.

8. **When a control tower located at an airport within Class D airspace ceases operation for the day, what happens to the lower limit of the controlled airspace?** (AIM 3-2-5)

   When a Class D surface area is part-time, the airspace may revert to either a Class E or Class G. When a part-time Class D surface area changes to Class G, the surface area becomes Class G airspace up to, but not including, the overlying controlled airspace.

9. **If the rotating beacon is on at an airport during daylight hours, what significance does this have?** (AIM 2-1-9)

   In Class B, Class C, Class D, and Class E surface areas, operation of the airport beacon during the hours of daylight often indicates that the ground visibility is less than 3 miles and/or the ceiling is less than 1,000 feet. ATC clearance in accordance with Part 91 is required for landing, takeoff, and flight in the traffic pattern. Pilots should not rely solely on the operation of the airport beacon to indicate if weather conditions are IFR or VFR. There is no regulatory requirement for daylight operation, and it is the pilot's responsibility to comply with proper preflight planning as required by Part 91.

10. What are the various types of runway markings (precision instrument runway) and what do they consist of? (AIM 2-3-3)

a. *Runway designators*—Runway number is the whole number nearest one-tenth the magnetic azimuth of the centerline of the runway, measured clockwise from the magnetic north.

b. *Runway centerline marking*—Identifies the center of the runway and provides alignment guidance during takeoff and landings; consists of a line of uniformly spaced stripes and gaps.

c. *Runway aiming point marking*—Serves as a visual aiming point for a landing aircraft; two rectangular markings consist of a broad white stripe located on each side of the runway centerline and approximately 1,000 feet from the landing threshold.

d. *Runway touchdown zone markers*—Identify the touchdown zone for landing operations and are coded to provide distance information in 500 feet increments; groups of one, two, and three rectangular bars symmetrically arranged in pairs about the runway centerline.

e. *Runway side stripe markings*—Delineate the edges of the runway and provide a visual contrast between runway and the abutting terrain or shoulders; continuous white stripes located on each side of the runway.

f. *Runway shoulder markings*—May be used to supplement runway side stripes to identify pavement areas contiguous to the runway sides that are not intended for use by aircraft; painted yellow.

g. *Runway threshold markings*—Used to help identify the beginning of the runway that is available for landing. Two configurations: either eight longitudinal stripes of uniform dimensions disposed symmetrically about the runway centerline, or the number of stripes is related to the runway width.

11. **What are the various types of taxiway markings and what do they consist of?** (AIM 2-3-4)

Markings for taxiways are yellow and consist of the following types:

a. *Taxiway centerline*—Single continuous yellow line; aircraft should be kept centered over this line during taxi; however, being centered on the centerline does not guarantee wingtip clearance with other aircraft or objects.

b. *Taxiway edge*—Used to define the edge of taxiway; two types, continuous and dashed.

c. *Taxiway shoulder*—Usually defined by taxiway edge markings; denotes pavement unusable for aircraft.

d. *Surface painted taxiway direction*—Yellow background with black inscription; supplements direction signs or when not possible to provide taxiway sign.

e. *Surface painted location signs*—Black background with yellow inscription; supplements location signs.

f. *Geographic position markings*—Located at points along low visibility taxi routes; used to identify aircraft during low visibility operations.

12. **What are the six types of signs installed on airports?** (AIM 2-3-7 through 2-3-13)

a. *Mandatory instruction signs*—Red background/white inscription; denotes hazardous areas.

b. *Location signs*—Black background/yellow inscription; used to identify either a taxiway or runway on which an aircraft is located.

c. *Direction signs*—Yellow background/black inscription; identifies designation(s) of intersecting taxiway(s) leading out of intersection that pilot would expect to turn onto or hold short of.

d. *Destination signs*—Yellow background/black inscription; signs have arrow showing direction of taxi route to that destination.

e. *Information signs*—Yellow background/black inscription; provide pilot information on such things as areas that cannot be seen by control tower, radio frequencies, noise abatement procedures, etc.

f. *Runway distance remaining signs*—Black background with white numeral inscription; indicates distance (in thousands of feet) of landing runway remaining.

13. **The acronym LAHSO refers to what specific air traffic control procedure?** (AIM 4-3-11)

Land and hold short operations (LAHSO)—at controlled airports, air traffic control may clear a pilot to land and hold short of an intersecting runway, an intersecting taxiway, or some other designated point on a runway other than an intersecting runway or taxiway. Pilots may accept such a clearance provided that the PIC determines that the aircraft can safely land and stop within the available landing distance (ALD). Student pilots or pilots not familiar with LAHSO should not participate in the program.

14. **Where can ALD data be found?** (AIM 4-3-11)

ALD data is published in the special notices section of the *Chart Supplement U.S.* Controllers will also provide ALD data upon request.

15. **Describe the visual aids that assist a pilot in determining where to hold short at an airport with LAHSO in effect.** (AIM 4-3-11)

The visual aids consist of a three-part system of yellow hold-short markings, red and white signage, and, in certain cases, in-pavement lighting. Pilots are cautioned that not all airports conducting LAHSO have installed any or all of the LAHSO markings, signage, or lighting.

16. Describe runway hold-short markings and signs.
(AIM 2-3-5, 2-3-8)

Runway holding position markings—These markings indicate where aircraft MUST STOP when approaching a runway. They consist of four yellow lines, two solid and two dashed, spaced six or twelve inches apart, and extend across the width of the taxiway or runway. The solid lines are always on the side where the aircraft must hold.

Runway holding position sign—Located at the holding position on taxiways that intersect a runway or on runways that intersect other runways. These signs have a red background with a white inscription and contain the designation of the intersecting runway.

17. Describe a displaced threshold. (AIM 2-3-3)

It is a threshold located at a point on the runway other than the designated beginning of the runway. Displacement of the threshold reduces the length of the runway available for landings. The portion of the runway behind it is available for takeoffs in either direction and landings from the opposite direction. A ten-foot-wide white threshold bar is located across the width of the runway at the displaced threshold. White arrows are located along the centerline in the area between the beginning of the runway and the displaced threshold. White arrowheads are located across the width of the runway just prior to the threshold bar.

18. Describe a tri-color light VASI system. (AIM 2-1-2)

A tri-color visual approach slope indicator (VASI) normally consists of a single light unit projecting a three-color visual approach path into the final approach area of the runway. The visual glide path provides safe obstruction clearance within plus or minus 10° of the extended runway centerline and to 4 NM from the runway threshold.

Red = Below glidepath
Amber = Above glidepath
Green = On glidepath

19. What is PAPI? (AIM 2-1-2)

The precision approach path indicator (PAPI) uses light units similar to the VASI but are installed in a single row of either two or four light units. These systems have an effective visual range of about 5 miles during the day and up to 20 miles at night. The row of light units is normally installed on the left side of the runway.

20. What is PVASI? (AIM 2-1-2)

Pulsating visual approach slope indicators (PVASI) normally consist of a single light unit projecting a two-color visual approach path into the final approach area of the runway upon which the indicator is installed. The useful range of the system is about 4 miles during the day and up to 10 miles at night.

Pulsating white light = Above glidepath
Steady white light = On glidepath
Steady red light = Slightly below glidepath
Pulsating red light = Well below glidepath

D. Runway Incursion Avoidance

1. Preflight planning for taxi operations should be an integral part of the pilot's flight planning process. What information should this include? (AC 91-73)

a. Review and understand airport signage, markings, and lighting.

b. Review the airport diagram, planned taxi route, and identify any hot spots.

c. Review the latest airfield NOTAMs and ATIS (if available) for taxiway/runway closures, construction activity, etc.

d. Conduct a pre-taxi/pre-landing briefing that includes the expected/assigned taxi route and any hold short lines and restrictions based on ATIS information or previous experience at the airport.

e. Plan for critical times and locations on the taxi route (complex intersections, crossing runways, etc.).

f. Plan to complete as many aircraft checklist items as possible prior to taxi.

2. What is a *hot spot* on a taxi diagram? (Chart Supplement)

A hot spot is a runway safety-related problem area on an airport that presents increased risk during surface operations. Typically, it is a complex or confusing taxiway/taxiway intersection or taxiway/runway intersection. The area of increased risk has either a history of or potential for runway incursions or surface incidents due to a variety of causes, such as but not limited to: airport layout, traffic flow, airport marking, signage and lighting, situational awareness, and training. Hot spots are depicted on airport diagrams as open circles or polygons designated as "HS 1," "HS 2," etc.

3. Why is use of sterile cockpit procedures important when conducting taxi operations? (AC 91-73)

Pilots must be able to focus on their duties without being distracted by non-flight-related matters unrelated to the safe and proper operation of the aircraft. Refraining from nonessential activities during ground operations is essential. Passengers should be briefed on the importance of minimizing conversations and questions during taxi as well as on arrival, from the time landing preparations begin until the aircraft is safely parked.

4. After completing your pre-taxi/pre-landing briefing of the taxi route you expect to receive, ATC calls and gives you a different route. What potential pitfall is common in this situation? (AC 91-73)

A common pitfall of pre-taxi and pre-landing planning is setting expectations and then receiving different instructions from ATC. Pilots need to follow the instructions that they actually receive. Short-term memory is of limited duration.

5. When issued taxi instructions to an assigned takeoff runway, are you automatically authorized to cross any runway that intersects your taxi route? (AIM 4-3-18)

No. Aircraft must receive a runway crossing clearance for each runway that their taxi route crosses. When assigned a takeoff runway, ATC will first specify the runway, issue taxi instructions, and state any hold short instructions or runway crossing clearances if the taxi route will cross a runway. When issuing taxi instructions to any point other than an assigned takeoff runway, ATC will specify the point to which to taxi, issue taxi instructions, and state any hold short instructions or runway crossing clearances if the taxi route will cross a runway. ATC is required to obtain a read back from the pilot of all runway hold short instructions. Additionally, ATC is not authorized to clear a pilot to cross more than a runway at a time. If a pilot has been issued a clearance across a runway that would require them to cross another one first, they should query ATC for clarification before proceeding.

6. **When receiving taxi instructions from a controller, pilots should always read back what information?** (AIM 4-3-18)

    a. The runway assignment.

    b. Any clearance to enter a specific runway.

    c. Any instruction to hold short of a specific runway or line up and wait.

7. **What are some recommended practices that can assist a pilot in maintaining situational awareness during taxi operations?** (AC 91-73)

    a. A current airport diagram should be available for immediate reference during taxi.

    b. Monitor ATC instructions/clearances issued to other aircraft for the big picture.

    c. Focus attention outside the cockpit while taxiing.

    d. Use all available resources (airport diagrams, airport signs, markings, lighting, and ATC) to keep the aircraft on its assigned taxi route.

    e. Cross-reference heading indicator to ensure turns are being made in the correct direction and that you're on the assigned taxi route.

    f. Prior to crossing any hold short line, visually check for conflicting traffic; verbalize "clear left, clear right."

    g. Be alert for other aircraft with similar call signs on the frequency.

    h. Understand and follow all ATC instructions and if in doubt—Ask!

(continued)

i. If available, use an EFB that shows aircraft position awareness or onboard aircraft navigation equipment that might display this information to additionally display position and confirm taxi compliance.

8. How can a pilot use aircraft exterior lighting to enhance situational awareness and safety during airport surface operations? (AC 91-73, SAFO)

To the extent possible and consistent with aircraft equipment, operating limitations, and pilot procedures, pilots should illuminate exterior lights as follows:

a. *Engines running*—Turn on the rotating beacon whenever an engine is running.

b. *Taxiing*—Prior to commencing taxi, turn on navigation/position lights and anti-collision lights.

c. *Crossing a runway*—All exterior lights should be illuminated when crossing a runway.

d. *Entering the departure runway for takeoff*—All exterior lights (except landing lights) should be on to make your aircraft more conspicuous to aircraft on final and ATC.

e. *Cleared for takeoff*—All exterior lights including takeoff/ landing lights should be on.

Note: If you see an aircraft in takeoff position on a runway with landing lights ON, that aircraft has most likely received its takeoff clearance and will be departing immediately.

9. During calm or nearly calm wind conditions, at an airport without an operating control tower, a pilot should be aware of what potentially hazardous situations? (AC 91-73)

Aircraft may be landing and/or taking off on more than one runway at the airport. Also, aircraft may be using an instrument approach procedure to runways other than the runway in use for VFR operations. The instrument approach runway may intersect the VFR runway. It is also possible that an instrument arrival may be made to the opposite end of the runway from which a takeoff is being made.

10. **When taxiing at a non-towered airport, what are several precautionary measures you should take prior to entering or crossing a runway?** (AC 91-73)

    Listen on the appropriate frequency (CTAF) for inbound aircraft information and always scan the full length of the runway, including the final approach and departure paths, before entering or crossing the runway. Self-announce your position and intentions and remember that not all aircraft are radio-equipped.

E. 14 CFR Part 91

1. **Can a commercial pilot allow a passenger to carry alcohol on board an aircraft for the purpose of consumption?** (14 CFR 91.17)

    The regulations do not specifically address this issue but do indicate that a person who is intoxicated (or becomes intoxicated) must not be allowed on board the aircraft. Except in an emergency, no pilot of a civil aircraft may allow a person who appears to be intoxicated or who demonstrates by manner or physical indications that the individual is under the influence of drugs (except a medical patient under proper care) to be carried in that aircraft. This does not expressly prohibit an individual who has had any amount of alcohol from boarding an aircraft or consuming alcohol during a flight. It leaves the decision to the pilot-in-command to determine if they are intoxicated and/or present a risk to the safety of flight.

2. **No person may act as a crewmember of a civil aircraft with a blood alcohol level of what value?** (14 CFR 91.17)

    No person may act or attempt to act as a crewmember of a civil aircraft while having .04 percent by weight or more alcohol in the blood.

3. **No matter the blood alcohol level, a pilot who has consumed any alcoholic beverage may not act or attempt to act as a crewmember for what period of time?** (14 CFR 91.17)

    No person may act or attempt to act as a crewmember of a civil aircraft within 8 hours after the consumption of any alcoholic beverage.

4. When are the operation of portable electronic devices not allowed on board an aircraft? (14 CFR 91.21)

No person may operate, nor may any operator or PIC of an aircraft allow the operation of, any portable device on any of the following U.S.-registered aircraft.

a. Aircraft operated by a holder of an air carrier operating certificate or an operating certificate; or

b. Any other aircraft while it is operated under IFR.

This regulation offers exemption for (1) portable voice recorders; (2) hearing aids; (3) heart pacemakers; (4) electric shavers; or (5) any other portable electronic device that the operator of the aircraft has determined will not cause interference with the navigation or communication system of the aircraft on which it is to be used. This leaves it up to the pilot to determine if a device will be allowed. Many devices such as tablets, cellular telephones, music players, or book readers are commonly accepted as not creating interference.

5. Preflight action as required by regulation for all flights away from the vicinity of the departure airport shall include a review of what specific information? (14 CFR 91.103)

For a flight under IFR or a flight not in the vicinity of an airport, all available information, including:

NOTAMs

Weather reports and forecasts

Known ATC traffic delays

Runway lengths at airports of intended use

Alternatives available if the planned flight cannot be completed

Fuel requirements

Takeoff and landing distance data

6. When are flight crewmembers required to wear their seatbelts? (14 CFR 91.105)

During takeoff, and landing, and while en route, each required flight crewmember shall keep the safety belt fastened while at the crewmember station (also, during takeoff and landing only, using the shoulder harness if installed).

7. **Is the use of safety belts and shoulder harnesses required when operating an aircraft on the ground?** (14 CFR 91.107)

Yes; each person on board a U.S.-registered civil aircraft must occupy an approved seat or berth with a safety belt, and if installed, shoulder harness, properly secured about him or her during movement on the surface, takeoff, and landing.

8. **If a formation flight has been arranged in advance, can passengers be carried for hire?** (14 CFR 91.111)

No; no person may operate an aircraft, carrying passengers for hire, in formation flight.

9. **What is the maximum speed allowed when operating inside Class B airspace, under 10,000 feet and within a Class D surface area?** (14 CFR 91.117)

Unless otherwise authorized or required by ATC, no person may operate an aircraft at or below 2,500 feet above the surface within 4 NM of the primary airport of a Class C or Class D airspace area at an indicated airspeed of more than 200 knots. This restriction does not apply to operations conducted within a Class B airspace area. Such operations shall comply with the "below 10,000 feet MSL" restriction:

"No person shall operate an aircraft below 10,000 feet MSL, at an indicated airspeed of more than 250 knots."

10. **What regulations pertain to altimeter setting procedures?** (14 CFR 91.121)

Below 18,000 feet MSL:

a. The current reported altimeter setting of a station along the route and within 100 NM of the aircraft.

b. If there is no station within the area described above, the current reported altimeter of an appropriate available station.

c. In the case of an aircraft not equipped with a radio, the elevation of the departure airport or an appropriate altimeter setting available before departure.

Note: If barometric pressure exceeds 31.00 inHg, set 31.00 inHg (*see* AIM).

At or above 18,000 feet MSL set to 29.92 inHg.

11. **What are the regulatory fuel requirements for both VFR and IFR flight (day and night)?** (14 CFR 91.151, 91.167)

   a. *VFR conditions*—No person may begin a flight in an airplane under VFR conditions unless (considering wind and forecast weather conditions) there is enough fuel to fly to the first point of intended landing and, assuming normal cruising speed:
   - During the day, to fly after that for at least 30 minutes; or
   - At night, to fly after that for at least 45 minutes.

   b. *IFR conditions*—No person may operate a civil aircraft in IFR conditions unless it carries enough fuel (considering weather reports and forecasts) to:
   - Complete the flight to the first airport of intended landing;
   - Fly from that airport to the alternate airport; and
   - Fly after that for 45 minutes at normal cruising speed.

   If an alternate is not required, complete the flight to the destination airport with a 45-minute reserve remaining.

12. **What minimum flight visibility and clearance from clouds are required for VFR flight in the following situations?** (14 CFR 91.155)

   Class C, D, or E Airspace (controlled airspace)
   - Less than 10,000 feet MSL:
     Visibility: 3 SM
     Cloud clearance: 500 feet below, 1,000 feet above, 2,000 feet horizontal
   - At or above 10,000 feet MSL:
     Visibility: 5 SM
     Cloud clearance: 1,000 feet below, 1,000 feet above, 1 statute mile horizontal

   Class G Airspace (uncontrolled airspace)
   - 1,200 feet or less above the surface (regardless of MSL altitude):
     Day
     Visibility: 1 SM
     Cloud clearance: clear of clouds
     Night
     Visibility: 3 SM
     Cloud clearance: 500 feet below, 1,000 feet above, 2,000 feet horizontal

- More than 1,200 feet above the surface but less than 10,000 feet MSL:
  Day
  Visibility: 1 SM
  Cloud clearance: 500 feet below, 1,000 feet above, 2,000 feet horizontal
  Night
  Visibility: 3 SM
  Cloud clearance: 500 feet below, 1,000 feet above, 2,000 feet horizontal

- More than 1,200 feet above the surface and at or above 10,000 feet MSL:
  Visibility: 5 SM
  Cloud clearance: 1,000 feet below, 1,000 feet above, 1 SM horizontal

13. **When conducting IFR flight operations, what minimum altitudes are required over surrounding terrain?** (14 CFR 91.177 and Part 95)

    Minimum altitudes are:

    Mountainous terrain—at least 2,000 feet above the highest obstacle within a horizontal distance of 4 NM from the course to be flown. Part 95 designates the location of mountainous terrain.

    Other than mountainous terrain—at least 1,000 feet above the highest obstacle within a horizontal distance of 4 NM from the course to be flown.

14. **What are several examples of situations in which an ELT is not required equipment on board the aircraft?** (14 CFR 91.207)

    Examples of operations where an ELT is not required are:

    a. Ferrying aircraft for installation of an ELT.

    b. Ferrying aircraft for repair of an ELT.

    c. Aircraft engaged in training flights within a 50 NM radius of an airport.

15. Where is a Mode C transponder and ADS-B Out equipment required? (AIM 4-1-20, 14 CFR 91.215, 91.225, 99.13)

In general, the regulations require aircraft to be equipped with an operable Mode C transponder and ADS-B Out equipment when operating:

a. In Class A, Class B, or Class C airspace areas;

b. Above the ceiling and within the lateral boundaries of Class B or Class C airspace up to 10,000 feet MSL;

c. In Class E airspace at and above 10,000 feet MSL within the 48 contiguous states and the District of Columbia, excluding the airspace at and below 2,500 feet AGL;

d. Within 30 miles of a Class B airspace primary airport, below 10,000 feet MSL (Mode C Veil);

e. In Class E airspace at and above 3,000 feet MSL over the Gulf of Mexico from the coastline of the United States out to 12 NM.

f. All aircraft flying into, within or across the contiguous United States ADIZ.

Note: Civil and military aircraft should operate with the transponder in the altitude reporting mode and ADS-B Out transmissions enabled (if equipped) at all airports, any time the aircraft is positioned on any portion of an airport movement area. This includes all defined taxiways and runways.

16. Where are aerobatic flight maneuvers not permitted? (14 CFR 91.303)

No person may operate an aircraft in aerobatic flight:

a. Over any congested area of a city, town, or settlement;

b. Over an open air assembly of persons;

c. Within the lateral boundaries of the surface areas of Class B, Class C, Class D, or Class E airspace designated for an airport;

d. Within 4 nautical miles of the center line of any Federal airway;

e. Below an altitude of 1,500 feet above the surface; or

f. When flight visibility is less than 3 statute miles.

For the purposes of this section, aerobatic flight means an intentional maneuver involving an abrupt change in an aircraft's attitude, an abnormal attitude, or abnormal acceleration, not necessary for normal flight.

17. When must each occupant of an aircraft wear an approved parachute? (14 CFR 91.307)

a. Unless each occupant of the aircraft is wearing an approved parachute, no pilot of a civil aircraft carrying any person (other than a crewmember) may execute any intentional maneuver that exceeds:

- A bank of 60° relative to the horizon; or
- A nose-up or nose-down attitude of 30° relative to the horizon.

b. This regulation does not apply to:

- Flight tests for pilot certification or rating; or
- Spins and other flight maneuvers required by the regulations for any certificate or rating when given by a CFI or an ATP.

18. What is required to operate an aircraft towing an advertising banner? (14 CFR 91.311)

No pilot of a civil aircraft may tow anything with that aircraft (other than under 14 CFR §91.309, "Towing gliders") except in accordance with the terms of a certificate of waiver issued by the Administrator.

19. What categories of aircraft cannot be used in the carriage of persons or property for hire? (14 CFR 91.313, 91.315, and 91.319)

a. Restricted category.
b. Limited category.
c. Experimental.

In some instances, a LODA (letter of deviation authority) may be secured to allow for exemption from this restriction.

20. Do regulations permit a pilot to drop objects from an aircraft in flight? (14 CFR 91.15)

In general, regulations prohibit pilots from dropping objects from an aircraft in flight unless specific conditions and authorizations are met. Dropping objects from an aircraft can pose hazards to people and property on the ground, as well as create a risk to the aircraft and other aircraft in the vicinity.

According to the 14 CFR §91.15, pilots are prohibited from dropping any object from an aircraft that creates a hazard to persons or property. This regulation allows for limited exceptions when objects are dropped in accordance with approved procedures during aerial application, firefighting, search and rescue operations, or other authorized activities. Furthermore, dropping objects from an aircraft without proper authorization may result in violations of other regulations, such as endangering people or property on the ground or violating airspace restrictions.

F. AIM (Aeronautical Information Manual)

Exam Tip: Be sure to obtain ASA's FAR/AIM app for your phone, tablet, or EFB. If the evaluator asks a FAR/AIM question you can't answer, you may reply "I don't know the answer, but I can quickly look it up." The ASA app will allow you to easily search and find the answer in seconds.

1. What is primary radar and secondary radar? (P/CG)

Primary radar—A radar system in which a minute portion of a radio pulse transmitted from a site is reflected by an object and then received back at that site for processing and display at an ATC facility.

Secondary radar—A radar system in which the object to be detected is fitted with a transponder. Radar pulses transmitted from the searching transmitter/receiver (interrogator) site are received in the transponder and used to trigger a distinctive transmission from the transponder. The reply transmission, rather than the reflected signal, is then received back at the transmitter/receiver site for processing and display at an ATC facility.

2. What is airport surveillance radar? (P/CG)

Airport surveillance radar (ASR) is approach control radar used to detect and display an aircraft's position in the terminal area. ASR provides range and azimuth information but does not provide elevation data. Coverage of ASR can extend up to 60 miles.

3. Describe the various types of terminal radar services available for VFR aircraft. (AIM 4-1-18, P/CG)

Basic radar service—Safety alerts, traffic advisories, limited radar vectoring (on a workload-permitting basis) and sequencing at locations where procedures have been established for this purpose and/or when covered by a letter of agreement.

TRSA service—Radar sequencing and separation service for participating VFR aircraft in a TRSA.

Class C service—This service provides, in addition to basic radar service, approved separation between IFR, and VFR aircraft, and sequencing of VFR arrivals to the primary airport.

Class B service—Provides, in addition to basic radar service, approved separation of aircraft based on IFR, VFR, and/or weight, and sequencing of VFR arrivals to the primary airport(s).

4. What frequencies other than 121.5 are monitored by most FSSs? (AIM 4-2-14)

FSS and supplemental weather service locations are allocated frequencies for different functions; for example, in Alaska, certain FSSs provide Local Airport Advisory on 123.6 MHz or other frequencies that can be found in the *Chart Supplement U.S.* If you are in doubt as to what frequency to use, 122.2 MHz is assigned to the majority of FSSs as a common enroute simplex frequency.

5. If operations are not being conducted in airspace requiring a transponder, can an aircraft equipped with a transponder leave it off? (AIM 4-1-20)

Unless otherwise requested by ATC, aircraft equipped with an ATC transponder maintained in accordance with 14 CFR §91.413, MUST operate with this equipment on the appropriate Mode 3/A code, or other code as assigned by ATC, and with altitude reporting enabled whenever in controlled airspace. If practical, aircraft

SHOULD operate with the transponder enabled in uncontrolled airspace. Aircraft equipped with ADS-B Out MUST operate with this equipment in the transmit mode at all times, unless otherwise requested by ATC.

6. **At what altitude would a pilot expect to encounter military aircraft when navigating through a military training route designated "VR1207"?** (AIM 3-5-2)

   Less than 1,500 AGL; Military training routes with no segment above 1,500 feet AGL shall be identified by four-digit characters; e.g., IR1206, VR1207.

   MTRs that include one or more segments above 1,500 feet AGL shall be identified by three-digit characters; e.g., IR206, VR207.

7. **When is a pilot required to file an International Flight Plan (FAA Form 7233-4)?** (faa.gov, AIM 5-1-6)

   The FAA prefers users to file an International Flight Plan for all flights. Use of an International Flight Plan (Form 7233-4) is mandatory for:

   a. Assignment of RNAV SIDs and STARs or other performance-based navigation (PBN) routing.

   b. All civilian IFR flights that will depart U.S. domestic airspace.

   c. Domestic IFR flights except military/DoD and civilians who file stereo route flight plans.

   d. All military/DoD IFR flights that will depart U.S. controlled airspace.

8. **What is an abbreviated IFR flight plan?** (P/CG)

   An abbreviated IFR flight plan is an authorization by ATC requiring pilots to submit only that information needed for the purpose of ATC. It is frequently used by aircraft which are airborne and desire an instrument approach or by an aircraft on the ground which desires to climb to VFR-on-top conditions.

9. **How long will a flight plan remain on file after the proposed departure time has passed?** (AIM 5-1-13)

To prevent computer saturation in the enroute environment, parameters have been established to delete proposed departure flight plans which have not been activated. Most centers have this parameter set so as to delete these flight plans a minimum of 2 hours after the proposed departure time or expect departure clearance time (EDCT).

10. **If you fail to report a change in arrival time or forget to close your flight plan, when will search and rescue procedures begin?** (AIM 5-1-14)

If you fail to report or cancel your flight plan within ½ hour after your ETA, search and rescue procedures are started.

11. **What constitutes a change in flight plan?** (AIM 5-1-12)

In addition to altitude or flight level, destination and/or route changes, increasing or decreasing the speed of the aircraft constitutes a change in flight plan. Therefore, anytime the average true airspeed at cruising altitude between reporting points varies or is expected to vary from that given in the flight plan by ±5 percent or 10 knots, whichever is greater, ATC should be advised.

12. **What is a DVFR flight plan?** (AIM 5-1-8)

VFR flights (except DOD or law enforcement flights) into an ADIZ are required to file DVFR flight plans for security purposes. Detailed ADIZ procedures can be found in AIM Chapter 5, Section 6. Also see 14 CFR Part 99, Security Control of Air Traffic.

13. **What is an ADIZ?** (AIM 5-6-3)

An Air Defense Identification Zone (ADIZ) is an area of airspace over land or water in which the ready identification, location, and control of all aircraft (except DOD and law enforcement aircraft) are required in the interest of national security.

14. **Where are Air Defense Identification Zones normally located?** (P/CG)

Domestic ADIZ—located within the United States along an international boundary of the United States.

Coastal ADIZ—located over the coastal waters of the United States.

Land-based ADIZ—located over U.S. metropolitan areas, which is activated and deactivated as needed, with dimensions, activation dates and other relevant information disseminated via NOTAM.

15. **What requirements must be satisfied prior to operations into, within, or across an ADIZ?** (14 CFR 99.13, AIM 5-6-4)

Operational requirements for aircraft operations associated with an ADIZ are as follows:

Flight plan—An IFR or DVFR flight plan must be filed with the appropriate aeronautical facility.

Two-way radio—An operating two-way radio is required.

Transponder—Aircraft must be equipped with an operable radar beacon transponder having altitude reporting (Mode C) capabilities. The transponder must be turned on and set to the assigned ATC code.

Position reports—For IFR flights, normal position reporting. For DVFR flights, an estimated time of ADIZ penetration must be filed at least 15 minutes prior to entry.

Land-based ADIZ—Activated and deactivated over U.S. metropolitan areas as needed, with dimensions, activation dates, etc., disseminated via NOTAM. Pilots unable to comply with all NOTAM requirements must remain clear of land-based ADIZ. Pilots entering a land-based ADIZ without authorization, or who fail to follow all requirements, risk interception by military fighter aircraft.

16. **What are the six classes of aircraft present in the United States?** (AIM 3-2-2 through 3-2-6, 3-3-1, P/CG)

Class A airspace—Generally, airspace from 18,000 feet MSL up to and including FL600, including airspace overlying the waters within 12 NM of the coast of the 48 contiguous states and Alaska; and designated international airspace beyond 12 NM of the coast of the 48 contiguous states and Alaska within areas of domestic radio navigational signal or ATC radar coverage, and within which domestic procedures are applied.

Class B airspace—Generally, airspace from the surface to 10,000 feet MSL surrounding the nation's busiest airports in terms of IFR operations or passenger enplanements. The configuration of each Class B airspace area is individually tailored and consists of a surface area and two or more layers, (some resemble upside-down wedding cakes), and is designated to contain all published instrument procedures once an aircraft enters the airspace. An ATC clearance is required for all aircraft to operate in the area, and all aircraft cleared as such receive separation services within the airspace. The visibility and cloud clearance requirement for VFR operations is 3 SM visibility and clear of clouds.

Class C airspace—Generally, airspace from the surface to 4,000 feet above the airport elevation (charted in MSL) surrounding airports that have an operational control tower, are serviced by a radar approach control, and that have a certain number of IFR operations or passenger enplanements. Although the configuration of each Class C airspace area is individually tailored, the airspace usually consists of a 5 NM radius core surface area that extends from the surface up to 4,000 feet above the airport elevation, and a 10 NM radius shelf area that extends from 1,200 feet to 4,000 feet above the airport elevation.

Class D airspace—Generally, airspace from the surface to 2,500 feet above the airport elevation (charted in MSL) surrounding airports that have an operational control tower. The configuration of each Class D airspace area is individually tailored and when instrument procedures are published, the airspace will normally be designed to contain those procedures.

(continued)

Class E (controlled) airspace—Generally, if the airspace is not Class A, B, C, or D, and it is controlled airspace, it is Class E airspace. Class E airspace extends upward from either the surface or a designated altitude to the overlying or adjacent controlled airspace. Examples include: Surface areas designated for an airport, extensions to a surface area, airspace used for transition, enroute domestic areas, Federal airways, offshore airspace areas.

Class G (uncontrolled) airspace—Class G airspace is that portion of the airspace that has not been designated as Class A, B, C, D, and E airspace.

17. Define the following types of airspace: Prohibited Area, Restricted Area, Military Operations Area, Warning Area, Alert Area, Controlled Firing Area, National Security Areas, Special Air Traffic Rules (SATR), Special Flight Rules Area (SFRA). (AIM 3-4-2 through 3-4-8, 3-5-7)

Prohibited Area—For security or other reasons, aircraft flight is prohibited.

Restricted Area—Contains unusual, often invisible hazards to aircraft, flights must have permission from the controlling agency, if VFR. IFR flights will be cleared through or vectored around it.

Military Operations Area—Designed to separate military training from IFR traffic. Permission is not required, but VFR flights should exercise caution. IFR flights will be cleared through or vectored around it.

Warning Area—Same hazards as a restricted area, it is established beyond the 3-mile limit of International Airspace. Permission is not required, but a flight plan is advised.

Alert Area—Airspace containing a high volume of pilot training or unusual aerial activity. No permission is required, but VFR flights should exercise caution. IFR flights will be cleared through or vectored around it.

Controlled Firing Areas—CFAs contain activities which, if not conducted in a controlled environment, could be hazardous to non-participating aircraft. The distinguishing feature of the CFA, as compared to other special use airspace, is that its activities are suspended immediately when spotter aircraft, radar or ground lookout positions indicate an aircraft might be approaching the area. CFAs are not charted.

National Security Areas—Airspace of defined vertical and lateral dimensions established at locations where there is a requirement for increased security and safety of ground facilities. Pilots are requested to voluntarily avoid flying through the depicted NSA. When it is necessary to provide a greater level of security and safety, flight in NSAs may be temporarily prohibited by regulation under the provisions of 14 CFR §99.7.

Special Air Traffic Rules (SATR)—Rules that govern procedures for conducting flights in certain areas listed in Part 93. The term "SATR" is used in the United States to describe the rules for operations in specific areas designated in the Code of Federal Regulations.

Special Flight Rules Area (SFRA)—Airspace of defined dimensions, above land areas or territorial waters, within which the flight of aircraft is subject to the rules set forth in Part 93, unless otherwise authorized by ATC. Not all areas listed in Part 93 are designated SFRA, but special air traffic rules apply to all areas described in Part 93.

Note: Current and scheduled status information on special use airspace can be found on the FAA's SUA website at sua.faa.gov.

Exam Tip: Be prepared to explain the type of airspace your planned route of flight will take you through from departure to arrival at your destination. Know the required visibility, cloud clearance, and communication requirements at any point and altitude along your route of flight. Also, expect the "what if you're here" questions concerning special use airspace, special VFR clearances, etc.

18. **What is the main difference between controlled airspace and uncontrolled airspace?** (AIM 3-2-1 and 3-3-1)

The main difference between controlled airspace and uncontrolled airspace lies in the presence or absence of air traffic control (ATC) services and the associated regulations governing aircraft operations within each type of airspace.

Controlled Airspace:

a. *ATC services*—In controlled airspace, ATC services are provided. ATC controllers monitor and manage the flow of aircraft, providing guidance, separation, and traffic information to ensure safe and efficient operations.

(continued)

b. *Communication*—Pilots are required to establish two-way radio communication and follow instructions from ATC when operating in controlled airspace.

c. *Separation standards*—ATC ensures appropriate separation between aircraft in controlled airspace, maintaining a safe distance both horizontally and vertically.

d. *Clearance requirements*—Pilots need to obtain clearances for various activities, including takeoff, landing, changes in altitude, and navigation within controlled airspace.

e. *Instrument flight rules (IFR)*—Controlled airspace is often associated with IFR operations, where pilots navigate and operate based on instrument procedures and ATC guidance.

f. *Specific designations*—Controlled airspace includes different classifications, such as Class A, B, C, D, and E airspace, each with specific regulations and requirements.

Uncontrolled Airspace:

a. *No ATC services*—Uncontrolled airspace does not have active ATC services. Pilots operate on a "see and avoid" principle, relying on visual scanning and communication with other pilots to maintain separation.

b. *Communication*—While radio communication is not mandatory in uncontrolled airspace, pilots are encouraged to communicate their intentions on designated frequencies to enhance situational awareness.

c. *Visual flight rules (VFR)*—Uncontrolled airspace is often associated with VFR operations, where pilots rely on visual references and operate according to VFR rules and regulations.

d. *Lower altitude limits*—Uncontrolled airspace generally starts at the surface and extends up to the base of controlled airspace above.

e. *General traffic awareness*—Pilots in uncontrolled airspace are responsible for their own navigation, traffic avoidance, and maintaining safe separation from other aircraft.

19. What is a TFR? (AC 91-63)

A temporary flight restriction (TFR) is a regulatory action issued via the U.S. NOTAM system to restrict certain aircraft from operating within a defined area, on a temporary basis, to protect persons or property in the air or on the ground. They may be issued due to a hazardous condition, a special event, or as a general warning for the entire FAA airspace. TFR information can be obtained from an FSS or on the internet at tfr.faa.gov.

Exam Tip: On the day of your practical test, verify that a last-minute TFR hasn't been issued for your area or along your planned route of flight.

20. Where can a pilot find information regarding TFRs and whether they will affect the pilot's area of flight or route? (AC 91-63)

Information about TFRs and their activity can be obtained from an official weather briefing source. The website tfr.faa.gov actively provides current and future scheduled TFR information. Many flight planning applications on EFBs also import current TFR information to help advise a pilot of their presence.

21. May a pilot operate their aircraft through a TFR? (AC 91-63)

A Temporary Flight Restriction (TFR) is a regulatory tool implemented by the FAA to restrict or prohibit aircraft operations within a defined airspace area due to specific events, emergencies, or hazardous conditions. Flying through a TFR without proper authorization or meeting the specified criteria is generally prohibited and can result in severe penalties, including enforcement actions or loss of pilot privileges. Typically, TFRs are established to keep pilots from flying in the area, and a pilot should not expect to be able to operate in the affected area during the time of effectiveness of the TFR. Some allowances are given for IFR traffic.

22. Can a pilot fly above a TFR? (AC 91-63)

Many TFRs have vertical and lateral limits. Staying outside of those limits is allowed. For example, if a firefighting TFR has a vertical limit of 10,000 feet MSL, a pilot may cross the lateral limits of the TFR above the vertical limits (for example, cruising at 12,000 feet MSL) without incurring a TFR violation. It is always best to operate on an IFR flight plan or with VFR flight following if operating near, above, or in a TFR.

23. What is a TRSA? (P/CG)

A terminal radar service area (TRSA) consists of airspace surrounding designated airports wherein ATC provides radar vectoring, sequencing, and separation on a full time basis for all IFR and participating VFR aircraft. Pilot participation is urged but not mandatory.

24. What procedures should be used in avoiding wake turbulence when landing? (AIM 7-4-6)

a. *Landing behind a larger aircraft, on the same runway*—Stay at or above the larger aircraft's final approach flight path. Note its touchdown point and land beyond it.

b. *Landing behind a larger aircraft, on a parallel runway closer than 2,500 feet*—Consider possible drift to your runway. Stay at or above the larger aircraft's final approach flight path and note its touchdown point.

c. *Landing behind a larger aircraft on a crossing runway*—Cross above the larger aircraft's flight path.

d. *Landing behind a departing larger aircraft on the same runway*—Note the larger aircraft's rotation point, and land well before the rotation point.

e. *Landing behind a departing larger aircraft on a crossing runway*—Note the larger aircraft's rotation point. If it is past the intersection, continue the approach, and land prior to the intersection. If the larger aircraft rotates prior to the intersection, avoid flight below the larger aircraft's flight path. Abandon the approach unless a landing is ensured well before reaching the intersection.

25. **What wind condition prolongs the hazards of wake turbulence on a landing runway for the longest period of time?** (AIM 7-4-4)

    A light quartering tailwind.

26. **What procedures should be used in avoiding wake turbulence when departing a runway and while enroute VFR?** (AIM 7-4-6)

    a. *Departing behind a larger aircraft*—Note the larger aircraft's rotation point, rotate prior to larger aircraft's rotation point. Continue climb above the larger aircraft's climb path until turning clear of its wake.

    b. *Intersection takeoffs on the same runway*—Be alert to adjacent larger aircraft operations, particularly upwind of your runway. If intersection takeoff clearance is received, avoid a subsequent heading which will cross below the larger aircraft's path.

    c. *Departing or landing after a larger aircraft executing a low approach, missed approach, or touch-and-go landing*—Ensure that an interval of at least 2 minutes has elapsed before you take off or land. Because vortices settle and move laterally near the ground, the vortex hazard may continue to exist along the runway, particularly in light quartering wind situations.

    d. *Enroute VFR (thousand-foot altitude plus 500 feet)*—Avoid flight below and behind a large aircraft's path. If a larger aircraft is observed above or on the same track (meeting or overtaking), adjust your position laterally, preferably upwind.

27. **Who is responsible for wake turbulence avoidance, the pilot or the air traffic controller?** (AIM 7-4-8)

    The pilot is responsible. Acceptance of instructions from ATC (traffic information, follow an aircraft, visual approach clearance), is acknowledgment that the pilot has accepted responsibility for his/her own wake turbulence separation.

28. **Define the term *hydroplaning*.** (FAA-H-8083-3)

    Hydroplaning occurs when the tires are lifted off a runway surface by the combination of aircraft speed and a thin film of water present on the runway.

29. What are the three basic types of hydroplaning?
(FAA-H-8083-3)

Dynamic—Occurs when there is standing water on the runway surface. Water about 1/10-inch deep acts to lift the tire off the runway. The minimum speed at which dynamic hydroplaning occurs has been determined to be about 8.6 times the square root of the tire pressure in pounds per square inch.

Viscous—Occurs as a result of the viscous properties of water. A very thin film of fluid cannot be penetrated by the tire and the tire consequently rolls on top of the film. Viscous hydroplaning can occur at much slower speeds than dynamic hydroplaning but requires a smooth acting surface.

Reverted rubber hydroplaning—Occurs when a pilot, during the landing roll, locks the brakes for an extended period of time while on a wet runway. The friction creates heat which, combined with water, creates a steam layer between the aircraft tire and runway surface.

30. What is the best method of speed reduction if hydroplaning is experienced on landing? (FAA-H-8083-3)

Touchdown speed should be as slow as possible consistent with safety. After the nosewheel is lowered to the runway, moderate braking should be applied. If deceleration is not detected and hydroplaning is suspected, the nose should be raised and aerodynamic drag utilized to decelerate to a point where the brakes become effective.

31. What are several types of illusions in flight that may lead to errors in judgment on landing? (AIM 8-1-5)

Runway width illusion—Narrower than usual runway creates illusion aircraft is higher than actual; pilot tends to fly a lower approach than normal.

Runway and terrain slope illusion—Upsloping runway/terrain creates illusion aircraft is higher than actual; pilot tends to fly a lower approach than normal. Downsloping runway/terrain has the opposite effect.

Featureless terrain illusion—An absence of ground features creates illusion that aircraft is higher than actual; pilot tends to fly a lower approach than normal.

Atmospheric illusions—Rain on windscreen creates illusion of greater height; atmospheric haze creates illusion of greater distance from runway; pilot tends to fly a lower approach than normal.

32. **What is the most effective method of scanning for other air traffic?** (AIM 8-1-6)

Effective scanning is accomplished with a series of short, regularly spaced eye movements that bring successive areas of the sky into the central vision field. Each movement should not exceed 10°, and each area should be observed for at least 1 second to enable detection. Although horizontal back and forth eye movements seem preferred by most pilots, each pilot should develop a comfortable scanning pattern and then adhere to it to ensure optimum scanning.

33. **Discuss recommended collision avoidance procedures and considerations in the following situations: before takeoff, climbs and descents, straight-and-level flight, traffic patterns, traffic at VOR sites, and training operations.** (FAA-H-8083-25)

a. *Before takeoff*—Before taxiing onto a runway or landing area in preparation for takeoff, scan the approach area for possible landing traffic, executing appropriate maneuvers to provide a clear view of the approach areas.

b. *Climbs and descents*—During climbs and descents in flight conditions that permit visual detection of other traffic, make gentle banks left and right at a frequency that allows continuous visual scanning of the airspace.

c. *Straight and level*—During sustained periods of straight-and-level flight, execute appropriate clearing procedures at periodic intervals.

d. *Traffic patterns*—Entries into traffic patterns while descending should be avoided.

e. *Traffic at VOR sites*—Due to converging traffic, maintain sustained vigilance in the vicinity of VORs and intersections.

f. *Training operations*—Maintain vigilance and make clearing turns before a practice maneuver. During instruction, the pilot should be asked to verbalize the clearing procedures (call out clear "left, right, above, below"). High-wing and low-wing aircraft have their respective blind spots: For high-wing aircraft, momentarily raise the wing in the direction of the intended turn and look for traffic prior to commencing the turn; for low-wing aircraft, momentarily lower the wing.

34. When transitioning busy terminal airspace, where can information be found concerning VFR flyways, corridors, and transition routes? (AIM 3-5-5)

Information regarding VFR flyways, corridors, and transition routes for transitioning busy terminal airspace can be found in various sources, including:

a. *Aeronautical charts*—Sectional charts, terminal area charts (TAC), and other aeronautical charts often depict VFR flyways, corridors, and transition routes. These charts highlight specific routes designed to facilitate the movement of VFR traffic through busy terminal airspace. Flyways and transition routes are typically depicted with specific symbols and labels to assist pilots in route planning.

b. *Chart Supplements*—*Chart Supplements* provide detailed information about airports and airspace facilities, including specific VFR flyways, corridors, and transition routes available in busy terminal areas. These publications contain information on recommended routes, altitudes, and any special procedures or considerations for flying through or around busy airspace.

c. *NOTAMs (Notices to Air Missions)*—NOTAMs may contain important information related to VFR flyways, corridors, and transition routes. Temporary changes or restrictions, such as airspace closures, specific routing instructions, or other pertinent information, may be communicated through NOTAMs.

d. *Air traffic control (ATC)*—Pilots can obtain information regarding VFR flyways, corridors, and transition routes by contacting air traffic control facilities serving the area. ATC can provide guidance, specific routing instructions, or any temporary restrictions or instructions in effect.

35. What is the width of a federal airway? (FAA-H-8083-15)

The width of a Federal airway, also known as a victor airway, is generally four nautical miles on each side of the centerline. This creates a total width of eight nautical miles for the airway.

G. Night Flight Operations

1. Explain the arrangement and interpretation of the position lights on an aircraft. (FAA-H-8083-3)

A red light is positioned on the left wingtip, a green light on the right wingtip, and a white light on the tail. If both a red and green light of another aircraft are observed, and the red light is on the left and the green to the right, the airplane is flying in the same direction. Care must be taken not to overtake the other aircraft and to maintain clearance. If a red light is observed on the right and a green light to the left on another aircraft, then the airplane could be on a collision course.

2. Position lights are required to be on during what period of time? (14 CFR 91.209)

No person may operate an aircraft during the period from sunset to sunrise unless the aircraft has lighted position lights.

3. When operating an aircraft in, or in close proximity to, a night operations area, what is required of an aircraft? (14 CFR 91.209)

The aircraft must:
- Be clearly illuminated;
- Have position lights; or
- Be in an area marked by obstruction lights.

4. When are aircraft that are equipped with an anti-collision light system required to operate that light system? (AIM 4-3-23, 14 CFR 91.209)

Aircraft equipped with an anti-collision light system are required to operate that light system during all types of operations (day and night). However, the anti-collision lights need not be lighted when the PIC determines that, because of operating conditions, it would be in the interest of safety to turn the lights off.

5. **What are the three definitions of *night*?** (14 CFR 1.1, 61.57, 91.209)

   14 CFR §1.1—the time between the end of evening civil twilight and the beginning of morning civil twilight, as published in the Air Almanac, converted to local time. Use this definition when logging night flight time.

   14 CFR §61.57—the period beginning one hour after sunset and ending one hour before sunrise. Use this definition when determining currency to act as PIC of an aircraft carrying passengers.

   14 CFR §91.209—the period from sunset to sunrise. Use this definition to determine when you are required to have position and anti-collision lights on.

6. **What are the different types of rotating beacons used to identify airports?** (AIM 2-1-9)

   a. White and green—lighted land airport.
   b. Green alone*—lighted land airport.
   c. White and yellow—lighted water airport.
   d. Yellow alone*—lighted water airport.
   e. Green, yellow, and white—lighted heliport.
   f. White (dual peaked) and green—military airport.

   * "Green alone" and "yellow alone" beacons are used only in connection with a white-and-green, or white-and-yellow beacon display, respectively.

7. **Describe several types of aviation obstruction lighting.** (AIM 2-2-3)

   a. *Aviation red obstruction lights*—Flashing aviation red beacons and steady burning aviation red lights.

   b. *High intensity white obstruction lights*—Flashing high intensity white lights during daytime with reduced intensity for twilight and nighttime operation.

   c. *Dual lighting*—A combination of flashing aviation red beacons and steady burning aviation red lights for nighttime operation and flashing high intensity white lights for daytime operation.

8. What color are runway edge lights? (AIM 2-1-4)

Runway edge lights are white. On instrument runways, however, yellow replaces white on the last 2,000 feet or half the runway length (whichever is less), to form a caution zone for landings.

9. What color are the lights marking the ends of the runway? (AIM 2-1-4)

The lights marking the ends of the runway emit red light toward the runway to indicate the end of the runway to a departing aircraft, and green light outward from the runway end to indicate the threshold to landing aircraft.

10. Describe runway end identifier lights (REIL). (AIM 2-1-3)

REILs are installed at many airfields to provide rapid and positive identification of the approach end of a particular runway. The system consists of a pair of synchronized flashing lights located laterally on each side of the runway threshold. REIL may be either omnidirectional or unidirectional facing the approach area.

11. What color are taxiway edge lights? (AIM 2-1-10)

Taxiway edge lights emit blue light and are used to outline the edges of taxiways during periods of darkness or restricted visibility conditions.

12. What color are taxiway centerline lights? (AIM 2-1-10)

Taxiway centerline lights are steady-burning, green light.

13. How does a pilot determine the status of a light system at a particular airport? (FAA-H-8083-3)

The pilot needs to check the *Chart Supplement U.S.* and any NOTAMs to find out about available lighting systems, light intensities and radio-controlled light system frequencies.

14. How does a pilot activate a radio-controlled runway light system while airborne? (AIM 2-1-8)

The pilot activates radio-controlled lights by keying the microphone on a specified frequency. The following sequence can be used for typical radio-controlled lighting systems:

a. On initial arrival, key the microphone seven times to turn the lights on and achieve maximum brightness;

b. If the runway lights are already on upon arrival, repeat the above sequence to ensure a full 15 minutes of lighting; then

c. The intensity of the lights can be adjusted by keying the microphone seven, five, or three times within 5 seconds.

Exam Tip: Be prepared to determine and explain the type and status of airport and runway lighting at your departure and destination airports.

15. What are some additional risks to flying at night that may not be present during day flight operations? (FAA-H-8083-3)

Some common additional risks of flying at night include the following:

a. Decreased visibility and situational awareness.

b. Decreased ability to see other traffic.

c. Decreased ability to see and choose an emergency landing location if any emergencies occur.

d. Inability to see and avoid clouds or storms that would be more visible during daylight operations.

e. Aeromedical effects on vision at altitudes where those effects are more readily noticed; primarily vision effects.

f. Fatigue if a pilot is operating at the end of a day in the dark having not rested prior to flight.

Each of these offers additional risk a pilot should be aware of and mitigate to any degree possible if they will be flying at night.

H. High-Altitude Operations

1. **What are some basic operational advantages when conducting high-altitude operations?**
   a. True airspeeds increase with altitude.
   b. Winds aloft are stronger providing tailwind opportunities.
   c. Capability to see and avoid thunderstorms.
   d. Better visibility.
   e. Less turbulence.
   f. Above the weather instead of in it.
   g. Reduced chance for icing.
   h. Conflicts with other air traffic reduced.

2. **What are the regulations concerning use of supplemental oxygen on board an aircraft? (14 CFR 91.211)**
   No person may operate a civil aircraft of U.S. registry:
   a. At cabin pressure altitudes above 12,500 feet MSL up to and including 14,000 feet MSL, unless, for that part of the flight at those altitudes that is more than 30 minutes, the required minimum flight crew is provided with and uses supplemental oxygen.
   b. At cabin pressure altitudes above 14,000 feet MSL, unless the required flight crew is provided with and uses supplemental oxygen for the entire flight time at those altitudes.
   c. At cabin pressure altitudes above 15,000 feet MSL, unless each occupant is provided with supplemental oxygen.

3. **What are the regulations pertaining to the use of supplemental oxygen on board a pressurized aircraft? (14 CFR 91.211)**
   Above FL250—At least a 10-minute supply of supplemental oxygen, in addition to any oxygen required to satisfy 14 CFR §91.211, is available for each occupant of the aircraft for use in the event that a descent is necessitated by loss of cabin pressurization.

   Above FL350—At least one pilot at the controls of the airplane is wearing and using an oxygen mask that is secured and sealed that either supplies oxygen at all times or automatically supplies oxygen whenever the cabin pressure altitude of the airplane exceeds 14,000 feet MSL.

   (continued)

Note: One pilot need not wear and use an oxygen mask while at or below FL410 if two pilots are at the controls and each pilot has a quick donning type of oxygen mask that can be placed on the face within 5 seconds. Also, if for any reason at any time it is necessary for one pilot to leave the controls of the aircraft when operating at altitudes above FL350, the remaining pilot at the controls shall put on and use an oxygen mask until the other pilot has returned to that crewmember's station.

4. **What are the requirements to operate within Class A airspace?** (14 CFR 91.135, 91.215, 91.225)

   a. Operated under IFR and in compliance with an ATC clearance received prior to entering the airspace;

   b. Equipped with instruments and equipment required for IFR operations;

   c. Flown by a pilot rated for instrument flight; and

   d. Equipped, when in Class A airspace, with:

   • A radio providing direct pilot/controller communication on the frequency specified by ATC in the area concerned; and

   • The applicable equipment specified in 14 CFR §91.215 (transponder regulation) and §91.225 (ADS-B Out regulation).

5. **What additional equipment is required when operating above flight level 240?** (14 CFR 91.205)

   For flight at and above 24,000 feet MSL: if VOR navigational equipment is required (appropriate to the ground facilities to be used) no person may operate a U.S.-registered civil aircraft within the 50 states and the District of Columbia at or above FL240 unless that aircraft is equipped with approved DME or a suitable RNAV system.

6. **What type of navigational charts are used when operating at altitudes above 18,000 feet?** (AIM 9-1-4)

   Enroute high altitude charts are designed for navigation at or above 18,000 feet MSL. This four-color chart series includes the jet-route structure; VHF NAVAIDs with frequency, identification, channel, geographic coordinates; selected airports, reporting points. These charts are revised every 56 days.

I. National Transportation Safety Board

1. When is immediate notification to the NTSB required?
(49 CFR Part 830)

The operator of an aircraft shall immediately, and by the most expeditious means available, notify the nearest NTSB field office when an aircraft accident or any of the following listed incidents occur:

a. Flight control system malfunction.

b. Crewmember unable to perform normal duties.

c. Turbine engine failure of structural components.

d. In-flight fire.

e. Aircraft collision in-flight.

f. Property damage, other than aircraft, estimated to exceed $25,000.

g. Overdue aircraft (believed to be in an accident).

h. Release of all or a portion of a propeller blade from an aircraft.

i. Complete loss of information (excluding flickering) from more than 50 percent of an aircraft's EFIS cockpit displays.

j. When compliance with ACAS resolution advisories issued to IFR aircraft is necessary to avert a collision.

k. Helicopter tail or main rotor blade damage that requires major repair or replacement of blades.

l. Air carrier aircraft lands or departs on a taxiway, incorrect runway, or area not designated as a runway.

m. A runway incursion that requires operator or crew of another aircraft or vehicle to take immediate corrective action to avoid a collision.

n. When an aircraft is overdue and is believed to have been involved in an accident.

2. After an accident or incident has occurred, how soon must a report be filed with the NTSB? (49 CFR Part 830)

The operator shall file a report on NTSB Form 6120.1 or 6120.2, available from NTSB field offices or from the NTSB, Washington D.C., 20594:

a. Within 10 days after an accident;

b. When, after 7 days, an overdue aircraft is still missing.

A report on an incident for which notification is required as described shall be filed only as requested by an authorized representative of the NTSB.

3. Define *aircraft accident*. (49 CFR 830.2)

An aircraft accident means an occurrence associated with the operation of an aircraft which takes place between the time any person boards the aircraft with the intention of flight and all such persons have disembarked, and in which any person suffers death or serious injury, or in which the aircraft receives substantial damage.

4. Define *aircraft incident*. (49 CFR 830.2)

An aircraft incident means an occurrence other than an accident associated with the operation of an aircraft, which affects or could affect the safety of operations.

5. Define the term *serious injury*. (49 CFR 830.2)

Serious injury means any injury which:

a. Requires hospitalization for more than 48 hours, commencing within 7 days from the date the injury was received;

b. Results in a fracture of any bone (except simple fractures of fingers, toes or nose);

c. Causes severe hemorrhages, nerve, muscle or tendon damage;

d. Involves any internal organ; or

e. Involves second- or third-degree burns affecting more than 5 percent of the body surface.

6. **Define the term *substantial damage*.** (49 CFR 830.2)

   Substantial damage means damage or failure which adversely affects structural strength, performance or flight characteristics of the aircraft and which normally requires major repair or replacement of the affected component.

7. **Will notification to the NTSB always be necessary in any aircraft accident even if there were no injuries?** (49 CFR Part 830)

   Refer to the definition of accident. An aircraft accident can be substantial damage and/or injuries, and the NTSB always requires a report if this is the case.

8. **Where are accident or incident reports filed?** (49 CFR Part 830)

   The operator of an aircraft shall file any report with the field office of the Board nearest the accident or incident. NTSB contact information can be found at ntsb.gov.

J. Aviation Security

1. **What are several actions you can take to enhance aircraft security?** (TSA)

   a. Always lock your aircraft.

   b. Keep track of door/ignition keys and don't leave keys in unattended aircraft.

   c. Use secondary locks (prop, tie down, throttle, and wheel locks) or aircraft disabler if available.

   d. Lock hangar when unattended.

2. **What type of airport security procedures should you review regularly to prevent unauthorized access to aircraft at your airport?** (49 CFR Part 1552)

   a. Limitations on ramp access to people other than instructors and students.

   b. Standards for securing aircraft on the ramp.

   c. Securing access to aircraft keys at all times.

(continued)

    d. New auxiliary security items for aircraft (prop locks, throttle locks, locking tie downs).

    e. After-hours or weekend access procedures.

3. When witnessing suspicious or criminal activity, what are three basic ways for reporting the suspected activity? (TSA)

If you determine that it's safe, question the individual. If their response is unsatisfactory and they continue to act suspiciously:

    a. Alert airport or FBO management.

    b. Contact local law enforcement if the activity poses an immediate threat to persons or property.

    c. Contact the 866-GA-SECURE hotline to document the reported event.

4. Are there any security programs or requirements established for Part 135, charter, or flight training operations? (49 CFR Part 1544)

Yes; The TSA has established several regulatory programs that include:

    a. *Twelve Five Standard Security Program (TFSSP)*—applies to aircraft with a MTOW of more than 12,500 punds that offer scheduled or charter service and carry passengers or cargo. The program requires watch list matching of passengers, aircraft access control procedures, background checks for flight crews, and reporting procedures.

    b. *Private Charter Standard Security Program (PCSSP)*—applies to Parts 121, 125, and 135 charter aircraft operations in aircraft over 100,309 pounds MTOW or with a seating configuration of 61 or more seats; requires the same security measures as TFSSP, but also requires screening of passengers and accessible property.

    c. *Alien Flight Student Program (AFSP)*—requires background checks for foreign flight candidates seeking flight training in the United States. Additional security awareness training is also mandated for flight training providers.

5. What is a Security Identification Display Area (SIDA)?
(AIM 2-3-15)

SIDAs are limited access areas that require a badge issued in accordance with procedures in 49 CFR Part 1542. A SIDA can include the Air Operations Area (AOA), which could be an aircraft movement area or parking area or a Secured Area, such as where commercial passengers enplane. The AOA may not be a SIDA, but a Secured Area is always a SIDA. Movement through or into a SIDA is prohibited without authorization and proper identification being displayed.

Human
Factors

8

A. Fitness for Flight

1. What regulations apply to medical certification?

Part 67, Medical Standards and Certification.

2. As a flight crewmember, you receive a new diagnosis for high blood pressure. You are in possession of a current medical certificate that was issued before your diagnosis. Can you continue to exercise the privileges of your certificate? (AIM 8-1-1)

No; the regulations prohibit a pilot who possesses a current medical certificate from performing crewmember duties while the pilot has a known medical condition or an increase of a known medical condition that would make the pilot unable to meet the standards for the medical certificate. A pilot would need to have a new medical issued on which this was disclosed and determined by the FAA if a new medical certificate issuance was possible.

3. Are flight crewmembers allowed the use of any medications while performing required duties? (AIM 8-1-1)

The regulations prohibit pilots from performing crewmember duties while using any medication that affects the faculties in any way contrary to safety. The safest rule is not to fly as a crewmember while taking any medication, unless approved to do so by the FAA.

4. Are there any over-the-counter medications that could be considered safe to use while flying? (AIM 8-1-1, FAA OTC Med Guide)

Only limited over-the-counter medications should be considered safe to use while flying. A key factor is if a medication indicates it "may cause drowsiness" or if it advises the user to "be careful when driving a motor vehicle or operating machinery," then it is not considered safe to use while flying. Pilot performance can be seriously degraded by both prescribed and over-the-counter medications, as well as by the medical conditions for which they are taken. Many medications have primary effects that may impair judgment, memory, alertness, coordination, vision, and the ability to make calculations. Also, any medication that depresses the central nervous system can make a pilot more susceptible to hypoxia.

5. **What are several factors that may contribute to impairment of a pilot's performance?** (AIM 8-1-1)

Illness

Medication

Stress

Alcohol

Fatigue

Emotion

B. Flight Physiology

1. **What is hypoxia?** (AIM 8-1-2)

Hypoxia is a state of oxygen deficiency in the body sufficient to impair functions of the brain and other organs.

2. **Give a brief explanation of the four forms of hypoxia.** (FAA-H-8083-25)

Hypoxic—The result of insufficient oxygen available to the body as a whole. The reduction in partial pressure of oxygen at high altitude is an example for pilots.

Hypemic—The blood is unable to transport a sufficient amount of oxygen to the cells; the result of oxygen deficiency in the blood, rather than a lack of inhaled oxygen, CO_2 poisoning is an example.

Stagnant—This results when the oxygen-rich blood in the lungs is not moving. It can result from shock, the heart failing to pump blood effectively, a constricted artery, and with excessive acceleration of gravity (Gs).

Histotoxic—Inability of the cells to effectively use oxygen; it can be caused by alcohol and other drugs.

3. **Where does hypoxia usually occur, and what symptoms should one expect?** (AIM 8-1-2)

Although a deterioration in night vision occurs at a cabin pressure altitude as low as 5,000 feet, other significant effects of altitude hypoxia usually do not occur in the normal healthy pilot below 12,000 feet. From 12,000 feet to 15,000 feet of altitude, judgment, memory, alertness, coordination, and ability to make calculations are impaired, and headache, drowsiness, dizziness and either a sense of well-being or belligerence occur.

4. What factors can make a pilot more susceptible to hypoxia? (AIM 8-1-2)

a. Carbon monoxide inhaled in smoking or from exhaust fumes.

b. Anemia (lowered hemoglobin).

c. Certain medications.

d. Small amounts of alcohol.

e. Low doses of certain drugs (antihistamines, tranquilizers, sedatives, analgesics, etc.).

Also, extreme heat or cold, fever, and anxiety increase the body's demand for oxygen, and hence its susceptibility to hypoxia.

5. How can hypoxia be avoided? (AIM 8-1-2, FAA-H-8083-25)

Hypoxia is prevented by heeding factors that reduce tolerance to altitude, by enriching the inspired air with oxygen from an appropriate oxygen system, and by maintaining a comfortable, safe cabin pressure altitude. For optimum protection, pilots are encouraged to use supplemental oxygen above 10,000 feet during the day, and above 5,000 feet at night. If supplemental oxygen is not available, a fingertip pulse oximeter can be very useful in monitoring blood O_2 levels.

6. What is hyperventilation? (AIM 8-1-3)

Hyperventilation is an abnormal increase in the volume of air breathed in and out of the lungs, and it can occur subconsciously when a stressful situation is encountered in flight. This results in a significant decrease in the carbon dioxide content of the blood. Carbon dioxide is needed to automatically regulate the breathing process.

7. What symptoms can a pilot expect from hyperventilation? (AIM 8-1-3)

As hyperventilation "blows off" excessive carbon dioxide from the body, a pilot can experience symptoms of lightheadedness, suffocation, drowsiness, tingling in the extremities, and coolness, and react to them with even greater hyperventilation. Incapacitation can eventually result from uncoordination, disorientation, and painful muscle spasms. Finally, unconsciousness can occur.

8. **How can a hyperventilating condition be reversed?** (AIM 8-1-3)

The symptoms of hyperventilation subside within a few minutes after the rate and depth of breathing are consciously brought back to normal. The buildup of carbon dioxide in the body can be hastened by controlled breathing in and out of a paper bag held over the nose and mouth.

9. **What is ear block?** (AIM 8-1-2)

As the aircraft cabin pressure decreases during ascent, the expanding air in the middle ear pushes open the Eustachian tube and escapes down to the nasal passages, thereby equalizing in pressure with the cabin pressure. But this is not automatic during descent, and the pilot must periodically open the Eustachian tube to equalize pressure. An upper respiratory infection or a nasal allergic condition can produce enough congestion around the Eustachian tube to make equalization difficult. Consequently, the difference in pressure between the middle ear and aircraft cabin can build to a level that holds the Eustachian tube closed, making equalization difficult if not impossible. An ear block produces severe pain and loss of hearing that can last from several hours to several days.

10. **How is ear block normally prevented from occurring?** (AIM 8-1-2)

Ear block can normally be prevented by swallowing, yawning, tensing muscles in the throat or, if these do not work, by the combination of closing the mouth, pinching the nose closed and attempting to blow through the nostrils (Valsalva maneuver). It is also prevented by not flying with an upper respiratory infection or nasal allergic condition.

11. **What is spatial disorientation?** (FAA-H-8083-15)

Orientation is the awareness of the position of the aircraft and of oneself in relation to a specific reference point. Spatial disorientation specifically refers to the lack of orientation with regard to position in space and to other objects.

12. What causes spatial disorientation? (FAA-H-8083-15)

Orientation is maintained through the body's sensory organs in three areas:

a. Visual: the eyes maintain visual orientation.

b. Vestibular: the motion sensing system in the inner ear maintains vestibular orientation.

c. Postural: the nerves in the skin, joints, and muscles of the body maintain postural orientation.

When human beings are in their natural environment, these three systems work well. However, when the human body is subjected to the forces of flight, these senses can provide misleading information resulting in disorientation.

13. What is the cause of motion sickness, and what are its symptoms? (AIM)

Motion sickness is caused by continued stimulation of the inner ear, which controls the pilot's sense of balance. The symptoms are progressive. First, the desire for food is lost. Then, saliva collects in the mouth and the person begins to perspire freely. Eventually, the person becomes nauseated and disoriented, and may have a headache and a tendency to vomit. If the air sickness becomes severe enough, the pilot may become completely incapacitated.

14. What action should be taken if a pilot or passenger suffers from motion sickness? (AIM)

If a passenger is suffering from airsickness, a pilot may attempt to help manage their condition in a few ways. First, provide the passenger with an airsickness bag. Many passengers are embarrassed to tell the pilot they are feeling ill and may wait longer than they should to advise the pilot, putting them closer to vomiting than might be desirable. It is a good practice to advise passengers prior to flight of the location and how to use airsickness bags. After that, while piloting the aircraft, the pilot may open air vents or potentially windows, have the passenger loosen clothing, or use supplemental oxygen if available. The pilot should have the passenger focus outside of the aircraft and limit head movements to minimize the effects of airsickness. If it persists or worsens, the pilot should divert to a nearby suitable landing location to allow the passenger to stabilize.

15. What regulations apply, and what common sense should prevail, concerning the use of alcohol? (AIM 8-1-1)

The regulations prohibit pilots from performing crewmember duties within 8 hours after drinking any alcoholic beverage or while under the influence of alcohol. However, due to the slow destruction of alcohol, a pilot may still be under its influence 8 hours after drinking a moderate amount of alcohol. Therefore, an excellent rule is to allow at least 12 to 24 hours from "bottle to throttle," depending on the amount of alcoholic beverage consumed.

16. What is carbon monoxide poisoning? (AIM 8-1-4)

Carbon monoxide is a colorless, odorless, and tasteless gas contained in exhaust fumes. When breathed, even in minute quantities over a period of time, it can significantly reduce the ability of the blood to carry oxygen. Consequently, effects of hypoxia occur.

17. How does carbon monoxide poisoning occur, and what symptoms should a pilot be alert for? (AIM 8-1-4)

Most heaters in light aircraft work by air flowing over the manifold. Use of these heaters while exhaust fumes are escaping through manifold cracks and seals is responsible for several nonfatal and fatal aircraft accidents from carbon monoxide poisoning each year. A pilot who detects the odor of exhaust or experiences symptoms of headache, drowsiness, or dizziness while using the heater should suspect carbon monoxide poisoning.

18. What action should be taken if a pilot suspects carbon monoxide poisoning? (AIM 8-1-4)

A pilot who suspects this condition exists should immediately shut off the heater and open all air vents. If symptoms are severe, or they continue after landing, the pilot should seek medical treatment.

19. Discuss the effects of nitrogen excesses from scuba diving upon a pilot or passenger in flight. (AIM 8-1-2)

A pilot or passenger who intends to fly after scuba diving should allow the body sufficient time to rid itself of excess nitrogen absorbed during diving. If not, decompression sickness due to evolved gas can occur during exposure to low altitude and create a serious inflight emergency. The recommended waiting times before flight are as follows:

Flight altitudes up to 8,000 feet:

a. Wait at least 12 hours after a dive that did not require a controlled ascent.

b. Wait at least 24 hours after a dive in which a controlled ascent was required.

Flight altitudes above 8,000 feet:

a. Wait at least 24 hours after any scuba dive.

Note: The recommended altitudes are actual flight altitudes above mean sea level and not pressurized cabin altitudes. This takes into consideration the risk of decompression of the aircraft during flight.

20. For a pilot who has been taking an over-the-counter (OTC) cold medication, how do the various environmental factors the pilot is exposed to in flight affect the drug's physiological impact on the pilot? (FAA-H-8083-25)

Drugs that cause no apparent side effects on the ground can create serious problems at relatively low altitudes. Even at typical general aviation altitudes, the changes in concentrations of atmospheric gases in the blood can enhance the effects of seemingly innocuous drugs and result in impaired judgment, decision-making, and performance.

Note: Information on the FAA's "Do Not Issue (DNI) Medications" can be found at: www.faa.gov/ame_guide/media/DNI_DNF_tables .pdf.

21. **What is the difference between acute fatigue and chronic fatigue?** (AIM 8-1-1)

Acute fatigue refers to a short-term state of fatigue that occurs as a result of recent sleep deprivation, extended wakefulness, or physical or mental exertion. It is a normal physiological response to extended periods of wakefulness or intense activity. Acute fatigue can typically be relieved by getting sufficient rest and sleep. While acute fatigue can impair performance, it is usually temporary and can be quickly remedied.

Chronic fatigue is characterized by persistent and long-lasting feelings of exhaustion, even after adequate rest and sleep. It is not relieved by short-term measures and may persist for weeks, months, or longer. Chronic fatigue can have various underlying causes, including medical conditions such as chronic fatigue syndrome, fibromyalgia, or sleep disorders. It can significantly impact daily functioning, productivity, and overall quality of life. Managing chronic fatigue often requires medical intervention and lifestyle adjustments to address the root cause and improve symptoms.

22. **What is stress? What are the two categories of stress?** (FAA-H-8083-25)

Stress can be defined as the body's response to any demand or challenge, whether physical, mental, or emotional. It is a natural and instinctive reaction that prepares individuals to cope with perceived threats or pressures. There are two main categories of stress: acute stress and chronic stress.

Acute Stress—A short-term and immediate form of stress that arises from specific events or situations. It is often associated with a time-limited period of pressure or a sudden demand. Examples include taking a test, public speaking, or handling an emergency situation. Acute stress triggers the body's fight-or-flight response, leading to physiological changes such as increased heart rate, elevated blood pressure, and heightened mental alertness. Once the stressor is removed or the situation is resolved, the body returns to its normal state.

Chronic Stress—Long-term and ongoing stress that persists over an extended period. It can be caused by continuous exposure to demanding circumstances, such as work-related pressures, relationship difficulties, financial problems, or chronic health conditions. Unlike acute stress, chronic stress can have detrimental effects on physical and mental well-being if left unaddressed. It can lead to various health issues, including anxiety, depression, cardiovascular problems, weakened immune system, and impaired cognitive function.

23. What is spatial disorientation? Give several examples of illusions that can lead to spatial disorientation.
(AIM 8-1-5)

Spatial disorientation refers to the phenomenon where a pilot's perception of their aircraft's position, motion, or orientation in relation to the Earth's surface becomes inaccurate or misleading. It occurs when the sensory information from the pilot's visual, vestibular (inner ear), and proprioceptive (body position) systems conflict or are insufficient to provide an accurate perception of spatial orientation. Several examples of illusions that can lead to spatial disorientation for a pilot include:

a. *The leans*—After a prolonged turn, the pilot may experience a sensation of banking in the opposite direction, leading to an incorrect perception of level flight.

b. *Graveyard spiral*—If a pilot enters a coordinated descending turn and then levels the wings, they may experience the illusion of climbing. This can lead to pulling back on the controls, exacerbating the descent.

c. *Coriolis illusion*—When a pilot makes a rapid head movement during a prolonged constant-rate turn, they may experience the false sensation of rotation in an entirely different axis.

d. *Somatogravic illusion*—During rapid acceleration, such as during takeoff, the pilot may perceive a nose-up attitude, leading to a tendency to push the aircraft's nose down.

e. *Inversion illusion*—After abrupt upward vertical acceleration, the pilot may perceive an inverted (upside-down) orientation, potentially leading to disorientation and incorrect control inputs.

f. *False horizon*—In poor visibility or dark conditions, pilots may misinterpret cloud formations, lights, or other visual cues as the horizon, resulting in an inaccurate perception of aircraft attitude.

These illusions can significantly affect a pilot's judgment and control inputs, potentially leading to spatial disorientation and loss of control.

24. **Optical or visual illusions can increase the risk of an incident or accident occurring to even the most experienced pilots. What can a pilot do to mitigate that risk?** (FAA-H-8083-2)

Pilots can mitigate the risk of optical or visual illusions by taking the following measures:

a. *Cross-check instruments*—Rely on flight instruments to supplement visual cues and cross-check information. Instruments provide objective data and can help pilots overcome misleading visual inputs. Regularly scan and interpret instrument indications to maintain accurate situational awareness.

b. *Visual scanning techniques*—Implement effective visual scanning techniques, such as the scan, identify, evaluate, and execute (SIEE) method. This involves systematically scanning the environment, identifying potential hazards or changes, evaluating their implications, and executing appropriate actions based on that evaluation.

c. *Maintain instrument proficiency*—Practice and maintain proficiency in instrument flying, even if primarily operating under visual flight rules (VFR). Proficiency in instrument flying enhances the ability to rely on instruments during challenging visual conditions or when facing optical illusions.

d. *Personal limitations and decision-making*—Be aware of personal limitations and exercise good judgment. Recognize when visibility or conditions exceed personal capabilities and make informed decisions accordingly. Consider delaying or diverting flights if visual illusions pose an excessive risk.

By being knowledgeable, vigilant, and proactive, pilots can effectively mitigate the risks associated with optical illusions. Remaining focused on the principles of airmanship, continuously improving skills, and making informed decisions based on accurate information are essential for flight safety.

25. Discuss the symptoms and corrective actions for dehydration and heatstroke. (FAA-H-8083-25)

Dehydration and heatstroke are serious conditions that can occur when the body is exposed to high temperatures and inadequate fluid intake. The symptoms and corrective actions for each are discussed below.

Dehydration—Symptoms of dehydration include increased thirst, dry mouth, fatigue, dizziness, headache, dark urine, and decreased urine output. If left untreated, it can progress to more severe symptoms such as confusion, rapid heartbeat, and low blood pressure. Corrective actions for dehydration involve replenishing fluids and electrolytes. Move to a cooler environment, rest, and slowly drink water or oral rehydration solutions. Avoid excessive intake of sugary or caffeinated beverages, as they can worsen dehydration. If symptoms persist or worsen, seek medical attention.

Heatstroke—Heatstroke is a life-threatening condition that occurs when the body's temperature regulation system fails, resulting in a dangerously high body temperature. Symptoms include high body temperature (above 104°F or 40°C), rapid and shallow breathing, hot and dry skin, confusion, agitation, seizures, and loss of consciousness. Immediate corrective actions for heatstroke are critical. Call emergency services and take immediate steps to cool the person down. Move them to a shaded or air-conditioned area, remove excess clothing, and cool their body with cool water or wet towels. Fan the person or apply ice packs to aid in cooling. Do not give fluids if the person is unconscious or unable to drink. Prompt medical attention is essential for heatstroke cases.

Prevention is key in avoiding dehydration and heatstroke. Stay hydrated by drinking plenty of fluids, especially in hot weather or during physical activity.

C. Single-Pilot Resource Management

1. Define the term *single-pilot resource management.* (FAA-H-8083-9)

Single-pilot resource management (SRM) is the art and science of managing all the resources (both on board the aircraft and from outside sources) available to a single pilot (prior to and during flight) to ensure that the successful outcome of the flight is never in doubt. SRM helps pilots learn to execute methods of gathering information, analyzing it, and making decisions.

2. What practical application provides a pilot with an effective method to practice SRM? (FAA-H-8083-9)

The Five P (5P) checklist consists of "the Plan, the Plane, the Pilot, the Passengers, and the Programming." It is based on the idea that the pilot has essentially five variables that impact his or her environment and that can cause the pilot to make a single critical decision, or several less critical decisions, that when added together can create a critical outcome.

3. Explain the use of the 5P model to assess risk associated with each of the five factors. (FAA-H-8083-2)

At key decision points, application of the 5P checklist should be performed by reviewing each of the critical variables:

Plan—weather, route, publications, ATC reroutes/delays, fuel onboard/remaining.

Plane—mechanical status, automation status, database currency, backup systems.

Pilot—illness, medication, stress, alcohol, fatigue, eating.

Passengers—pilots/non-pilots, nervous or quiet, experienced or new, business or pleasure.

Programming—autopilot, GPS, MFD/PFD; anticipate likely reroutes/clearances; questions to ask—What is it doing? Why is it doing it? Did I do it?

4. When is the use of the 5P checklist recommended?
(FAA-H-8083-9)

The 5P concept relies on the pilot to adopt a scheduled review of the critical variables at points in the flight where decisions are most likely to be effective. These key decision points include preflight, pre-takeoff, hourly or at the midpoint of the flight, pre-descent, and just prior to the final approach fix (or, for VFR operations, just prior to entering the traffic pattern). They also should be used anytime an emergency situation arises.

D. Aeronautical Decision Making

1. Define the term *aeronautical decision making*.
(FAA-H-8083-9)

Aeronautical decision making (ADM) is a systematic approach to the mental process used by aircraft pilots to consistently determine the best course of action in response to a given set of circumstances. The two most commonly used models for practicing ADM are the DECIDE model and the 3P model.

2. The DECIDE model of decision-making involves which elements? (FAA-H-8083-9)

Detect a change needing attention.

Estimate the need to counter or react to a change.

Choose the most desirable outcome for the flight.

Identify actions to successfully control the change.

Do something to adapt to the change.

Evaluate the effect of the action countering the change.

3. How is the 3P model different from the DECIDE model of ADM? (FAA-H-8083-2)

The Perceive, Process, Perform (3P) model is a continuous loop of the pilot's handling of hazards. The DECIDE model and naturalistic decision-making focus on particular problems requiring resolution. Therefore, pilots exercise the 3P process continuously, while the DECIDE model and naturalistic decision-making result from the 3P process.

4. **How will you use the 3P model to recognize and mitigate risks throughout a flight?** (FAA-H-8083-9)

Once a pilot has completed the 3P decision process and selected a course of action, the process begins again because the circumstances brought about by the course of action requires analysis. The decision-making process is a continuous loop of perceiving, processing and performing.

5. **Name five hazardous attitudes that can affect a pilot's ability to make sound decisions and properly exercise authority over a flight. How would you mitigate them?** (FAA-H-8083-9)

Attitude	Antidote
Anti-authority ("Don't tell me.")	Follow the rules—they are usually right.
Impulsivity ("Do it quickly.")	Think first—not so fast.
Invulnerability ("It won't happen to me.")	It could happen to me.
Macho ("I can do it.")	Taking chances is foolish.
Resignation ("What's the use?")	I can make a difference; I am not helpless.

6. **What is the first step in neutralizing a hazardous attitude, and what strategies can pilots use to neutralize common hazardous attitudes?** (FAA-H-8083-25)

The first step in neutralizing a hazardous attitude is to recognize and acknowledge its presence. Awareness is crucial because it allows pilots to catch and address any negative thought patterns or tendencies that may compromise safety. By acknowledging the hazardous attitude, pilots can take appropriate actions to counteract it. The identification of a hazardous attitude is often facilitated by training and self-reflection.

The FAA has identified five hazardous attitudes that can affect pilot decision-making and safety: anti-authority, impulsivity, invulnerability, macho, and resignation. Once a hazardous attitude is recognized, pilots can utilize strategies to neutralize it:

(continued)

a. *Antidote application*—Each hazardous attitude has a corresponding antidote recommended by the FAA. For example, the antidote for impulsivity is "Not so fast, think first!" Pilots can mentally apply the antidote to counteract the negative mindset associated with the hazardous attitude.

b. *Thought replacement*—Replace negative or hazardous thoughts with positive and safe thoughts. Focus on the importance of following regulations, making rational decisions, and prioritizing safety over other considerations.

c. *Self-awareness and monitoring*—Continuously monitor thoughts, emotions, and attitudes during flight operations. Be vigilant for signs of hazardous attitudes and take immediate action to neutralize them when they arise.

d. *Seek input and support*—Engage with fellow pilots, instructors, or other aviation professionals to discuss and gain perspectives on hazardous attitudes. Seek input and support to reinforce safe decision-making and foster a positive safety culture.

By recognizing the presence of a hazardous attitude and taking proactive steps to counteract it, pilots can mitigate risks, make safer decisions, and enhance overall flight safety.

7. **Explain the risks associated with becoming fixated on a problem to the exclusion of other aspects of the flight.** (FAA-H-8083-2)

Becoming fixated on a problem to the exclusion of other aspects of the flight can introduce significant risks and compromise flight safety. Here are some of the risks associated with fixation:

a. *Loss of situational awareness*—Fixation on a single problem can cause pilots to lose sight of the broader situational awareness. By focusing solely on the issue at hand, they may neglect to monitor other critical factors such as navigation, weather changes, traffic, or system malfunctions that could contribute to an unsafe situation.

b. *Delayed decision-making*—Excessive fixation can lead to delayed decision-making. Pilots may spend an excessive amount of time trying to solve a particular problem, leading to a delay in taking necessary actions to address other evolving risks or emergencies.

c. *Tunnel vision*—Fixation can create tunnel vision, narrowing a pilot's field of attention and perception. They may overlook important cues or warning signs outside their immediate focus, increasing the likelihood of missing critical information or hazards.

d. *Ineffective problem-solving*—Focusing excessively on a single problem may limit a pilot's ability to consider alternative solutions or strategies. They may become locked into a single course of action, even if it proves ineffective or inappropriate given the circumstances.

e. *Neglected flight parameters*—Fixation can cause pilots to neglect important flight parameters such as altitude, airspeed, or fuel levels. Failure to monitor and adjust these parameters in a timely manner can result in a loss of control or fuel exhaustion.

To mitigate these risks, pilots should maintain a comprehensive situational awareness, regularly scan instruments and outside references, and allocate attention to multiple critical aspects of the flight. They should also prioritize effective decision-making, seeking assistance from other crew members or ATC if needed. By avoiding fixation and maintaining a well-rounded focus, pilots can better respond to changing conditions, manage risks, and ensure the overall safety of the flight.

E. Risk Management

1. Define the term *risk management*. (FAA-H-8083-9)

Risk management is a decision-making process designed to systematically identify hazards, assess the degree of risk, and determine the best course of action. It is a logical process of weighing the potential costs of risks against the possible benefits of allowing those risks to stand uncontrolled.

2. What is the definition of a *hazard*? (FAA-H-8083-2)

A hazard is a present condition, event, object, or circumstance that could lead to or contribute to an unplanned or undesired event such as an accident.

3. **What are several examples of aviation hazards?**
   (FAA-H-8083-2)
   a. A nick in the propeller blade.
   b. Improper refueling of an aircraft.
   c. Pilot fatigue.
   d. Use of unapproved hardware on aircraft.
   e. Weather.

4. **What is the definition of *risk*?** (FAA-H-8083-2)
   Risk is the future impact of a hazard that is not controlled or eliminated.

5. **How can the use of the PAVE checklist during flight planning help you to assess risk?** (FAA-H-8083-9)
   Use of the PAVE checklist provides pilots with a simple way to remember each category to examine for risk during flight planning. The pilot divides the risks of flight into four categories:

   Pilot-In-Command—general health, physical/mental/emotional state, proficiency, currency.

   Aircraft—airworthiness, equipment, performance capability.

   enVironment—weather hazards, terrain, airports/runways to be used, conditions.

   External pressures—meetings, people waiting at destination, desire to impress someone, etc.

6. **Explain the use of a personal minimums checklist and how it can help a pilot control risk.** (FAA-H-8083-9)
   One of the most important concepts that safe pilots understand is the difference between what is "legal" in terms of the regulations and what is "smart" or "safe" in terms of pilot experience and proficiency. One way a pilot can control the risks is to set personal minimums for items in each risk category. These are limits unique to that individual pilot's current level of experience and proficiency.

7. **What is one method you can use to identify risk before departure?** (FAA-H-8083-2)

One way a pilot can limit exposure to risks is to set personal minimums for items in each risk category. These are limits unique to that individual pilot's current level of experience and proficiency.

Pilot—experience/recency (takeoffs/landings, hours in make/model), physical/mental condition (IMSAFE).

Aircraft—fuel reserves, VFR day/night, aircraft performance (W&B, density altitude, etc.), aircraft equipment (avionics familiarity, charts, survival gear).

EnVironment—airport conditions (runway condition/length), weather (winds, ceilings, visibilities).

External pressures—allowance for delays, diversion, cancellation, alternate plans, personal equipment available for alternate plans (phone numbers, credit cards, medications).

8. **Explain the use of a personal checklist such as "I'M SAFE" to determine personal risks.** (FAA-H-8083-9)

Personal, self-assessment checklists assist pilots in conducting preflight checks on themselves, reviewing their physical and emotional states that could have an effect on their performance. The "I'M SAFE" checklist reminds pilots to consider the following:

Illness—Do I have any symptoms?

Medication—Have I been taking prescription or over-the-counter drugs?

Stress—Am I under psychological pressure from my job? Do I have money, family, or health problems?

Alcohol—Have I been drinking alcohol within 8 hours? Within 24 hours?

Fatigue—Am I tired and not adequately rested?

Emotions—Am I fully recovered from any extremely upsetting events?

9. **Describe how the 3P model can be used for practical risk management.** (FAA-H-8083-2)

The 3P model for risk management offers a simple, practical, and systematic approach that can be used during all phases of flight. To use it, pilots will:

Perceive the hazards for a flight, which are present events, objects, or circumstances that could contribute to an undesired future event. Think through circumstances related to the PAVE risk categories. The fundamental question to ask is, "what could hurt me, my passengers, or my aircraft?"

Process the hazards by evaluating their impact on flight safety. Think through the Consequences of each hazard, Alternatives available, Reality of the situation, and External pressures (CARE) that might influence their analysis.

Perform by implementing the best course of action. Transfer (Can the risk decision be transferred to someone else? Can you consult someone?); Eliminate (Is there a way to eliminate the hazard?); Accept (Do the benefits of accepting risk outweigh the costs?); Mitigate (What can you do to reduce the risk?) (TEAM)

10. **Explain how often a pilot should use the 3P model of ADM throughout a flight.** (FAA-H-8083-9)

Once a pilot has completed the 3P decision process and selected a course of action, the process begins again because the circumstances brought about by the course of action require analysis. The decision-making process is a continuous loop of perceiving, processing and performing.

11. **What is a risk assessment matrix?** (FAA-H-8083-2, FAA-H-8083-25)

A risk assessment matrix is a tool used to assess the likelihood of an event occurring and the severity or consequences of that event. The matrix assists a pilot in differentiating between low-, medium-, and high-risk flights.

12. What is a Flight Risk Assessment Tool (FRAT)?
(go.usa.gov/xkhJK)

A FRAT is a preflight planning tool that uses a series of questions in each of the major risk categories (PAVE) to help a pilot identify and quantify risk for a flight. The tool enables proactive hazard identification, is easy to use, and can visually depict risk. It is an invaluable tool in helping pilots make better go/no-go decisions and should be a part of every flight. A FRAT Fact Sheet is available at https://www.faa.gov/newsroom/safety-briefing/flight-risk-assessment-tools.

F. Task Management

1. Define the term *task management*. (FAA-H-8083-9)

Task management is the process by which pilots manage the many, concurrent tasks that must be performed to safely and efficiently operate an aircraft.

2. What are several factors that can reduce a pilot's ability to manage workload effectively? (FAA-H-8083-25)

Environmental conditions—Temperature and humidity extremes, noise, vibration, and lack of oxygen.

Physiological stress—Fatigue, lack of physical fitness, sleep loss, missed meals (leading to low blood sugar levels), and illness.

Psychological stress—Social or emotional factors, such as a death in the family, a divorce, a sick child, or a demotion at work. This type of stress may also be related to mental workload, such as analyzing a problem, navigating an aircraft, or making decisions.

3. What are several options that a pilot can employ to decrease workload and avoid becoming overloaded? (FAA-H-8083-25)

Stop, think, slow down, and prioritize. Tasks such as locating an item on a chart or setting a radio frequency may be delegated to another pilot or passenger; an autopilot, if available, may be used; or ATC may be enlisted to provide assistance.

4. What is one method of prioritizing tasks to avoid an overload situation? (FAA-H-8083-25)

During any situation, and especially in an emergency, remember the phrase "aviate, navigate, and communicate."

5. How can tasks be completed in a timely manner without causing a distraction from flying? (FAA-H-8083-9)

By planning, prioritizing, and sequencing tasks, a potential work overload situation can be avoided. As experience is gained, a pilot learns to recognize future workload requirements and can prepare for high workload periods during times of low workload.

6. What are two common methods of checklist usage? (drs.faa.gov)

a. *Do-Verify (DV) method*—consists of the checklist being accomplished in a variable sequence without a preliminary challenge. After all of the action items on the checklist have been completed, the checklist is then read again while each item is verified. The DV method allows the pilot/flight crew to use flow patterns from memory to accomplish a series of actions quickly and efficiently.

b. *Challenge-Do-Verify (CDV) method*—consists of a pilot/ crewmember making a challenge before an action is initiated, taking the action, and then verifying that the action item has been accomplished. The CDV method is most effective in two-pilot crews where one crewmember issues the challenge and the second crewmember takes the action and responds to the first crewmember, verifying that the action was taken.

7. What are several examples of common errors that can occur when using a checklist?

a. Checklist items are missed because of distraction or interruption (by passengers, ATC, etc.).

b. Checklist items are incorrectly performed (hurrying checklist; reading item but not verifying or setting).

c. Failure to use the appropriate checklist for a specific phase of flight.

d. Too much time is spent with head down, reading the checklist and compromising safety.

e. Checklist is not readily accessible in cockpit.

f. Emergency/abnormal procedures checklist is not readily available.

g. Memory items are accomplished but not confirmed with the checklist.

8. **What are several recommended methods for managing checklist accomplishment?** (drs.faa.gov)

a. The pilot should touch/point at each control, display or switch.

b. Verbally state the desired status of the checklist item.

c. When complete, announce that "_____ checklist is complete."

9. **What are immediate action items?** (drs.faa.gov)

An immediate action item is an action that must be accomplished so expeditiously (in order to avoid or stabilize a hazardous situation) that time is not available for the pilot/crewmember to refer to a manual or checklist. Once the emergency has been brought under control, the pilot refers to the actual checklist to verify that all immediate action items were accomplished. Only after this is done should the remainder of the checklist be completed.

Exam Tip: Demonstrate use the appropriate checklists throughout the test, especially while on the ground during preflight, before taxi, before takeoff and after landing. The evaluator will be watching for this. While inflight, in situations where use of a checklist would be unsafe or impractical, completion of the checklist items first and then a review of the appropriate checklist would be appropriate.

10. **Discuss the importance of understanding the procedure for the positive exchange of flight controls.** (FAA-H-8083-16)

On flights with more than one pilot in the cockpit, accidents occur due to a lack of communication or a misunderstanding as to who actually has control of the aircraft. When control of the aircraft is transferred between two pilots, it is important to acknowledge this exchange verbally. The pilot relinquishing control of the aircraft should state, "You have the flight controls." The pilot assuming

(continued)

control of the aircraft should state, "I have the flight controls," and then the pilot relinquishing control should restate, "You have the flight controls." Following these procedures reduces the possibility of confusion about who is flying the aircraft at any given time.

11. Explain how you will use the aircraft checklists during flight. Should you use the checklists in an emergency or just depend on your memory? (FAA-H-8083-25)

During flight, aircraft checklists are vital tools that help ensure safe and efficient operations. They serve as a systematic guide to performing critical tasks, procedures, and checks in a consistent and accurate manner. Pilots typically use checklists as described below.

Pre-flight—Prior to departure, pilots use pre-flight checklists to verify the aircraft's condition, systems, and equipment. This includes conducting a thorough inspection, confirming fuel quantity, checking control surfaces, verifying instrument functionality, and more. By following the checklist, pilots ensure that all necessary checks are completed before initiating flight.

Normal procedures—Throughout the flight, pilots refer to checklists to perform routine tasks and procedures. This includes pre-takeoff checks, climb and cruise checklists, approach and landing checklists, and other specific procedures as outlined in the aircraft's operating manual or standard operating procedures (SOPs). Using checklists helps maintain consistency and reduces the likelihood of overlooking critical items.

Abnormal and emergency procedures—In the event of abnormal or emergency situations, pilots rely heavily on emergency checklists. These checklists provide step-by-step instructions for addressing specific emergencies or abnormal conditions, such as engine failure, fire, electrical malfunctions, or loss of communication. Using checklists in emergencies helps pilots respond in a structured and efficient manner, ensuring appropriate actions are taken and critical steps are not missed.

It is essential to use checklists even in emergency situations. During emergencies, stress and time pressure can impair memory and judgment. Checklists provide a reliable and systematic approach to manage emergencies, helping pilots maintain focus and complete necessary actions accurately. Depending solely on memory in emergencies increases the risk of missing critical steps or making errors.

12. Once information flow exceeds a person's ability to mentally process and act on it, what two alternatives exist? (FAA-H-8083-9)

When information flow exceeds a person's ability to mentally process and act on it, two alternatives exist: prioritization and delegation.

Prioritization involves identifying and focusing on the most critical and immediate tasks or information while temporarily setting aside or filtering out non-essential elements. By prioritizing, individuals can allocate their mental resources effectively and address the most pressing issues first. This allows for a more manageable workload and ensures that the most important actions are taken promptly.

Delegation involves entrusting certain tasks or responsibilities to others who are capable and available to handle them. When faced with an overwhelming amount of information or tasks, individuals can delegate specific duties to qualified individuals or team members. Delegation enables a more efficient distribution of workload and ensures that tasks are completed by those best suited to handle them, thereby preventing cognitive overload and promoting effective decision-making.

Both prioritization and delegation help individuals cope with information overload and prevent mental saturation, which can lead to errors, stress, and impaired performance. By employing these strategies, individuals can better manage their workload, maintain situational awareness, and ensure that critical tasks are addressed in a timely manner.

G. Situational Awareness

1. **Define the term** *situational awareness.* (FAA-H-8083-25)

   Situational awareness (SA) is the accurate perception and understanding of all the factors and conditions within the four fundamental risk elements (PAVE) that affect safety before, during, and after the flight.

2. **What are some of the elements inside and outside the aircraft that a pilot must consider to maintain situational awareness?** (FAA-H-8083-9)

   Inside the aircraft—the status of aircraft systems, pilot, and passengers.

   Outside the aircraft—awareness of where the aircraft is in relation to terrain, traffic, weather, and airspace.

3. **What are several factors that reduce situational awareness?** (FAA-H-8083-15)

   Factors that reduce SA include fatigue, distractions, unusual or unexpected events, complacency, high workload, unfamiliar situations, and inoperative equipment.

4. **When flying a technically advanced aircraft (TAA), what are several procedures that help ensure that situational awareness is enhanced, not diminished, by the automation?** (FAA-H-8083-25)

   Two basic procedures are to always double-check the system and to use verbal callouts. At a minimum, ensure the presentation makes sense. Was the correct destination fed into the navigation system? Callouts, even for single-pilot operations, are an excellent way to maintain situational awareness as well as manage information.

5. **What additional procedures can be used for maintaining situational awareness in technically advanced aircraft?** (FAA-H-8083-25)

   a. Perform verification checks of all programming prior to departure.

   b. Check the flight routing—ensure all routing matches the planned route of flight.

c. Always verify waypoints.

d. Make use of all onboard navigation equipment—use VOR to backup GPS, and vice versa.

e. Match the use of the automated system with pilot proficiency—stay within personal limitations.

f. Plan a realistic flight route to maintain situational awareness—ATC doesn't always give you direct routing.

g. Be ready to verify computer data entries—incorrect keystrokes can lead to loss of situational awareness.

H. CFIT Awareness

1. A majority of controlled flight into terrain (CFIT) accidents have been attributed to what factors? (AC 61-134)

a. Lack of pilot currency.

b. Loss of situational awareness.

c. Pilot distractions and breakdown of SRM.

d. Failure to comply with minimum safe altitudes.

e. Breakdown in effective ADM.

f. Insufficient planning, especially for the descent and arrival segments.

2. A pilot can decrease the likelihood of a CFIT accident at the destination by identifying what risk factors prior to flight? (FAA-H-8083-16)

Factors such as airport location, runway lighting, weather/ daylight conditions, approach specifications, ATC capabilities and limitations, type of operation, departure procedures, controller/ pilot phraseology, and crew configuration should all be considered prior to flight.

3. **Describe several operational techniques that will help you avoid a CFIT accident.** (AC 61-134)

   a. Maintain situational awareness at all times.

   b. Adhere to safe takeoff and departure procedures.

   c. Familiarize yourself with surrounding terrain features and obstacles.

   d. Adhere to published routes and minimum altitudes.

   e. Fly a stabilized approach.

   f. Understand ATC clearances and instructions.

   g. Don't become complacent.

4. **What is the sterile cockpit rule and how can adherence to this rule prevent CFIT accidents?** (FAA-H-8083-9)

   Commonly known as the sterile cockpit rule, 14 CFR §121.542 (and §135.100) require flight crewmembers to refrain from nonessential activities (eating, chatting, reading a newspaper, etc.) during critical phases of flight. Critical phases of flight are all ground operations involving taxi; takeoff and landing; and all other flight operations below 10,000 feet, except cruise flight. A series of accidents caused by flight crews who were distracted from their flight duties during critical phases of flight caused the FAA to propose the rule. While the regulation grew out of accidents in the airline industry, it holds true for the entire aviation community. Pilots can improve flight safety significantly by reducing distractions during critical phases of flight.

I. Automation Management

1. **What does the term *automation management* refer to?** (FAA-H-8083-9)

   Automation management is the demonstrated ability to control and navigate an aircraft by means of the automated systems installed in the aircraft. It includes understanding whether and when to use automated systems, including, but not limited to, the GPS and the autopilot.

   Exam Tip: To assist in management of the aircraft during the practical test, the applicant is expected to demonstrate automation management skills by utilizing installed, available, or airborne equipment such as autopilot, avionics and systems displays, and/or the flight management system (FMS). The evaluator is expected to test the applicant's knowledge of the systems that are installed and operative during both the oral and flight portions of the practical test.

2. **In what three areas must a pilot be proficient when using advanced avionics or any automated system?** (FAA-H-8083-25)

The pilot must know what to expect, how to monitor the system for proper operation, and be prepared to promptly take appropriate action if the system does not perform as expected.

3. **What is the most important aspect of managing an autopilot/FMS?** (FAA-H-8083-9)

Knowing at all times which modes are engaged, which modes are armed to engage, and being capable of verifying that armed functions (e.g., navigation tracking or altitude capture) engage at the appropriate time.

4. **At a minimum, the pilot flying with advanced avionics must know how to manage what three primary items?** (FAA-H-8083-25)

The course deviation indicator (CDI), the navigation source, and the autopilot.

5. **Explain what is meant by the term *automation bias* and discuss how it can increase risk.** (FAA-H-8083-2)

Automation bias is the relative willingness of a pilot to trust and use automated systems. By failing to monitor the systems and failing to check the results of the processes of those systems, the pilot becomes increasingly detached from aircraft operation, which significantly increases risk.

6. **Automation management is a good place to practice the standard callout procedures. What are standard callouts?** (FAA-H-8083-16)

To assist in maintaining situational awareness, professional flight crews often use standard callouts. For example, the non-flying pilot may call 2,000 and 1,000 feet prior to reaching an assigned altitude. The callout may be "two to go" and "one to go." Single-pilot operations can also benefit from this practice by adopting standard, set callouts that can be used in the different segments of a flight. Examples of standard callouts are: "Power set"; "airspeed alive"; "rotate"; "positive rate—gear up"; "localizer alive"; "glideslope alive"; "nav source verified"; "approach mode armed"; "approach mode active"; "final approach fix"; etc.

Commercial
Flight
Maneuvers

Exam Tip: Remember to always perform clearing turns prior to beginning any flight maneuver.

A. Steep Turns

1. What is a steep turn? (FAA-H-8083-3)

Steep turns are those resulting from a degree of bank (more than approximately 45°) at which the overbanking tendency of an airplane overcomes stability, and the bank tends to increase unless pressure is applied to the aileron controls to prevent it. Maximum turning performance is attained and relatively high load factors are imposed.

2. What is the desired bank angle in a steep turn? (FAA-S-ACS-7)

A bank angle of at least 50° (±5°) is desired.

3. What is the recommended entry speed for a steep turn? (FAA-S-ACS-7)

Establish the manufacturer's recommended airspeed or if one is not stated, a safe airspeed not to exceed V_A.

4. How do you maintain altitude in a steep turn? (FAA-H-8083-3)

To maintain bank angle and altitude, as well as orientation, requires an awareness of the relative position of the horizon to the nose and the wings. If the altitude begins to increase or decrease, changing elevator back pressure can be used to alter the altitude; however, a more effective method is a slight increase or decrease in bank angle to control small altitude deviations. If the altitude is decreasing, reducing the bank angle a few degrees helps recover or stop the altitude loss trend; if the altitude is increasing, increasing the bank angle a few degrees will help recover or stop the altitude increase trend.

5. What are the altitude, airspeed, bank, and heading tolerances for a steep turn? (FAA-S-ACS-7)

Maintain the entry altitude, ±100 feet, airspeed, ±10 knots, bank, ±5°; and roll out on the entry heading, ±10°.

6. **Why does the airplane have a tendency to overbank in a steep turn?** (FAA-H-8083-3)

An airplane has a tendency to overbank in a steep turn due to the interaction between the lift and the banking angle. When an airplane is banked into a turn, the wing generates both vertical lift (to support the weight of the aircraft) and horizontal lift (to change the aircraft's direction). As the bank angle increases, the vertical component of lift decreases while the horizontal component increases. This means that the total lift available to counteract the aircraft's weight is reduced, which can lead to a decrease in altitude if not compensated for.

To maintain a constant altitude in a turn, the pilot needs to increase the back pressure on the elevator to increase the angle of attack and the lift generated by the wings. Failure to apply sufficient back pressure can result in a loss of altitude or a descent. This increased back pressure is required because the vertical component of lift is reduced in the steeply banked turn.

If the pilot does not adequately compensate for the reduced vertical lift, the aircraft can overbank, meaning the bank angle increases beyond the desired or intended angle. This can lead to a steeper turn, increased load factor on the aircraft, and potentially exceeding the aircraft's structural limits. To prevent overbanking, pilots need to be aware of the aircraft's bank angle and make the necessary control inputs to maintain the desired bank angle and altitude. Proper coordination of aileron, elevator, and rudder controls is crucial to ensure a coordinated and controlled turn without overbanking.

7. **What effect will a steep turn have on an airplane's stall speed and load factor? Why?** (FAA-H-8083-3)

A steep turn in an airplane will have the following effects on stall speed and load factor:

Stall speed—The stall speed of an airplane increases in a steep turn. As the bank angle increases, the load factor on the wings also increases. The load factor is the ratio of the lift being generated to the aircraft's weight. In a coordinated level turn, the load factor increases with the square of the bank angle. Since stall speed is directly proportional to the square root of the load factor, an increased load factor results in a higher stall speed. Therefore, the airplane will need a higher airspeed to maintain sufficient lift and avoid stalling during a steep turn.

Load factor—In a steep turn, the load factor on the airplane increases. The load factor is the additional force experienced by the aircraft's structure and occupants due to the change in direction and the resulting centrifugal force. In a coordinated level turn, the load factor is equal to the reciprocal of the cosine of the bank angle. For example, in a 60-degree bank angle, the load factor is 2, meaning the total load on the aircraft is twice its weight. Higher load factors increase the stress on the wings, control surfaces, and airframe. Therefore, the structural integrity of the aircraft must be considered when performing steep turns to avoid exceeding the maximum design load limits.

B. Chandelles

1. What is a chandelle? (FAA-H-8083-3)

A chandelle is a maximum performance climbing turn beginning from approximately straight-and-level flight, and ending at the completion of 180° of turn in a wings-level, nose-high attitude at the minimum controllable airspeed.

2. What altitude and airspeed will you use when entering a chandelle? (FAA-H-8083-3)

The specific altitude and airspeed to use when entering a chandelle maneuver may vary depending on factors such as the aircraft type, weight, and performance capabilities, but the altitude must be no lower than 1,500 feet AGL.

Altitude—When entering a chandelle, it is typically recommended to begin the maneuver from a safe altitude that provides an adequate margin above the minimum safe altitude for the area. The altitude chosen should also consider any applicable airspace restrictions and local regulations. A typical altitude range for entering a chandelle might be between 1,500 to 3,000 feet AGL, depending on the situation and airspace considerations.

Airspeed—The recommended airspeed for entering a chandelle is usually based on the aircraft's maneuvering speed (V_A), which is the maximum speed at which full deflection of the flight controls can be applied without exceeding the aircraft's design limitations. It provides a safety margin against structural stress during aggressive maneuvers. Pilots should maintain a speed close to or slightly above maneuvering speed to ensure proper control authority and structural integrity during the maneuver.

3. **In a chandelle, constant bank and changing pitch occur in what part of the maneuver?** (FAA-H-8083-3)

   The first 90° of turn require a constant 30° of bank and a gradual and constant change in pitch attitude.

4. **In a chandelle, constant pitch and changing bank occur in what part of the maneuver?** (FAA-H-8083-3)

   The last 90° of turn requires a very gradual change in bank from 30° to 0° and a constant pitch attitude so as to arrive at minimum airspeed as the airplane is rolled out to a wings-level attitude.

5. **What is the maximum amount of bank in the chandelle?** (FAA-S-ACS-7)

   30° of bank.

6. **What should your speed be upon completion of the chandelle?** (FAA-S-ACS-7)

   You should begin a coordinated constant-rate rollout from the 90° point to the 180° point, ±10° just above a stall airspeed, and maintaining that airspeed momentarily avoiding a stall.

7. **At what two points will your wings be level in a chandelle?** (FAA-S-ACS-7)

   Immediately before entering the chandelle and upon rollout at the 180° point.

8. **Discuss the potential outcome of the chandelle maneuver if you use too much pitch initially.**
   (FAA-H-8083-3)

   Pitching too much initially in a chandelle maneuver can have several effects on the outcome:

   a. *Altitude loss*—Pitching too much initially can result in a significant altitude loss during the maneuver. The chandelle is a climbing maneuver where the aircraft rolls into a bank and simultaneously pitches up to maintain a constant rate of climb while executing a 180-degree change in heading. If the initial pitch is too aggressive, it can cause a rapid climb rate, leading to excessive drag and increased deceleration. This can result in a loss of altitude during the maneuver, making it difficult to achieve the desired altitude at the completion of the chandelle.

   b. *Airspeed decay*—Excessive initial pitching can cause the aircraft's airspeed to decay. The chandelle maneuver requires maintaining a constant rate of climb while rolling into the bank. If the pitch is too aggressive, it can cause the aircraft to slow down and potentially approach the stall speed. This can lead to a loss of control, reduced maneuverability, and compromised safety.

   c. *Difficulty in maneuver execution*—Over-pitching initially can make it challenging to smoothly transition into the bank and maintain the correct coordination of controls throughout the maneuver. It can result in an unstable flight condition, requiring excessive control inputs to correct the aircraft's attitude and heading.

   To execute a chandelle maneuver successfully, it is important to apply smooth and coordinated control inputs. Gradual pitching allows for a controlled climb, maintaining airspeed and minimizing altitude loss.

C. Lazy Eights

1. What is a lazy eight? (FAA-H-8083-3)

A lazy eight consists of two 180° turns, in opposite directions, while making a climb and a descent in a symmetrical pattern during each of the turns.

2. What procedures are recommended prior to beginning a lazy-eight maneuver? (FAA-H-8083-3)

Prior to performing a lazy eight, the airspace behind and above should be clear of other air traffic. The maneuver should be entered from straight-and-level flight at normal cruise power and at the airspeed recommended by the manufacturer or at the airplane's design maneuvering speed.

3. Where should the highest pitch attitude occur in a lazy eight? (FAA-H-8083-3)

At the 45° point the pitch attitude should be at a maximum and the angle of bank continuing to increase. Also, at the 45° point, the pitch attitude should start to decrease slowly toward the horizon at the 90° reference point.

4. Where should the lowest nose-down attitude occur in a lazy eight? (FAA-H-8083-3)

When the airplane has turned 135°, the nose should be at its lowest pitch attitude.

5. What are the altitude, airspeed and heading tolerances allowed when performing a lazy eight? (FAA-S-ACS-7)

You should achieve the following throughout the maneuver:

a. Approximately 30° bank at the steepest point.

b. Constant change of pitch, roll rate, and airspeed.

c. Altitude tolerance at 180° points, ±100 feet (30 meters) from entry altitude.

d. Airspeed tolerance at the 180° point, ±10° knots from entry airspeed.

e. Heading tolerance at the 180° point, ±10°.

6. To summarize, describe the appropriate values to be obtained in a lazy eight at the entry, 45-, 90-, 135- and 180-degree points. (FAA-H-8083-3)

Entry:
- Level flight
- Maneuvering or cruise speed (whichever is less) or manufacturer's recommended speed

45° point:
- Maximum pitch-up attitude
- Bank angle at 15°

90° point:
- Bank angle approximately 30°
- Minimum airspeed
- Maximum altitude
- Level pitch attitude

135° point:
- Maximum pitch-down attitude
- Bank approximately 15°

180° point:
- Level flight
- Original heading (±10°)
- Entry airspeed (±10 knots)
- Entry altitude (±100 feet)

7. When entering a lazy eight, will you establish the bank first, pitch first, or both at the same time? (FAA-H-8083-3)

When entering a lazy eight maneuver, the general technique is to establish the bank angle first before making any significant changes in pitch. The sequence typically involves the following steps:

a. *Establish the bank*—Begin by smoothly rolling into the desired bank angle. The bank angle chosen should be appropriate for the maneuver and consider factors such as aircraft type, weight, and performance capabilities. The roll should be initiated smoothly and progressively to the desired bank angle.

b. *Coordinate the controls*—As the bank is established, coordinate the controls by applying rudder input to maintain coordination throughout the maneuver. Proper coordination helps prevent sideslip and ensures the aircraft maintains a coordinated turn.

c. *Manage the pitch*—Once the desired bank angle is achieved, make slight and gradual adjustments in pitch to smoothly transition from level flight to the climbing and descending phases of the lazy eight. Pitch inputs are typically used to control the altitude changes and maintain a consistent altitude during each half of the maneuver.

While bank is established first and pitch adjustments follow, it is important to note that the entire maneuver should be flown smoothly and without abrupt control inputs. Pilots should maintain a coordinated and controlled flight throughout the lazy eight, ensuring that changes in bank and pitch are gradual and coordinated.

8. **Discuss the reference point selection for the lazy eight maneuver.** (FAA-H-8083-3)

In the lazy eight maneuver, selecting appropriate reference points is crucial for maintaining precise control and executing the maneuver accurately. Reference points serve as visual cues to help pilots maintain consistent bank angles, pitch attitudes, and coordination throughout the maneuver. Here are some considerations for reference point selection in the lazy eight:

a. *Horizon line*—The horizon line can serve as a primary reference point for maintaining a level pitch attitude during the straight and level portions of the maneuver. By aligning the aircraft's nose with the horizon, pilots can ensure a consistent pitch attitude and avoid unintentional climbs or descents.

b. *Wingtip reference*—Using a wingtip as a reference point can assist in maintaining a constant bank angle throughout the maneuver. Pilots can visually align the wingtip with specific points on the horizon or other external references to ensure consistent bank angles on both sides of the maneuver.

c. *Leading edge of the wing*—The leading edge of the wing can also serve as a reference point for maintaining consistent bank angles. By visually aligning the leading edge with external references, pilots can monitor the bank angle and make necessary adjustments to ensure symmetry and accuracy in the maneuver.

(continued)

d. *Ground references*—Selecting fixed ground references, such as landmarks or points on the ground, can help pilots maintain the desired size and shape of the lazy eight. By referencing these fixed points, pilots can ensure that the maneuver is performed within a defined area and avoid unintentional deviations or drift.

Note: The selection of reference points may vary based on individual pilot preference, aircraft type, and environmental conditions. Pilots should practice and refine their reference point selection through training and experience to achieve consistent and precise execution of the lazy eight maneuver.

9. **When performing a lazy eight, why is more right rudder required in the right turn than in the left turn?** (FAA-H-8083-3)

In a lazy eight maneuver, more right rudder is typically required in the right turn than in the left turn due to several factors related to the aircraft's design and the forces acting on it during the maneuver.

a. *P-factor*—P-factor, also known as propeller factor, is a phenomenon that affects an aircraft's yawing motion during different angles of attack. In the lazy eight maneuver, as the aircraft rolls into a right turn, the descending blade of the propeller (right side) generates more thrust compared to the ascending blade (left side). This creates an imbalance in thrust, causing a left yawing moment. To counteract this yawing motion and maintain coordinated flight, additional right rudder input is required.

b. *Gyroscopic precession*—This is another factor that influences the yawing motion during a turn. When the aircraft pitches up or down (as it does during the lazy eight), the spinning propeller acts like a gyroscope and generates a force that is felt 90 degrees later in the direction of the rotation. In the case of a right turn, the gyroscopic precession produces a yawing moment to the right, necessitating increased right rudder input to maintain coordination.

c. *Slipstream effect*—The slipstream or propeller wash airflow created by the rotating propeller affects the airflow over the aircraft's vertical stabilizer (rudder). The slipstream tends to push the tail of the aircraft to the left, requiring more right rudder input to counteract this leftward force and maintain coordinated flight.

Overall, these factors contribute to the need for increased right rudder input during a right turn in a lazy eight maneuver.

D. Eights-On-Pylons

1. What are eights-on-pylons? (FAA-H-8083-3)

Eights-on-pylons is a training maneuver that involves flying the airplane in circular paths, alternately left and right, in the form of a figure-8 around two selected points or pylons on the ground. No attempt is made to maintain a uniform distance from the pylon. Instead, the airplane is flown at such an altitude and airspeed that a line parallel to the airplane's lateral axis, and extending from the pilot's eye appears to pivot on each of the pylons.

2. How do you determine pivotal altitude for eights-on-pylons? (FAA-H-8083-3)

A rule of thumb for estimating pivotal altitude using true airspeed in no-wind conditions, or ground speed when the wind is blowing, is to square the speed and divide by 15 for miles per hour or 11.3 for knots.

3. Does the pivotal altitude change in eights-on-pylons? (FAA-H-8083-3)

Yes, the pivotal altitude is critical and will change with variations in ground speed. Since the headings throughout the turns continually vary from directly downwind to directly upwind, the ground speed will constantly change. This will result in the proper pivotal altitude varying slightly throughout the eight. Therefore, adjustment must be made for this by climbing and descending as necessary to hold the reference line or point on the pylons. This change in altitude will be dependent on how much the wind affects the ground speed.

Remember:
Ground speed goes UP, pivotal altitude goes UP.
Ground speed goes DOWN, pivotal altitude goes DOWN.

4. How far should one pylon be from the other pylon in eights-on-pylons? (FAA-S-ACS-7)

They should be of sufficient distance apart to permit straight-and-level flight between pylons.

5. At the steepest point, the bank angle in an eights-on-pylon maneuver should be what value? (FAA-S-ACS-7)

Establish the correct bank angle for the conditions, not to exceed 40°.

6. Where is the highest pivotal altitude likely to occur in eights-on-pylons? (FAA-H-8083-3)

As the airplane turns downwind the ground speed increases; consequently the pivotal altitude is higher and the airplane must climb to hold the reference line on the pylon.

7. Where is the lowest pivotal altitude likely to occur in eights-on-pylons? (FAA-H-8083-3)

As the airplane heads into the wind, the ground speed decreases; consequently the pivotal altitude is lower and the airplane must descend to hold the reference line on the pylon.

8. What action should you take if your wing reference point appears to move ahead of the pylon? Move behind the pylon? (FAA-H-8083-3)

If the reference line appears to move ahead of the pylon, the pilot should increase altitude. If the reference line appears to move behind the pylon, the pilot should decrease altitude. Varying rudder pressure to yaw the airplane and force the wing and reference line forward or backward to the pylon is a dangerous technique and must not be attempted.

9. When performing an eights-on-pylon maneuver, where will the steepest angle of bank occur? (FAA-H-8083-3)

In the eights-on-pylon maneuver, the steepest angle of bank occurs at the midpoint of each half-loop or figure-eight pattern around the pylons. This is when the aircraft transitions from the climbing portion to the descending portion of the maneuver.

During the maneuver, the aircraft follows a path around two pylons in a figure-eight pattern. As the aircraft approaches each pylon, it enters a climbing turn while maintaining a constant radius around the pylon. As the aircraft reaches the midpoint between the two pylons, it reaches the steepest angle of bank. At this point, the aircraft is transitioning from the climbing turn to the descending turn. The steepest angle of bank occurs as the aircraft changes its direction and begins to descend towards the other pylon. The pilot needs to maintain a consistent bank angle while adjusting the pitch and power to maintain the desired altitude and airspeed throughout the maneuver.

10. **Will the pivotal altitude change when changing the angle of bank in an eights-on-pylon maneuver?** (FAA-H-8083-3)

The pivotal altitude in an eights-on-pylon maneuver does not change when adjusting the angle of bank. The pivotal altitude remains constant throughout the maneuver. The pivotal altitude is the altitude at which, for a given ground speed, the projection of the visual reference line to the pylon appears to pivot. The pivotal altitude does not vary with the angle of bank unless the bank is steep enough to affect the ground speed.

When changing the angle of bank during the eights-on-pylon maneuver, the pilot must adjust the pitch and power to maintain the desired altitude and airspeed while keeping the pivotal altitude constant. The bank angle adjustment should be made smoothly and gradually to avoid abrupt changes in the aircraft's flight path.

11. **What initial altitude and airspeed will you use when entering an eights-on-pylon maneuver?** (FAA-H-8083-3)

The specific initial altitude and airspeed to use when entering an eights-on-pylon maneuver may vary depending on factors such as the aircraft type, weight, performance capabilities, and maneuvering speed. When entering an eights-on-pylon maneuver, it is typically recommended to begin from a safe altitude that provides an adequate margin above the minimum safe altitude for the area. Pivotal altitude can be computed in reference to an aircraft's maneuvering speed that will be used.

The pivotal altitude in an eights-on-pylon maneuver can be calculated using the formula:

(continued)

$$Pivotal\ altitude = \frac{(ground\ speed)^2}{11.3 \times tangent(bank\ angle)}$$

Where:

Ground speed is the speed of the aircraft over the ground, typically measured in knots.

Bank angle is the angle of bank used during the maneuver, typically measured in degrees.

To calculate the pivotal altitude, follow these steps:

a. Determine the ground speed of the aircraft. This can be obtained from the aircraft's instruments or GPS.

b. Determine the bank angle that will be used during the eights-on-pylon maneuver. The bank angle is typically set according to the desired turn radius and maneuver precision.

c. Convert the bank angle from degrees to radians if necessary. This can be done by multiplying the bank angle by ($\pi \div 180$).

d. Apply the values to the formula shown above:

  • Calculate the tangent of the bank angle (in radians).

  • Divide the ground speed squared by the product of 11.3 and the tangent of the bank angle.

E. Power-Off 180° Accuracy Approach and Landing

1. What is a power-off 180° accuracy approach and landing? (FAA-H-8083-3)

Power-off accuracy approaches and landings are made by gliding, with the engine idling, from a specific point on downwind to touchdown, in a normal landing attitude at or within 200 feet beyond the specified touchdown point.

2. State the objective of learning a power-off 180° accuracy approach and landing. (FAA-H-8083-3)

The objective is to instill the judgment and procedures necessary for accurately flying the airplane, without power, to a safe landing. The ability to estimate the distance an airplane will glide and maintain the proper glide path while maneuvering the airplane is the real basis of all power-off accuracy approaches and landings.

3. **What are the standards expected of a student when executing this type of approach and landing?** (FAA-S-ACS-7)

   a. Complete the appropriate checklist.

   b. Make radio calls as appropriate.

   c. Plan and follow a flightpath to the selected landing area taking into consideration altitude, wind, terrain, and obstructions.

   d. Select the most suitable touchdown point based on wind, landing surface, obstructions, and aircraft limitations.

   e. Position airplane on downwind leg, parallel to landing runway.

   f. Correctly configure the airplane.

   g. As necessary, correlate crosswind with direction of forward slip and transition to side slip for landing.

   h. Touch down at a proper pitch attitude within 200 feet beyond, or on the specified point, with no side drift, and with the airplane's longitudinal axis aligned with and over the runway centerline or landing path, as applicable.

4. **Can I go around on a power-off 180° landing and try it again?**

   In a July 5, 2022, response from AFS-810,[1] the FAA responded to the Airman Testing Standards Group indicating the following:

   1. If the applicant chooses to go around on the Power-Off 180° Accuracy Approach and Landing, is that ALWAYS unsatisfactory? *Answer:* No. However, the intent of the evaluation is for the applicant to successfully complete the 180 degree accuracy landing on the first attempt. If the applicant were to execute a [go-around/rejected landing] without a risk mitigation justification (such as a deer on the runway or some other reason making the landing area unsafe), the applicant would normally be disqualified for that landing task.

   2. If no, under what conditions (or in what situations) is a go-around allowed? *Answer:* Executing a go-around during training or during a practical test is necessary, if conducting the 180 degree power-off approach and landing maneuver will create an unsafe condition. During practice, the pilot gets

   ---
   1. https://dperesources.com/wp-content/uploads/2022/10/180-degree-landing-response_July-2022.pdf.

better at judging the landing spot and how to deal with various conditions and go-arounds can and should occur during that practice. However, executing a go-around during the practical test (when not caused by issues outside of the control of the pilot) indicates the pilot does not have the skill or proficiency to complete the maneuver successfully, and should be disqualified.

F. Steep Spirals

1. What is a steep spiral? (FAA-H-8083-3)

A steep spiral is nothing more than a constant gliding turn, during which a constant radius around a point on the ground is maintained similar to the turns around a point maneuver. The radius should be such that the steepest bank will not exceed 60°.

2. What is the objective of a steep spiral? (FAA-H-8083-3)

The objective of this maneuver is to improve pilot techniques for airspeed control, wind drift control, planning, orientation, and division of attention. The steep spiral is not only a valuable flight training maneuver, but has practical application by providing a procedure for dissipating altitude while remaining over a selected spot in preparation for landing, especially for emergency forced landings.

3. During the steep spiral, how will you maintain a turn of constant radius around the selected spot on the ground? (FAA-H-8083-3)

Maintaining a constant radius during the maneuver will require correction for wind drift by steepening the bank on downwind headings and shallowing the bank on upwind headings. During the descending spiral, the pilot must judge the direction and speed of the wind at different altitudes and make appropriate changes in the angle of bank to maintain a uniform radius.

4. What standards must you maintain when executing a steep spiral? (FAA-S-ACS-7)

Start at an altitude that will allow a series of three 360°-turns. Maintain the specified airspeed ±10 knots, roll out toward object or specified heading ±10°, and do not exceed 60° of bank while applying wind drift correction to track a constant radius circle around a defined reference point.

G. Accelerated Stalls

1. What is an accelerated stall? (FAA-H-8083-3)

Accelerated stalls are stalls that occur at higher indicated airspeeds and/or lower than anticipated pitch attitudes as a result of excessive loads being suddenly imposed on an aircraft during improperly executed steep turns, stall and spin recoveries, and pull-ups from steep dives.

2. What is the objective of performing an accelerated stall? (FAA-H-8083-3)

The objective of demonstrating accelerated stalls is not to develop competency in setting up the stall, but rather to learn how they may occur and to develop the ability to recognize such stalls immediately, and to take prompt, effective recovery action.

3. If an airplane is skidding towards the outside of a steep turn, which wing will stall first? (FAA-H-8083-3)

It will have a tendency to roll to the inside of the turn because the inside wing stalls first.

4. What standards must you maintain when executing an accelerated stall? (FAA-S-ACS-7)

a. Clear the area.

b. Select an entry altitude that will allow the task to be completed no lower than 3,000 feet AGL.

c. Establish the configuration as specified by the evaluator.

d. Set power appropriate for the configuration, such that the airspeed does not exceed V_A or any other applicable POH/AFM limitation.

e. Establish and maintain a coordinated turn in a 45° bank, increasing elevator back pressure smoothly and firmly until an impending stall is reached.

f. Acknowledge the cues and recover promptly at the first indication of an impending stall (e.g., aircraft buffet, stall horn, etc.).

g. Execute a stall recovery in accordance with procedures set forth in the POH/AFM.

(continued)

h. Configure the airplane as recommended by the manufacturer, and accelerate to V_X or V_Y.

i. Return to the altitude, heading, and airspeed specified by the evaluator.

H. Emergency Descent

1. What is an emergency descent? (FAA-H-8083-3)

In general, emergency descent procedures are high drag, high airspeed procedures requiring a specific airplane configuration (such as power to idle, propellers forward, landing gear extended, and flaps retracted), and a specific emergency descent airspeed. Emergency descent maneuvers often include turns. The need for this maneuver may result from an uncontrollable fire, a sudden loss of cabin pressurization, or any other situation demanding an immediate and rapid descent.

2. What is the objective of performing an emergency descent? (FAA-H-8083-3, FAA-S-ACS-7)

The purpose in the ACS of an emergency descent is to determine that the applicant exhibits satisfactory knowledge, skills, and risk management associated with an emergency descent.

3. While conducting an emergency descent, it's recommended that a pilot initiate what maneuver? (FAA-H-8083-3, FAA-S-ACS-7)

When initiating an emergency descent, a pilot should use bank angle between 30° and 45° to maintain positive load factors during the descent.

Scenario-Based Training

10

by Arlynn McMahon

Introduction

During the oral portion of the Commercial Practical Exam, expect questions to include scenarios focused on typical jobs and flight assignments that new commercial pilots are normally hired for. These may include (as a few examples) banner towing, parachute operations, passenger sightseeing flights, and cargo flights. The examiner/inspector will expect you to be able to anticipate flight handling characteristics of an aircraft you have not flown before, based on your understanding of systems and aerodynamics.

Scenario-based questions often have more than one correct answer. Be certain that your answers include the content identified as the "must" items listed in the answers below. Additionally, be generous in showing the examiner your aeronautical decision making by examining the elements and sharing your thought process aloud.

As a commercial pilot and a professional, the FAA, the industry, and your future passengers expect you to take a larger view of things. You must see the "big picture" in addition to the details. In answering oral exam questions, you must look for and recognize the underlying elements presented by the scenarios. Be prepared to include risk management aspects in your answer whenever possible.

Scenario-Based Questions

1. **How will you determine if your flight is for compensation or hire?**

   Your answer must delve into the legalities of commercial pilot privileges. This requires you to understand several legal terms. Your answer must include:

   A flight is for compensation or hire if:

   * There is not a common purpose. Common purpose is defined as the pilot and passengers each having a reason to fly to a particular destination.

   AND

   * I am exercising "operational control"—that is, I am the one making the go/no-go decision, and decisions to revise or terminate the flight.

   OR

   * There is compensation or reimbursement in excess of my pro-rata share.

     1. Compensation is commonly thought of as money or other exchange of services. However, no money and no profit are required in the FAA's definition of compensation. The FAA considers free flight time as pilot compensation.

     2. Pro Rata is each person's evenly divided share of the flight. If the flight includes the pilot and two passengers, the pilot must also pay ⅓ the cost of the flight.

2. **Your flight assignment is a commercial sightseeing flight for two passengers. Your flight will be around the city and last about 30 minutes. What requirements must you meet to be PIC on this flight for hire?**

   Your answer must include the required pilot currency items and drug-testing requirements.

   To be the PIC for this flight, I must meet the normal pilot currency requirements:

   * A flight review completed within the last 24 calendar months.

   * A current Second Class Medical Certificate.

   * Three takeoffs and landings performed within the previous 90 days.

   (continued)

Drug testing is required for pilots of any passenger-carrying flight for compensation or hire. To meet this requirement, I must:

- Be enrolled in an FAA-approved anti-drug program either as an independent pilot or as part of my employer's program.
- Have passed a drug test within that program.
- Keep a copy of the drug test results for my files.

3. **During preflight of your single-engine aircraft you find that the carminix is inoperative. What must you do to legally fly the aircraft with inoperative equipment?**

"What is a carminix?" you ask. It doesn't matter, so don't let that bother you. Your thought process should be the same, and make sure your answer demonstrates your thought process.

If the aircraft has an approved MEL, then I would follow the procedures outlined. If the aircraft does not have an MEL, then to fly with the carminix inoperative, the following conditions must be met:

- Is it on the list of required equipment (ATOMATOEFLAMES)? If no, then
- Is it required for the type certificate? If no, then
- Is it required on the kinds of operation list? If no, then
- Is it required by an AD? If no, then
- Do I feel that I can fly safely without it? If yes, then I would:
  1. Deactivate and placard it.
  2. Have it removed and update the weight and balance data.

4. **Your assignment is a solo flight to reposition the aircraft to the company's maintenance base at Tiny City Airport, 25 NM away, for a 100-hour inspection. You will overfly the 100-hour inspection during the reposition for maintenance. Does this concern you in any way?**

Your answer must demonstrate your knowledge of 100-hour inspections and when they are due as well as an understanding of airworthiness directives.

- This is not a flight for compensation or hire; therefore, having this flight within the 100-hour inspection is not required.
- The hours flown beyond this 100-hour interval will affect future flights as the hours-over will be deducted from the next 100-hour due time.

- I am concerned about possible reoccurring airworthiness directives, as many ADs come due "coinciding with the next regularly scheduled inspection." I would research the possibility of an applicable reoccurring AD and if one exists, this flight will require a special flight permit. The 10-hour grace period for the 100-hour inspection does not apply to the AD.

5. **The company's maintenance base Is at Tiny City Airport, 25 NM away. Your assignment is a solo reposition flight to Tiny City to have an inoperative landing light fixed. Your landing is expected to be at sunset. NOTAMS indicate that runway lights are out. It is an asphalt runway. What are your thoughts about this flight?**

Your answer must demonstrate your understanding of requirements for flight with inoperative equipment. This question is also testing your ability to recognize possible risk factors. You should show your thought process by identifying these risk factors and possible steps you could take to mitigate them, and discussing your tolerance for handling multiple simultaneous risk factors.

I would have to meet the requirements for flight with inoperative equipment (such as disconnecting and placarding of the inoperative equipment).

This flight presents a number of risk factors, including the external factor of rushing to try to arrive before dark versus landing after dark on a dark runway without a landing light, and a possible night landing on a runway without runway lights. I would need to be confident in my ability to handle these (and potentially other) multiple simultaneous risk factors.

I would research ways to mitigate or reduce the risk factors with this flight. For example, is the problem with the landing light due only to a burnt-out bulb? If so, what is required to replace the bulb? Can I drive to Tiny City to pick up the maintenance technician to repair the light, and then fly him back home on the aircraft with the landing light operative?

I would also consider refusing the flight assignment if appropriate mitigation actions can't be taken.

6. Your boss has dispatched you to pick up an airplane just "returned-to-service." The plane has had an engine overhaul, and a new interior and full suite of new next-generation avionics installed. What will you do?

Your answer must demonstrate your understanding of flying a returned to service aircraft. You should also discuss the risk associated with the first few hours of flight after an aircraft has had extensive maintenance and your possible limitations with unfamiliar avionics. Specifically:

- Before takeoff, I'll ensure that the aircraft maintenance records are fully signed off and all required inspections are signed off:

  1. A new pitot-static/altimeter and transponder inspection may be required.
  2. A GPS manual/quick reference is required to be on board for flights under IFR.
  3. Portions of this work (avionics suite) may require an FAA Form 337.

- I will interview the technician about possible differences I should use in power settings and oil usage during the engine break-in time.

- The first hours after major alterations are the riskiest. I will plan to fly with alternative airports close by all along the route, and I will fly at higher altitudes to give me more time to respond in the event that a problem should develop.

- During all phases of flight, I will pay particular close attention in monitoring engine gauges.

- I will complete online research and download manuals for the new avionics to familiarize myself as best as possible with their operations before flight. I will also look for online simulators and tutorials.

- I will depart and fly day VFR on the trip home. This will give me more confidence during flight with unfamiliar avionics.

7. On a VFR night flight, the weather includes scattered, isolated thunderstorms. You are on a 1-mile final to Big City Regional Airport when a lightning strike from an approaching thunderstorm hits the ground control box, disabling airport lights. Beacon, runway, and taxiway lights are all dark. However, the FBO, ramp and terminal area is clearly illuminated. What will you do?

There is no right answer, except of course include that you will remain clear of the thunderstorm. This question is designed to put you in a bad situation to see what you'll do. On a 1-mile final you have very little time, so you must think fast. Show your aeronautical decision making by evaluating the elements aloud. A few things to consider in your discussion:

- I would test to confirm radio communications with ATC.
- If I decide to land:
  1. Negative: Landing in the face of a thunderstorm is generally not the best idea. I must be prepared for possible wind gusts and wind shear.
  2. Positive: Landing will get the aircraft on the ground as soon as possible and out of the path of the approaching thunderstorm. There is probably a centerline and other runway markings that will be illuminated by my landing light.
  3. Lights from the terminal may blind me—or help me.
- If aborting the landing:
  1. Good: I could re-enter the traffic pattern and evaluate the situation from traffic pattern altitude. This assumes I can remain clear of the thunderstorm.
  2. Better: I would circle in the clear sky outside of the thunderstorm until it passes, and then land. This assumes that I can remain clear of other traffic that may be doing the same thing. Because my plane was not hit by lightning, I can probably still communicate with other pilots even if I can't communicate with ATC.
  3. Best: I would depart the area and land someplace else. This option assumes that I have radio communications and am equipped with an alternate.

8. **The aircraft is not inspected for flight under IFR. You are not current to fly IFR. Your flight is from Big City Regional Airport located in Charlie airspace, to Tiny City Airport located in Golf airspace, 25 miles away. You carry cargo for compensation. Current METARs and TAFs call for clear skies and 2 SM visibility in haze. Legally, how will you conduct the flight?**

Because the examiner has asked how you can conduct this flight legally, your answer must demonstrate knowledge of the SVFR regulation and procedures, but you can still acknowledge the risk involved in flying low during periods of low visibility. CFIT awareness is key to this part of the discussion.

To conduct this flight legally, I will:

- Request a SVFR from ATC to depart Big City. I will choose an altitude that will allow me to remain in Golf airspace once cleared of the Charlie 5 NM ring.
- Remain at an altitude in Golf airspace while en route (most likely below 1,200 feet AGL).
- Being mindful of a possible transition area around Tiny City, I will remain in Golf Airspace (may be below 700 feet AGL).
- Land as usual.

I may not have radar coverage or flight following at those low altitudes. I must plan carefully and maintain awareness of obstacles and terrain along my flight, and maintain situational awareness to avoid CFIT.

9. **It's a very hot summer day with very high humidity. The six-place single-engine aircraft you are to fly is loaded to maximum gross weight with your employer's computer equipment and accessories. Talk me through your expectations for this takeoff and any deviations from a normal takeoff you might choose to use.**

Your answer must demonstrate your understanding of the effects of atmospheric conditions on the airplane's takeoff performance, and what actions you would take in terms of calculations or procedures as a result.

- Atmospheric conditions can adversely affect ground roll and takeoff performance. I will calculate takeoff performance with due diligence.

- I might choose to perform a short-field takeoff procedure to ensure runway length is sufficient.
- I will ensure that the computer equipment is secured. A short-field takeoff attitude may cause items to shift, and I anticipate the possibility of turbulence on a hot, humid day. I don't want shifting cargo.

10. **On a late night VFR flight, about 50 miles from your destination, you notice the ammeter is discharging and your interior lights are beginning to fade. Calls to ATC go answered. There are two possible alternative airports near your route; both are very small and without services of any kind. You have two paying passengers on board, both in the back seat. Weather is clear and calm. What will you do?**

Your answer must include an understanding of the electrical system and the underlying implication of an ammeter discharging.

With the ammeter discharging, I am about to lose electrical power and with it, electrical accessories. I would:

- Move my flashlights to within easy reach.
- Recycle the master switch (alternator side on a split switch) to reset a possible overvoltage relay problem.
- Prepare for possible complete electrical failure.
- Turn off all unnecessary electrical equipment.
- If the transponder is to be left on (airspace requirements), tune it to 7600.
- Inform passengers of the situation and how they may be of assistance to me.
- Obtain a VFR sectional chart and be prepared to navigate without radio systems.
- Maintain my situational awareness.
- Obtain the POH and review electrical system checklists.
- Choose between continuing to my destination versus landing as soon as practical:
  1. If I do not have VFR charts available, the best choice is to land as soon as practical. However, if I land as soon as

(continued)

practical I risk having stranded passengers and having no way to repair the aircraft.

2. If I have VFR charts, the weather is clear and calm, and I'm flying under VFR, continuing to the destination is an acceptable choice. If I continue to the destination, I'll consider how I will navigate there, activate pilot-controlled lighting, enter the traffic pattern, and land without flaps and landing light.

11. **You land for fuel at Tiny City Airport. To remain within aircraft max gross weight, you can only fuel to a total of 30 gallons. A 30-gallon load will just enable you to make it home with the required reserve without another fuel stop. What are your thoughts for accurately measuring fuel?**

Your answer must reflect your understanding of fuel measurement and consumption, and risk factors related to calculation of minimum fuel reserves.

- A safe pilot does not depend on aircraft fuel gauges or leave the responsibility for fueling to the line attendants.

- Risk increases if I have only "just enough" fuel to meet minimum fuel reserves. Am I familiar enough with this plane to accurately calculate fuel burn?

- I could use a calibrated fuel stick (if available) to determine the fuel based on time rather than gallons. Ideally I could use a visual indication—such as fueling to the top or to the tabs, and then draining down as needed from there.

12. **You've been hired by a banner tow organization to fly a C-172. Flying straight and level while towing a banner normally results in a slower-than-normal airspeed, higher-than-normal angle of attack, and higher-than-normal power settings. What engine-gauge indications would you expect to see and how will you control the engine?**

Your answer must include the following elements. Be prepared to discuss what the engine gauges tell you about the health of the engine.

- I would be concerned about possible engine overheating. A high angle of attack restricts air flow in and around the engine. Higher power settings also add to engine heat.
- I would pay close attention to engine gauges available in the plane, specifically exhaust gas temperature (EGT), oil temperature, and engine temperature.
- I would control engine cooling by using the highest possible airspeed, lowest possible angle of attack, and lowest possible power settings. I would also open all engine vents and richen the fuel/air mixture.

13. You've been hired by a parachute operator to fly a six-place single-engine airplane. Your job is to climb to 10,000 feet MSL and level off, at which point parachuters will climb outside the aircraft and hang on to your strut before free-falling. You'll make about five such flights each day. The aircraft is within max gross weight, but the passenger seats have been removed so that ten passengers with parachutes can sit on the floor during flight. They will scoot along the floor to the front-door opening to exit. What are your thoughts about aircraft handling characteristics?

Your answer must include considerations and effects related to center of gravity and aircraft performance of flight under the described scenario.

I anticipate:

- Possible CG variances as the passengers move around and exit the aircraft. This will affect stall speed, stability and performance.
- A lateral CG imbalance when passengers are hanging on the wing strut. This may require me to switch fuel tanks.
- The weight change when passengers exit the aircraft will affect aircraft performance, especially at 10,000 feet MSL.
- A change in aircraft performance, assuming that the door has been removed.
- Flight at slow speeds while passengers are hanging on the strut.

After parachuters exit the aircraft, I would descend quickly, without overcooling the engine, so that I am ready to pick up the next load of passengers.

14. It's 3:00 a.m. You are three hours into a late night cross-country. You are returning home, solo. The weather is clear and calm, and you are VFR at 9,500 feet MSL and getting massive tailwinds. But you are very sleepy and having difficulty staying awake. It's another hour flight time home. What will you do?

Your answer must include the risk factors associated with not being mentally alert, demonstrate an understanding of possible physiological effects of flight, and discuss possible mitigation actions.

Too many accidents occur in the last miles of a long trip because the pilot was unwilling to divert or land knowing they were so close to home. If I'm flying while tired or not mentally alert, my risk increases due to reduced situational awareness, hindered ADM, and possible physiological consequences (such as falling asleep while piloting).

The physiological aspects of flight at 9,500 feet for long durations include possible hypoxia. Many pilots start to feel slightly hypoxic at altitudes below those required for supplemental oxygen.

Actions I can take to counter these effects:

- Descend to a lower altitude. Breathe supplemental oxygen if available.
- Direct air vents into my face, sing, keep busy—anything I can do to regain mental alertness.
- Land as soon as practical, walk around, drink coffee, and then take off and continue the trip.
- Land as soon as practical; call it a night even if I have to nap on the FBO couch or in the plane.

Proper preflight planning could have helped me in this situation. I should consider carrying a portable oxygen bottle anytime I have a late night flight, or any night flight after a long day, when flying above 5,000 feet.

15. **You are on downwind at Big City Regional with paying passengers on board when suddenly you hear strange noises from the engine and feel a serious vibration. Holes in the engine cowl confirm a failed cylinder. Winds on the ground are about 10 knots. What will you do?**

    Your answer must demonstrate your understanding of engine operations, the underlying implication of a failed cylinder, emergency procedures for your aircraft, and actions you will consider (and their associated risk factors).

    A failed cylinder means the aircraft has an engine failure.

    I would follow the correct emergency procedure for my aircraft per the POH/AFM. I would declare an emergency. A commercial pilot must not hesitate to gather all possible resources to aid in handling an emergency, including contacting other available crew members and ground personnel.

    I would consider other possible closer landing areas, such as another runway or taxiway. Other options might be the grassy area between runways, or even an emergency field off the airport.

    If I end up making a crosswind and/or downwind landing, this presents additional risk and aircraft performance implications.

16. **You have 5 hours logged in the make and model of aircraft flown by your new employer. The aircraft will be loaded to max gross weight, but not over. On board will be the boss's wife, elderly mother-in-law, and two-year-old daughter. The weather is generally VFR but typical afternoon thunderstorms are forecasted all along your route. What are your thoughts about this flight assignment?**

    This question is testing your ability to recognize possible risk factors. Your answer should discuss your tolerance for handling multiple simultaneous risk factors, and ways to mitigate or reduce these risk factors.

    I would first make an honest assessment of my ability to handle multiple simultaneous risk factors, including unfamiliarity with the plane, flight at max gross weight, passengers who may become a distraction, and possible weather. I could mitigate/reduce these risk factors by arranging the takeoff time for early morning to avoid thunderstorms, or arranging to get more time in the aircraft at gross weight before the departure day, etc.

I might also consider refusing the flight assignment if appropriate mitigation actions can't be taken.

17. You have 400 hours total time. You completed a one hour checkout yesterday in your new employer's aircraft, resulting in your high performance endorsement. Your assignment is a sightseeing flight around town for three large business men. You will be at max gross weight. With the hot, humid summer day, your aircraft will require about half of the available runway for liftoff. Will you accept this flight assignment? Why or why not?

Most pilots give an answer they think the examiner wants to hear: "No, because there are several risk factors." However, that may not be the best answer. Let the examiner hear your thought processes. Specifically:

- Assuming the aircraft is somewhat similar to what I am used to flying (for example, C-182 versus C-172) then the one hour checkout for a 400-hour pilot should be safe. However, if the aircraft is very different (glass cockpit Cirrus versus standard cockpit C-172), then the one hour checkout may not be sufficient.

- If the checkout was performed at max gross weight, then this flight should be no problem.

- If I carefully calculate the takeoff distance and feel confident in the available runway, then takeoff should be no problem for me as a pilot with 400 hours.

- My short answer is that if I have similar flight experiences, then yes, I will accept this flight assignment. This is a good flight to stretch my comfort level.

18. **You are on a close-in base at Tiny City Airport with paying passengers on board when suddenly you see another aircraft on final, which will conflict. What will you do?**

Your answer must discuss right-of-way rules as well as specific actions you will take in this situation.

I would follow right-of-way rules. However, a commercial pilot is always prepared to give up right of way for the safety of flight.

If I encountered this situation, I would:

• Add full power and perform a maximum climb either straight ahead or to the right, or do a level left 360° turn if spacing permits.

• Attempt to communicate with the other pilot, in a professional manner, after both planes are out of harm, to inform them of my intentions to follow.

19. **You have flown through eight states and have made 18 IFR IAPs in the past three days. The weather is now clear and cold. A blanket of snow completely covers the ground. Upon arrival to Tiny City Airport, you notice the runway has not been cleared. What will you do?**

Your answer must include the soft-field landing procedure for your aircraft, and discussion of risk factors and possible mitigations.

If I proceed with landing at Tiny City Airport, I would follow the soft-field landing procedure for my aircraft. This includes keeping the nose wheel off the ground as long as possible, and minimizing braking.

I would attempt to mitigate the risk factors associated with a soft-field, potentially deep, slippery runway by:

• Attempting to call UNICOM to see if the attendant can tell me how deep the snow is.

• Considering a low approach over the runway to see what I can see and to look for possible drifts or snow banks.

• Calling FSS to inquire about runway conditions at nearby airports for a possible diversion.

(continued)

I will give myself plenty of time to evaluate alternatives and set up the airplane properly. I won't hesitate to fly out of my way to where runway and services are better.

This scenario reveals insufficient preflight planning. By making a phone call to FSS or the FBO to learn about local airport conditions, I can avoid this situation in the future. Perhaps the reason for poor planning is my fatigue—I've flown a lot of hours in the past three days. This is risky. Did I pass the "I'M SAFE" checklist?

20. Tell me about the emergency equipment and survival gear you normally carry on board for routine flights?

Your answer should show your understanding of where most accidents occur, how quickly you could expect rescue operations, and the specific emergency equipment and survival gear you carry.

Most accidents occur close to the home airport (which is where most flights occur). Rescue could easily take 48 hours or longer if I am not on a flight plan, and as a result, I would carry survival gear on routine flights. Specifically:

- Water and shelter are required.
- Basic first aid supplies are necessary.
- A fire extinguisher is more than a luxury item.
- The ELT battery may be activated manually.

21. As a professional commercial pilot, in what ways do you think you should alter your normal flight procedures when you are carrying passengers on board for hire?

Your answer should display your understanding of what it means to be a professional. Perhaps you do feel that normal flight procedures should be altered; however, most examiners want to hear that you always act professionally when flying, not just when carrying passengers for hire. Your answer could include:

Theoretically, I would make no changes to my normal flight procedures. I fully prepare for every flight. I fully utilize all available resources, maintain my skills, and fly to the best of my abilities.

Having said that, paying passengers expect me to be aware of their needs during flight and to communicate with them during the flight. They expect me to make in-flight decisions conservatively.

FAA Advisory
Circular
120-12   Appendix 1

U.S. Department
of Transportation
**Federal Aviation
Administration**

Advisory
Circular

SUBJECT: Private Carriage Versus Common Carriage of Persons or Property	DATE: 4/24/86 INITIATED BY: AFS-820	AC NO: 120-12A CHANGE:

1. **PURPOSE.** This advisory circular furnishes Federal Aviation Administration (FAA) personnel and interested segments of industry with general guidelines for determining whether current or proposed transportation operations by air constitute private or common carriage. If the operations are in interstate or foreign commerce, this distinction determines whether or not the operator needs economic authority as an "air carrier" from the Department of Transportation. Operations that constitute common carriage are required to be conducted under Federal Aviation Regulations (FAR) Parts 121 or 135. Private carriage may be conducted under FAR Parts 125 or 91, Subpart D. Operations conducted under FAR Section 91.181, which permits certain charges to be made, may also be subject to these guidelines, particularly the "time sharing" provisions of FAR Section 91.181(c)(1). It should also be noted that lease agreements entered into under FAR Section 91.181 are subject to FAR Section 91.54, "Truth in leasing clause requirement in leases and conditional sales contracts."

2. **CANCELLATION.** Advisory Circular 120-12, Private Carriage Versus Common Carriage By Commercial Operators Using Large Aircraft, dated June 24, 1964, is canceled.

3. **BACKGROUND.** "Common carriage" and "private carriage" are common law terms. The Federal Aviation Act of 1958 uses the term "common carriage" but does not define it. It has therefore been determined that guidelines giving general explanations of the term "common carriage" and its opposite, "private carriage," would be helpful.

4. **GUIDELINES.** A carrier becomes a common carrier when it "holds itself out" to the public, or to a segment of the public, as willing to furnish transportation within the limits of its facilities to any person who wants it. Absence of tariffs or rate schedules, transportation only pursuant to separately negotiated contracts, or occasional refusals to transport, are not conclusive proof that the carrier is not a common carrier. There are four elements in defining a common carrier; (1) a holding out of a willingness to (2) transport persons or property (3) from place to place (4) for compensation. This "holding out" which makes a person a common carrier can be done in many ways and it does not matter how it is done.

a. Signs and advertising are the most direct means of "holding out" but are not the only ones.

b. A "holding out" may be accomplished through the actions of agents, agencies, or salesmen who may, themselves, procure passenger traffic from the general public and collect them into groups to be carried by the operator. It is particularly important to determine if such agents or salesmen are in the business of selling transportation to the traveling public not only through the "group" approach but also by individual ticketing on known common carriers.

c. Physically holding out without advertising where a reputation to serve all is gained is sufficient to constitute an offer to carry all customers. There are many means by which physical holding out may take place. For example, the expression of willingness to all customers with whom contact is made that the operator can and will perform the requested service is sufficient. The fact that the holding out generates little success is of no consequence. The nature and character of the operation are the important issue.

d. Carriage for hire which does not involve "holding out" is private carriage. Private carriers for hire are sometimes called "contract carriers," but the term is borrowed from the Interstate Commerce Act and legally inaccurate when used in connection with the Federal Aviation Act. Private carriage for hire is carriage for one or several selected customers, generally on a long-term basis. The number of contracts must not be too great, otherwise it implies a willingness to make a contract with anybody. A carrier operating pursuant to 18 to 24 contracts has been held to be a common carrier because it held itself out to serve the public generally to the extent of its facilities. Private carriage has been found in cases where three contracts have been the sole basis of the operator's business. Special adaptation of the transportation service to the individual needs of shippers is a factor tending to establish private carriage but is not necessarily conclusive.

e. A carrier holding itself out as generally willing to carry only certain kinds of traffic is, nevertheless, a common carrier. For instance, a carrier authorized or willing only to carry planeloads of passengers, cargo, or mail on a charter basis is a common carrier, if it so holds itself out. This is, in fact, the basic business of supplemental air carriers.

f. A carrier flying charters for only one organization may be a common carrier if membership in the organization and participation in the flights are, in effect, open to a significant segment of the public. Similarly, a carrier which flies planeload charters for a common carrier, carrying the latter's traffic, engages in common carriage itself.

g. Occasionally, offers of free transportation have been made to the general public by hotels, casinos, etc. In such cases, nominal charges have been made which, according to the operators, bear the expense of gifts and gratuities. However, the operators maintain that the transportation is free. The courts have held that such operations are common carriage based on the fact that the passengers are drawn from the general public and the nominal charge constituted compensation.

h. Persons admittedly operating as common carriers in a certain field (for instance, in intrastate commerce) sometimes claim that transportation for hire which they perform in other fields (for instance, interstate or foreign commerce) is private carriage. To sustain such a claim, the carrier must show that the private carriage is clearly distinguishable from its common carriage business and outside the scope of its holding out. The claimed private carriage must be viewed in relation to and against the background of the entire carrying activity. Historically, Civil Aeronautics Board decisions have concluded that only in rare instances could carriage engaged in by a common carrier be legitimately classified as private.

i. In summary, persons intending to conduct only private operations in support of other business should look cautiously at any proposal for revenue-generating flights which most likely would require certification as an air carrier.

j. Persons who have questions concerning intended operation of their aircraft are encouraged to discuss their proposed operation with the Regional Counsel of the FAA region in which it intends to establish its principal business office. Such early interviews will materially assist the applicant in avoiding many of the "pitfalls" which could result in illegal common carriage operations.

William T. Brennan
Acting Director of Flight Standards

FAA Safe
Air Charter
Appendix 2

FAA Safe Air Charter

 Federal Aviation Administration

 SAFE AIR CHARTER

Q You just got your private pilot certificate...the ink is still wet. A buddy wants you to fly him and his girlfriend to Key West, he says he will pay for the rental of the aircraft. Can you take this flight?

A No. This flight requires a commercial operating certificate and a higher level pilot certificate because it is air transportation. Note: earning flight-time is compensation too.

Q What is a demonstration flight and what isn't?

A The purpose of a "true" demonstration flight is to demonstrate an aircraft to a prospective customer. Demonstration flights cannot be used to provide air transportation, unless the operator is certified under part 119. A typical illegal 'demonstration' flight is one where the operator is not demonstrating the aircraft to a prospective customer or the passenger is not considering purchase of the aircraft but rather has obtained air transportation.

Q Where can I find regulations on what I can do with my commercial pilot certificate without a Part 119 certificate?

A 14 CFR §119.1 (e) lists exceptions to the need for a Part 119 certificate. Be careful though...119.1 (e) has some conditions and limitations that you must follow to be legal. Additionally, 61.113 addresses private pilot privileges and limitations.

Q Can I fly Part 91 for the owner of an aircraft as a commercial pilot?

A Yes, as long as the owner does not receive compensation for the transportation of passengers or property on any of the flights. Although the 'owner' delegates functions of operational control to you —the corporate pilot, the 'owner' still has full legal responsibility for your actions.

Q So... you have just (today) earned your commercial pilot certificate! Congratulations! I (the Designated Pilot Examiner (DPE) that just issued your new pilot certificate) need to fly to an airport 25 miles away. I will only be there for 1 hour, and will need you to fly me back. I will pay you $100 plus the cost of the rental airplane. What will you say?

A No. While a commercial pilot certificate grants you the privilege to carry persons or property for compensation or hire, you must also meet the requirements of the applicable parts (e.g. Part 119; 133, 135, 137 etc.) of the regulation. This means that you might need to obtain an operating certificate or fly for someone with an operating certificate (e.g., an air carrier).

Q You are a flight instructor and also an air tour pilot. The 'boss' of the air tour says you can conduct a tour and give flight instruction at the same time. That way, you are not limited to the 25 mile limitation of the tour. What will you say?

A No. Part 119.1 (e) allows for flight instruction or air tours operated in conjunction with 91.147, however mixing is not allowed. The test will be what the passengers' purpose was...a tour...or flight instruction...cannot be both.

Q While talking about a flight you are planning to take to Las Vegas from Van Nuys, CA, a friend of yours asks if you can fly him/her to Phoenix on your way to KLAS. He/she offers to share expenses per 61.113 for the flight to Phoenix and then you can continue to Las Vegas. What will you say?

A No. Part 61, 61.113 (c) allows sharing costs only if there is a common purpose for the flight. I, the pilot, do not have a purpose to go to Phoenix. FAA Advisory Circular 61-142 is a great resource for this question!

And...the graduation question!

(continued)

Q In an attempt to earn money to afford his/her aircraft, the owner decides to dry-lease the aircraft to other local businesses. The owner hires the best aviation attorney money can buy and the dry-lease(s) are rock solid. The aircraft owner tells you that it appears things will be picking up and a couple leases have been signed. The owner tells you that you have a trip, tomorrow at 8:00am in a dry leased aircraft. Are you safe/legal to take the flight?

A No. The purpose of a lease agreement is to transfer operational control and legal responsibility to the lessee. The 'test' would be whether the lessee truly has operational control, or if operational control remained with the owner/lessor. An additional problem would be the apparent lack of independent pilot selection by the lessee. This scenario appears to describe a wet-lease, whereby the lessor provides/ schedules the aircraft AND provides/schedules you, the pilot. A Part 119 certificate would be required. See FAA Advisory Circular 91-37B.

Additional Resources

Safe Air Charter Resources: www.faa.gov/charter

AC 91-37B Truth in Leasing: www.faa.gov/documentLibrary/media /Advisory_Circular/AC_91-37B.pdf

AC 120-12A Private Carriage Versus Common Carriage of Persons or Property: www.faa.gov/documentLibrary/media/Advisory_Circular /AC%20120-12A.pdf

AC 61-142 Sharing Aircraft Operating Expenses in Accordance with 14 CFR §61.113(c): www.faa.gov/documentLibrary/media /Advisory_Circular/AC_61-142.pdf

Applicant's Practical Test Checklist

Appendix 3

Applicant's Practical Test Checklist

Appointment with Examiner

Examiner's Name: _____

Location for test (airport): _____

Date of test: _____

Start time for test: _____

Examiner's fee: _____

Documents to Bring to the Practical Test

___ *Aircraft Maintenance Records*
Logbook record of airworthiness and inspections for engine, aircraft, propeller, and AD compliance:
- Annual inspection
- 100-hour inspection (if applicable)
- VOR test (if applicable)
- Altimeter, pitot static test
- Transponder test
- ELT inspection and battery
- AD compliance documentation
- Current GPS database (if applicable)

___ *Aircraft Required Documents:*
- Supplemental documents
- Placards
- Airworthiness certificate
- Current aircraft registration
- Radio station license
- Owner's manual (AFM/POH)
- Weight and balance documentation

Personal Documents
___ Government-issued photo identification
___ Pilot certificate
___ Aviation Medical Certificate or BasicMed qualification (when applicable)
___ FAA Knowledge Test results
___ Completed FAA Form 8710-1, Airman Certificate and/or Rating Application, with instructor's signature, or completed IACRA form (a best practice is to have both in case of an IACRA system outage)

Training Documentation
___ Log of ground training meeting FAR requirements*
___ Log of flight training meeting FAR requirements
___ Log of experience requirements meeting FAR requirements
___ Endorsements signed by instructor for practical test eligibility
___ Graduation certificate if test will be conducted based on graduation
     from a Part 141 approved training provider
___ Log of experience indicating currency for flight (flight review
     endorsement or current solo endorsement; complex, high-
     performance, or tailwheel endorsement if applicable)
___ Copy of previous Notice of Disapproval (if the test is a retest)
___ Endorsement for retest (if the test is a retest)

A best practice is to have all of these items tabbed or identified to be
able to demonstrate eligibility for the practical test to the examiner.
The examiner is required to determine and confirm eligibility prior to
beginning the test. If they are unable to determine eligibility or you are
missing documentation, they may be unable to begin the test and it may
need to be rescheduled.

Equipment and Materials to Bring to the Test

___ View-limiting device
___ Current aeronautical charts (printed or electronic)
___ Flight computer, calculator, and/or plotter
___ Flight plan form and flight logs (printed or electronic)
___ *Chart Supplement*, airport diagrams, or other charting resources
___ Current FAR/AIM

** Note that ground training as logged by an online ground school for
the FAA Knowledge Test typically does not meet the requirements for
ground training for a certificate or rating. Be sure that you have logged
ground training for the practical test and that you have it documented
and available for review for the practical test.*